Also by Julia Child

*Mastering the Art of French Cooking,
Volume I,* 1961 (with Simone Beck and Louisette
Bertholle)

The French Chef Cookbook, 1968

*Mastering the Art of French Cooking,
Volume II,* 1970 (with Simone Beck)

From Julia Child's Kitchen, 1975

❧

These are Borzoi Books, published in New
York by Alfred A. Knopf

Julia Child & Company

by Julia Child

In collaboration with
E. S. Yntema

Photographs by
James Scherer

Alfred A. Knopf, New York
1978

Julia Child & Company

"Lo-Cal Banquet," "Dinner for the Boss,"
and "Birthday Dinner" appeared in somewhat shorter form in the October 1978
issue of *McCall's*.

Library of Congress Cataloging in Publica-
tion Data

Child, Julia.
    Julia Child & Company.

    Includes index.
    1. Cookery. 2. Menus. I. Title.
TX715.C5455   641.5   78-54922
ISBN 0-394-50200-0

Manufactured in the United States of America

First Edition

Contents

*The WGBH kitchen for Julia Child & Company,
designed by Fran Mahard.*

How This Book Began

It didn't take too much persuasion to induce me to do another television cooking series, particularly since my husband, Paul, approved, my friend and collaborator Ruth Lockwood was willing, as was my chief associate cook, Elizabeth Bishop, and our original producer of *The French Chef,* Russell Morash. But, we all decided, it was time to be entirely different, with a new title, a new musical theme (this one—which I describe as an elephant walk by bassoons—was developed by Robert J. Lurtsema, host of Boston's WGBH-Radio's *Morning Pro-Musica* program), and a real kitchen rather than a take-away set. We wanted a big room of our own where we could open the door, walk in, and start cooking... and then walk out again, closing the door behind us (our set designer, Fran Mahard, gave us this blue, green, and white beauty that you'll be seeing in the photographs throughout). Also, after over 200 programs on *The French Chef,* we felt it was time to get away from the purely French tradition. We would go in for general cooking where we could draw from anywhere and everywhere, since that really is the American way of doing things. A further decision was that we'd show a whole menu rather than just a single dish or subject. After all, one is not cooking in limbo. A dish belongs in a meal, and the cook has to plan the meal so that what goes with what makes gastronomic sense.

Let us have, said we, a series of shows featuring menus for special occasions—the special kind that most of us run into most of the time. For example, you suddenly find that your guest list has swelled to 19 people. You can't sit them down at your table; you'll have to serve them buffet style. Anyway, stand-up or sit-down, what do you feed to 19 people when you're the cook and butler combined? How do you shop for the meal? What staples do you have on hand? How do you time the cooking and then, of course, how do you cook everything? Or, on another occasion, the big boss is coming to dinner; you don't know him (or her!) very well but you do know they're a pretty conservative meat-and-potatoes couple. So what do you plan for them? Or you are to have a comfortable family-style Sunday night supper, with both grown-ups and children. What would be fun for all? What do you have ready, and what can everyone join in on? Or you've planned a barbecue but it looks like rain, or you just want a cozy and delicious meal for intimate friends.

But how can you cook a whole menu in a TV half hour? We did full menus a few times on *The French Chef,* but they were *tour-de-force* fast-food operations that actually did take only half an hour to cook. These would be more normal and leisurely meals. Even so, I'd be able to do only two or three of the dishes in the allotted 30 minutes, and I would simply have to show the rest already finished. Obviously we needed a book to complete the picture, and this is it. Here are not only all the recipes shown on television, but all the recipes for every dish displayed or mentioned but not cooked for you. Thus, whether or not you witnessed the event on the air, this book tells the whole story for each one of 13 occasions, from the planning and buying to the timing and the actual cooking of each dish on the menu. Also, because the best food is the freshest, there is a series of other choices for every dish—in case the ingredients for the main recipe are not available or a particular item of food does not appeal to you. And, since the occasions we have chosen are ones that frequently crop up in one's life, there is an appendix of alternate menus for the same situations, made up of recipes drawn from each of my other books. So you should never be at a loss for what to serve.

Words are not enough, however, when one is reading about a meal rather than seeing it being prepared. We therefore vowed to have color photographs not only taken during the actual television performances, but specially taken to show the whole menu displayed as an ensemble. In addition, we wanted photographs for each finished dish so that you can look at your eventual goal before starting to prepare it. We also wanted clear color photographs of such how-to procedures as the boning of a chicken, the stemming of a spinach leaf, the making of French puff pastry. You can describe them in words, but a good photograph explains what words cannot. This is particularly true when the photographs are taken from the cook's point of view—rather than the observer's (as almost all food illustration is done). Thus when you place your ingredients and equipment in front of you, everything will look exactly as it is positioned in the photograph, enabling you to work directly from the illustration. Thanks to the talent and patient devotion of our photographer, Jim Scherer, I think we are presenting some of the most distinguished and interesting food photography I have seen anywhere.

We are fortunate not only in photographers, but in my writing collaborator.

Left to right: Russell Morash, Ruth Lockwood, Julia Child, and make-up artist Louise Miller.

Because this book, for once, was to appear at the same time as the airing of the first television program, both the book and the taping of the programs had to occur simultaneously. Obviously I could not be both TV cook and book producer. We needed a fast professional writer with literary dash who could also organize and who knows and likes food. Heaven has sent us a perfect gem in Peggy Yntema. We have worked most happily and enthusiastically together and I must say that even I sometimes find it hard to tell where one leaves off and the other begins.

Writing collaboration was not enough, however, since if the only cook around were the one to be seen on the television screen we'd not have had much to look at. You should see what goes on behind the scenes! In addition to having enough food for the recipes themselves, we must have many of the dishes prepared in several stages of readiness. In other words, the meringue layers that you see going into the oven must have a ready-baked set of twins to come out of the oven, and then a triplet group of ready-baked on hand just in case something happens to the first and we have to do the scene over. We can't wait for them to bake; we've got to shoot right away. Again, if I am serving the elaborate fish dish at the end of the program, but the timing is wrong, we've got to do it over. In this case we either bring in a standby cooked and ready, or we patch up the first one and serve it again. (That happened to the Choulibiac on page 82; you'll note that the top covering, the yellow layer, is a bit thick. No wonder! We had to scrape off the top, put on a new one, rebake rapidly, and reshoot half a dozen times. Every time we did over that very short episode, something went wrong. The cameras bumped into each other one time; on another take I sneezed. The next time the plate tipped and the serving slipped off, and so forth and so on. At last the scene was done, but I'm surprised anything was left of that splendid dish and that it photographed so attractively except for the slightly too thick—and not quite cooked!—pastry layer on top.)

There's lots of cooking behind the scenes, then, and not only for the food on the air, but for the final display of the whole menu and additional dishes to be prepared for photographing. We needed a real cooking team under the leadership of our major domo and chief associate cook, Elizabeth Bishop. Rosemary Manell, also a longtime friend, cooking companion, and co-demonstrator, was in charge of backstage preparations for standby and final scene items. Assisting in these preparations was Wendy Davidson, talented cake decorator and imaginative dresser-up of dishes, as well as able assistant during our photography sessions. Among the volunteers was our faithful and charming Bonnie Eleph, tucked away in the offstage ready-room area, sautéing dozens and dozens of turkey breast slices for the Orloff, simmering tons of beans for a bonus recipe, trimming vegetables for the boiled dinner, and dicing mounds of potatoes for corned beef hash in four stages. Our jolly and stalwart volunteer cooks, Gladys Christopherson, Bess Coughlin, Jo Ford, Pat Pratt, and Bev Semens, were on hand for many rehearsals and all tapings (often aided by John Reardon), dishing out lunch, washing constant piles of pots and pans, peeling and chopping on demand, rushing out for emergency items, and ready for anything. They made a marvelous team. We ate well, cooked like fury, and had a good time throughout.

The cooks, Ruthie Lockwood and her two dedicated office assistants, Avis DeVoto and Marilyn Ambrose, our make-up artist, Louise Miller Philippe, and I are "our" side of the team, the so-called talent. "They" are the television technicians who do the sound, the lighting, and the camera work, the control room people who put it all together, the floor manager, who is the performer's connection to the director, and, of course, the all-important director himself, who is in charge of all that is seen and heard. Finally, there is the producer, who in turn is the boss of everything—talent, camera, food, director, and all. One of the happy aspects of this new series of programs is that we were working with so many of our original crew. Russell Morash, our producer, was our first producer-director when he was 28 years old and *The French Chef* pilot program lurched into the airwaves in July of 1962.

Left to right: Bess Coughlin, Liz Bishop, Peggy Yntema, Gladys Christopherson, Wendy Davidson, Bonnie Eleph, John Reardon, Julia Child, Bev Semens, and Rosemary Manell.

Willie Morton, then as now, was our sound man, and Chas Norton did the lighting. Kathy Smith was our switcher in the control room, Greg Macdonald was on camera, and Connie White was frequently our floor manager. Dave DeBarger, our director for this series, was also floor manager in the latter part of the old series. Working together was like old times.

And again like old times, our most frequently asked question was about what happens to all that food after the show. We used to eat it all up, all of us, as soon as the director gave us the all-clear sign that the tape was good. If there was sometimes too much, or if it had been so expensive as to strain the budget, we would auction it off among us. This time, alas, except for the first two shows, we had to save almost all of the food for the photographer. There it was, beautifully displayed at the end of the program, hot and tempting and ready to eat—and there it sat, and sat, and was moved around, and lit this way and that, and moved again, and reheated and fussed with, and finally most carefully photographed by Jim Scherer.

Wednesdays, after our cook-through rehearsal, he came in to photograph how-to techniques from over my shoulder. I remember his delight when he saw the human hand so clearly outlined under the chicken skin (page 22), dislodging it from the breast before boning the bird. Such time we spent over the right light and the right look for the shelling of peas to show peas, shells, and the funny little machine that did the work (page 180). Chris

Pullman and Gaye Korbet, the designers of this book, were on hand one evening when Jim and I and Wendy Davidson were laboriously changing lights and angles and reflectors for the delicate operation of pulling the vein from the end of a shrimp (page 114). Chris observed that he found it hard to believe five grown people could spend more than an hour most earnestly bent over something like a shrimp's intestine.

Attention to such detail, even that small part of a shrimp, is what makes working on a good team so rewarding. And we have been a team, a most happy one. "Harmony Inc. Complete Food Productions," we decided to call ourselves one late afternoon after a long taping, cooking, and photography session. But I've said very little so far about my alter ego and collaborator, Ruth Lockwood. Together we have worked out the framework of the shows, but it is she who has written the scripts and has calculated the complicated staging and timing involved. She has advised and rehearsed me before each scene and has been ever alert for each word and gesture during the performances. Ruth is a real TV genius in her field, and I am forever grateful to her. Nor have I spoken of our favorite editor, Judith Jones, who has been our leader in this whole book operation, getting those people to write their copy on time and those others to set it up on time, and always looking at words and type with her expert eye. Judith is another authentic genius in her field, and one with whom we are ever fortunate to be associated. Finally there is my dear husband, Paul, who was on hand with his own camera during all of the tapings, who has fetched and carried and chopped, and who has encouraged me and held my hand through every television show since the beginning and through every stage of every book. My most loving thanks to him.

So, that's all for a beginning. On to the meat of the matter! And, as ever, *bon appétit*.

J.C.
Cambridge, Mass., May 12, 1978

Paul Child.

❷ *indicates stop here.*
▼ *indicates further discussion under Remarks.*

Julia Child
& Company

A menu designed around duck, with a special roasting method which guarantees perfect cooking and easy carving. Herewith, also, a sumptuous apricot and hazelnut cake.

Birthday Dinner

Menu

Chesapeake Lump Crabmeat Appetizer

❧

Roast Duck with Cracklings
Purée of Parsnips in Zucchini Boats
Broccoli with Brown Butter and Lemon

❧

The Los Gatos Gâteau Cake

❧

Suggested wines:
Chablis with the crab; Burgundy or
Pinot Noir with the duck; Sauternes or
Champagne with the gâteau

Whenever anyone asks me what I want for a birthday dinner, I always say, "Roast duck and a big gooey cake." I love to eat duck when the skin is crisp and mahogany red-brown, the legs and wings just tender through, the breast meat moist, rosy, and tender. And guests always feel it's a special treat. You don't see duck too often at dinner parties. It does pose problems, and I've been giving them some thought.

Even a carver as adept as my husband finds that the docile duck becomes as stubborn as an ostrich on the carving board; that's the first problem. Second is the fact that roasted the usual way the breast meat is done much sooner than the leg and wing. Fat is problem number three: for perfect flavor, the fat must be drained off during cooking. But if you want a crisp skin, you can't cook it in the normal manner because the meat will be overdone. Many a cook is resigned to ruining the meat in order to enjoy a crackling skin.

A famous Chinese solution to these problems is Peking duck, the glory of Mandarin cuisine, for which one starts way ahead by forcing air between the duck's skin and flesh and hanging up the inflated carcass to dry. For the fine Norman ducks of Rouen, which are a cross between wild and domestic strains and are sold unbled, the French have thought up the duck press and produce a carnal feast indeed. Here the partly roasted bird is peeled of its skin, the breast is carved, the legs and wings are removed, and the carcass is crushed for its juices. The breast is then warmed in these juices, a rich dark red, laced with Burgundy wine. The legs and wings finish cooking while you eat the more delicate breast, and they come in as an encore. This requires expert servers, a chafing dish, and a duck press. But when we filmed the process at the Dorin brothers' restaurant in Rouen, I also showed a less elaborate alternative. With that in mind, I decided to continue with the roast-peel idea that I used then to produce another and simpler dish.

This way of dealing with duck involves neither sideboard antics nor fancy paraphernalia; and it solves all three of the problems I mentioned. The duck can be beautifully presented, since it is carved in the kitchen, and served before its redolence evaporates. I like to contrast its rich flavor, crisp skin, and succulent meat with a velvety purée of parsnips. Their very special flavor, earthy and sweetish—so compatible with duck—is transformed by puréeing. People who think they don't like parsnips are almost always enchanted with them this way, wondering happily, "What can it be?" I like to serve the parsnip purée in baked zucchini shells—chosen for their unobtrusive taste and their jade and emerald color—an easy and elegant vegetable accompaniment. I'd hate to disturb the rapport of these congenial flavors with anything else, so I serve another vegetable as a separate course.

Like opposite primary and secondary colors, fruit flavors seem to balance duck. So I've chosen a fruit-layered cake for the birthday dessert: crisp strips of nut meringue spread with a luscious apricot filling flavored with orange liqueur and a touch of Cognac, plus a discreet amount of butter cream, just enough to mediate the contrast in taste and texture.

I like this luxurious menu; and I also like to feel rested as well as hospitable when I call my best friends in to the table. No damp brow or hot hands for the birthday cook! I prepare most of this very posh dinner well in advance, and the work itself isn't difficult. The gorgeous cake is not only more fun to make than the sponge-layer kind, it's easier. And in the privacy of my kitchen, nobody can see me subduing the duck.

Preparations

Marketing and Storage:
Staples to have on hand

Salt
Peppercorns
Sugar (both granulated and confectioners)
Pure vanilla extract
Almond extract
Cream of tartar
Stick cinnamon
Bay leaves
Thyme or sage
Mustard (the strong Dijon type or Düsseldorf)▼
Apricot preserves or jam (optional)
All-purpose flour
Olive oil and cooking oil
Wines and liqueurs: dry white French vermouth, Cognac or rum, dry Port or Sercial Madeira, orange or apricot liqueur
Vegetables and fruits: a few carrots, onions, shallots or scallions, an orange, and lemons
Eggs (12)
Cream (½ pint [225 g] or so)
Fresh bread crumbs (in the freezer) ▼

Specific ingredients for this menu

Crab (enough for 6 as a first course; see recipe) ▼
Ducklings (two 4- to 5-pound or 2- to 2½-kg) ▼
Zucchini (6, about 6 inches or 15 cm long)
Parsnips (1½ to 2 pounds or ¾ to 1 kg)
Broccoli (2 bunches)
Parsley (1 bunch; or 1 or 2 of watercress)
Unsalted butter (about 1 pound or 450 g)
Dried apricots (1 pound or 450 g)
Whole shelled hazelnuts and blanched almonds (about 4 ounces or 120 g of each) ▼
Shaved (thinly sliced) almonds, toasted (about 8 ounces or 240 g)

▶ *Remarks:*

Staples

Mustard: always store prepared mustard in the refrigerator, otherwise it goes off in flavor; most supermarkets carry several varieties of strong European-type mustard, and the ball-park variety is not meant here. *Bread crumbs:* it's useful to have these always on hand in the freezer, and crumbs from fresh bread are best. To make them easily, cut crusts off nonsweet white bread, such as French, Italian, and Viennese, and crumb either in the blender or with the grating disk of a food processor; store in a plastic bag in the freezer where they will keep for weeks.

Specific ingredients for this menu

Crab: if you buy frozen crab, allow a day for it to defrost in the refrigerator, and see notes on crab in "Fish Talk," page 111.) *Ducks:* frozen ducks, like all frozen poultry, should be defrosted in the refrigerator to minimize juice loss since too quick defrosting can cause the ice crystals to pierce the flesh. Your best alternative is to defrost them in a sinkful of water. In either case, leave ducks in their plastic wrapping, and allow 2 to 3 days in the refrigerator, several hours in water. *Hazelnuts and almonds:* nuts are perishable, especially hazelnuts (called filberts by some people); taste them to be sure they are fresh, and store them in the freezer. To skin hazelnuts, place in a roasting pan in a 350°F/180°C oven, tossing about every 5 minutes or so, for 15 to 20 minutes, or until the nuts are lightly browned; rub in a towel to remove as much skin as you easily can. Toasting also gives them added flavor. Toast whole blanched shaved almonds in the same manner.

Chesapeake Lump Crabmeat Appetizer

Since how much you season your crabmeat depends entirely on its quality, I can only make suggestions. Freshly boiled crabmeat needs nothing on it, I think, only lemon, salt, and a peppermill passed at the table, and to each his own. Frozen and canned crab are very much up to you and your tastebuds as you fix your appetizer. Lemon juice, certainly, and often you will need very finely minced shallot or scallion, sometimes a little minced celery, and fresh minced drill or fragrant bottled dill weed, plus salt and pepper, and perhaps a tossing with good olive oil; I like to pass mayonnaise separately, for those who wish it. Arrange the crab on a bed of either shredded lettuce or romaine, or surround it with watercress, or wreathe it in seasoned ripe tomato pulp or red pimiento. You could also include quartered hard-boiled eggs, but that would be dictated by how much crab you were serving per person—and since crab is a luxury, ⅓ cup (¾ dL) for each guest is generous enough, even for a birthday party.

Roast Duck with Cracklings

In this method, the duck is given a preliminary or partial roasting, then a skin peeling and carving; half an hour before serving, the legs finish cooking along with the skin, cut into strips which render their fat and crisp in the oven. The breast meat is warmed briefly in wine and seasonings just before being arranged on the platter with the browned legs and crackling skin. All but the final cooking may be done in advance.

For 6 people

Two 4- to 5-pound (2 to 2¼-kg) ducklings
1 Tb cooking oil
1 medium-size carrot, roughly chopped
1 medium-size onion, roughly chopped
Salt, thyme or sage, 1 bay leaf, ½ cup (1 dL) strong prepared mustard, Dijon type
Generous 1 cup (¼ L) lightly pressed down, fresh nonsweet white bread crumbs
2 Tb duck-roasting fat or melted butter
1 Tb minced shallots or scallions
Pepper
¼ cup (½ dL) or so dry Port or Sercial Madeira

Preliminaries to roasting

Chop the ducks' wings off at the elbows and brown them in cooking oil with the neck, gizzard, and vegetables, in a heavy saucepan, then simmer in water to cover and ½ teaspoon salt for an hour. Drain, degrease, and reserve liquid for sauce later; you should have about ½ cup (1 dL) strong meaty liquid.

Meanwhile, here's a good trick for easy carving (you won't be carving at table with this recipe, but it still makes the duck easier to disjoint): working from inside the duck, sever ball joints where wings join shoulders (as illustrated opposite, top left) and second joints join small of back (opposite, lower left). Again for easy carving, remove wishbone from inside of neck opening and add to duck stock.

Sprinkle inside of duck with ¼ teaspoon salt and a pinch of thyme or sage, and tuck in the bay leaf. Pull out any loose fat from inside neck and cavity. Prick the skin all over on the back and sides (where you see the yellow fat under the skin) with a sharp-pronged fork or trussing needle, but do not go too deep where rosy flesh shows through skin, or the duck juices will seep out and stain the skin as the duck is roasting. To truss the duck, first, push needle through carcass underneath the wings, then come up around one wing, catch the neck skin flap against the backbone (upper right pic-picture); come out over opposite wing, and tie. For the second truss (middle right picture), push needle through underside of drumstick ends, catching the tail piece as you go, come back over tops of drumsticks, and tie. The neatly trussed duck will look like the one in the bottom picture.

🕐 May be prepared for roasting a day in advance.

A preliminary roasting
Preheat oven to 350°F/180°C. Place ducks breast up in roasting pan and set in middle level of preheated oven. Roast 30 to 35 minutes, or until breast meat is just springy to the touch (rather than squashy like raw duck)—this means the breast meat is just rosy and easy to carve, but the legs and thighs (which will cook more later) are still rare.

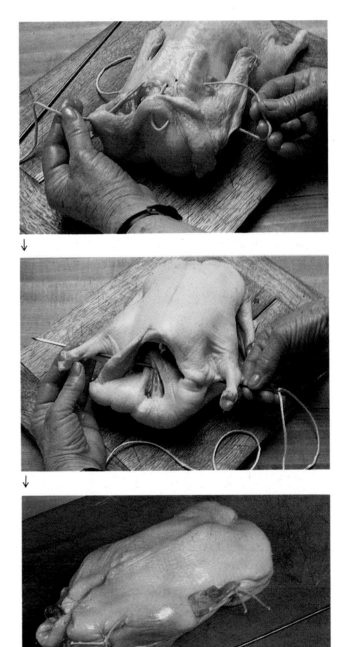

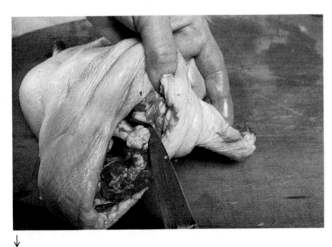

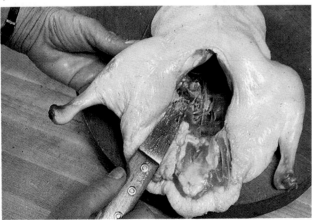

Skinning and carving—preliminaries to final cooking

While the duck is still warm, peel off its skin as follows: cut a slit down the length of the duck on either side of the breastbone, as I've done in the picture below, and remove skin from breast and thighs.

Then cut up the duck as shown in the lower right picture. Remove leg-thigh sections and separate legs from thighs; peel as much skin off them as you easily can, and cut off visible fat. Cut fat and skin into strips ¼ inch (¾ cm) wide and place in a baking dish. Paint legs and thighs with a thin coating of mustard, roll in crumbs, and arrange in another baking dish; sprinkle tops with a dribble of duck-roasting fat or melted butter.

Film a frying pan (not of cast iron) with duck fat or melted butter, sprinkle in half the shallots or scallions, carve the breast meat into neat slices, as illustrated, and arrange in the pan. Season lightly with salt and pepper and sprinkle with the remaining shallots or scallions. Pour in the Port or Madeira and the duck stock from the first paragraph. (You may wish to roast the carcasses and wings—which have little meat—a few minutes more and save for the cook's lunch the next day; that's what I do, at least.)

🕐   May be prepared to this point several hours before serving.

Finishing the ducks

Preheat the oven to 400°F/200°C, and half an hour before you plan to serve dinner, set dishes with crumbed legs and thighs and skin strips in the upper-third level. Roast skin until the pieces have browned nicely and rendered their fat; remove with a slotted spoon to a plate covered with paper toweling to drain; then toss with a sprinkling of salt and pepper. Roast legs until just tender when pressed—about 20 to 25 minutes. Keep both warm in turned-off oven, door ajar, until you are ready to serve. Between courses, as you are changing plates, bring the pan with the duck breast slices barely to the simmer, to poach the meat but keep it the color of a deep blush. Then arrange it on a hot platter and rapidly boil down the cooking juices until syrupy while you arrange the legs and the skin cracklings on the platter; pour the reduced pan juices over the breast meat and serve at once.

Remarks:

I was discussing duck the other day with a restaurant owner who serves a lot of duck to his clientele. He says he puts his in a 250°F/130°C oven and lets them roast slowly for 3 or 4 hours, pricking them several times to drain out the fat. The meat emerges a nice medium rare, the birds exude a lot of fat, and when he is ready to serve he pops them back in the oven, at 550°F/290°C, to brown and crisp the skin. I haven't tried the final crisping, since I fear so hot an oven and its effect on the rosy meat, but the slow roast is certainly easy and painless.

Purée of Parsnips

To go with roast duck, goose, pork, or turkey

For 4 to 6 servings (more than you need for the zucchini boats, but the purée is so good and reheats so well, I am suggesting almost double the necessary amount)

2 pounds (1 kg) parsnips

Salt

5 Tb cream

2 Tb butter

Pepper

Trim and peel the parsnips and cut into slices about ⅓ inch (1 cm) thick. Place in a saucepan with water barely to cover and a teaspoon of salt. Bring to the boil, cover pan, and boil slowly 20 to 30 minutes or until parsnips are tender and water has almost entirely evaporated. Using a vegetable mill or food processor, purée, and return to saucepan. Beat in the cream and butter, and season to taste with salt and pepper. Set pan in another containing simmering water, cover, and let cook 20 to 30 minutes more—note the subtle change in taste that takes place. Correct seasoning before serving.

🕐   May be cooked in advance and reheated over simmering water.

Zucchini Boats

To hold a purée of parsnips or other cooked filling

6 zucchini of uniform size, about 6 inches (15 cm) long

Salt

2 to 3 Tb melted butter

Pepper

Trim stem ends off zucchini and cut zucchini in half lengthwise. Hollow out the centers with a grapefruit knife, leaving a 3/16-inch (scant ¾-cm) border of flesh all around. (Save removed centers for soup.) Drop the boat-shaped zucchini in a large pan of lightly salted boiling water and boil slowly 4 to 5 minutes, or until barely tender—they must hold their shape. Brush with melted butter, season lightly with salt and pepper, and arrange in a roasting pan. Shortly before serving, pour in ¼ inch (¾ cm) water, and bake 4 to 5 minutes in the upper third of a preheated 425°F/220°C oven—to give them a little more flavor, but without letting them overcook and lose their shape.

Assembling

Arrange the hot zucchini boats in a serving dish, and with a pastry bag and cannelated tube, rapidly pipe the hot parsnip purée into them—much more attractive than when they are filled with a spoon. Serve at once.

Broccoli Flowerettes

For 6 people have a good 2 quarts or 2 liters of prepared broccoli—1½ bunches

This doesn't need a full-scale recipe, since broccoli is so easy to cook, but for the freshest-tasting, greenest, slightly crunchy, beautiful broccoli, you do have to peel the stems. Then the broccoli cooks in less than 5 minutes. Here's how to go about it: cut the stems off the broccoli, leaving the bud ends about 2½ inches (6½ cm) long; quarter the bud ends to make them all about 3/16 inch (scant ¾ cm) in diameter. From the cut end, pull off the skin up to the bud section. Peel the stems with a knife, going down to the tender white. Refrigerate in a covered bowl until you are ready to cook the broccoli.

To cook, you may blanch the broccoli ahead, and plunge into boiling water just before serving; or boil between courses, since it cooks so quickly. Bring a very large kettle with 5 to 6 quarts or liters lightly salted water to the rapid boil, drop in the broccoli, cover the kettle, and bring to the boil again over highest heat; as soon as the water boils, remove cover and boil slowly 4 to 5 minutes, just until broccoli is cooked through, slightly crunchy, and a beautiful bright green. Remove at once from the boiling water—a large perforated scoop is useful here. If you are serving immediately, arrange quickly on a platter, seasoning lightly with salt and pepper, the Brown Butter Sauce (see following recipe)—or use melted butter—and drops of lemon juice. (Or you may pre-cook the broccoli until barely tender before dinner and spread it out on a towel to cool rapidly; keep a kettle of fresh salted water at the boil between courses, and plunge the broccoli into the boiling water just before serving, to reheat for a moment; then dress it on the platter as described.)

Brown Butter Sauce:
For 6 servings

Cut 1 stick (4 ounces or 115 g) butter into fairly thin slices—for even melting—and place in a small saucepan over moderate heat, bringing the butter to a boil. Skim off foam as it collects and cook until butter turns a nice nutty brown—this will take only 2 to 3 minutes in all. If serving immediately, spoon over the food, leaving speckled particles in bottom of pan. For later serving, spoon into a clean pan and either reheat or keep over hot water.

The Los Gatos Gâteau Cake

A Dacquoise type of apricot-filled torte

For a 12-by-4-inch cake about 2 inches high, serving 12 to 14

The Meringue-Nut Layers:

¾ cup (1⅓ dL) each toasted and skinned hazelnuts and blanched toasted almonds

1 cup (¼ L) sugar

¾ cup (1¾ dL or 5 to 6) egg whites

Pinch salt and ¼ tsp cream of tartar

3 Tb additional sugar

1 Tb pure vanilla extract

¼ tsp almond extract

Equipment

A blender or food processor; 2 pastry sheets about 12 by 15 inches (30 x 37 cm) each (non-stick recommended); a 14-inch (35-cm) pastry bag with ½-inch (1½-cm) tip opening (recommended); a flexible-blade spatula

Using a blender or food processor, pulverize the hazelnuts with half the sugar, then the almonds with the remaining sugar. Preheat oven to 250°F/120°C, placing racks in upper- and lower-third levels. Butter and flour the pastry sheets, and trace 4 rectangles on them 12 by 4 inches (30 x 10 cm), as I have done here.

Beat the egg whites at slow speed until they have foamed, then beat in the salt and cream of tartar; increase speed gradually to fast, and beat until egg whites form stiff shining peaks. Immediately sprinkle in the remaining 3 tablespoons sugar while beating, add the vanilla and almond extracts, and continue for 30 seconds more. Remove beater from stand and at once sprinkle on the pulverized nuts and sugar, folding them in rapidly with a rubber spatula as you do so. Scoop the meringue into the pastry bag and squeeze out onto the traced rectangles, starting at the edges of each and working inward; smooth with a flexible-blade spatula. (Or spread and smooth with a spatula.) Set in oven and bake about an hour, switching levels every 20 minutes or so. The meringue layers are done when you can gently push them loose; do not force them, since they break easily and will budge only when they are ready to do so. Remove to a rack.

🕐 If not used within an hour or so, keep in a warming oven at 120°F/50°C, or wrap airtight and freeze.

The Apricot Filling:

About 2½ cups (6 dL)

1 pound (450 g) dried apricots

1 cup (¼ L) dry white French vermouth

2 cups (½ L) water

1 stick cinnamon

Zest (colored part of peel) of 1 orange

⅔ cup (1½ dL) sugar

2 Tb orange or apricot liqueur and 1 Tb Cognac or rum

Place the apricots in a saucepan and soak in vermouth and water several hours or overnight until tender. Then simmer with cinnamon and zest of orange for 10 minutes; add the sugar and simmer 10 minutes more or until very tender. Drain thoroughly and purée, using food processor or vegetable mill. Boil down cooking liquid (if any) to a thick syrup, and stir into the purée along with the liqueur.

🕐 May be completed a week or more in advance; cover and refrigerate.

Confectioners Butter Cream:
For 1 to 1½ cups
Make just before using

8 ounces (225 g) unsalted butter

10 ounces (285 g; 2 cups sifted directly into cup) confectioners sugar

2 egg yolks

1 Tb pure vanilla extract

3 to 4 Tb orange or apricot liqueur, Cognac, or rum

Equipment
An electric mixer

Beat the butter in a bowl over hot water just until softened, then beat in the sugar and continue for a minute or so until light and fluffy. Add the egg yolks, beating for 1 minute, then beat in the vanilla and liqueur. If too soft, beat over cold water until of easy spreading consistency.

Assembling the cake
(and additional ingredients)

About 1 cup (¼ L) confectioners sugar in a sieve or shaker

2 cups (about 8 ounces or 240 g) shaved almonds, lightly toasted

Lightly whipped and sweetened cream to pass with the cake (optional)

Equipment
A serving board or tray to hold the cake; wax paper; a flexible-blade spatula; rubber spatulas

The meringue layers break easily, but don't worry if they do; breaks—or San Andreas faults, as one California friend terms them—can be disguised. Save the best one for the top of the cake, 2 more for layers, and the final one is there just in case. Place double layers of wax paper strips on the serving board in such a way that they can be slipped out from sides and ends of cake after icing.

Set the least attractive of the meringue layers on the board, adjusting the wax paper to fit just under its edges. Reserving almost two thirds of the butter filling to ice the sides of the cake, spread half of what remains on the meringue layer, then cover with half of the apricot purée. Set a second meringue layer on top, and repeat with a spreading of butter cream and the remaining apricot. Top with a final meringue layer, and if it is unblemished dust with a coating of confectioners sugar. (If it is irreparably cracked, too much so to be disguised with sugar, ice it with butter cream and later sprinkle with almonds.)

Spread butter cream all around the sides of the cake. Then, with the palm of one hand, brush almonds all around to make an informal decoration. (Scatter almonds also on top, if you have the San Andreas fault to deal with.) Chill the cake—you may wish to cover it with a long box.

🕐   May be refrigerated for a day or two; the meringue layers gradually soften as the cake sits. Cake may be frozen; thaw in the refrigerator for several hours.

Serving

Cut cake into serving pieces from one of the small ends; a dollop of lightly whipped cream on the side goes nicely with the tart apricot filling.

Remarks:

This recipe allows for a good amount of butter cream, and you may wish to set a little aside. Then, if a reasonable amount of cake is left over, you can refrost the cut end and present, for all the world, a fresh new cake for its next go-around. As an aid to keeping the meringue-nut layers more crisp, you could paint the top of the bottom one, both sides of the middle one, and the bottom of the top layer with the following apricot glaze, letting it set for several minutes before filling the cake.

Apricot Glaze:

Boil up the contents of a 12-ounce (340-g) jar of apricot preserves with 3 tablespoons sugar, stirring, until last drops from a spoon are thick and sticky—and glaze reaches 238°F/115°C. Push through a sieve and use while still warm; return any left over to jar and keep for future glazings.

The fourth meringue layer

If you are sure of your layer stability, you can pulverize this one and either stir it into your apricot purée, or save it for a dessert topping as in the Floating Island, page 58. Or freeze it, and when you want finger cookies, cut it into crosswise strips with a serrated knife, sawing gently; cover with a sifting of confectioners sugar, or the icing of your choice.

🕐 Timing

This is a relatively fancy meal and involves quite a bit of work, but not much has to be done at the last minute. You can accomplish most of your marketing days in advance. The meringue-nut layers can be baked months beforehand if you freeze them, and the apricots can be cooked a week or more ahead. Just don't forget to thaw your ducks.

You'll need only about five minutes between first and second courses to crisp the duck cracklings and warm the breast slices; and just a moment before the third course to finish the broccoli if you have blanched it in advance.

Not long before announcing dinner, slip the dishes containing legs and skin strips into the oven. They can have sat an hour all prepared, and so can the breasts in their frying pan. You should get your wine bottles ready for evening, chill your whites, two hours before dinner.

Pre-roast, peel, and carve the ducks, if you're doing them the slow way, in the afternoon.

Early on the day of the party, you can assemble the cake and refrigerate it, purée the parsnips, and blanch the broccoli and the zucchini boats.

Menu Variations

The appetizer: Rather than crab you could serve caviar, or any shellfish: mussels, oysters, clams, scallops, shrimp, lobster. (See "Fish Talk," page 111.)

The main course: The ragout with garlic (bonus recipe) is wonderful, and very easy to serve, but you'd have to change your vegetables accordingly, as the recipe suggests. With the roast, you could omit the zucchini boats and just serve a plain parsnip purée in a dish, but no other way of cooking parsnips would suit roast duck so well. You might substitute a purée of turnips, celery root, or potatoes for the parsnips.

The vegetable course: This is probably the ideal way to cook broccoli. Any sauce but butter and lemon would be too rich on this menu, and a Polonaise garnish of browned crumbs and sieved egg would repeat the crumbs on the duck parts.

The dessert: You could fill your baked layers with puréed dried prunes. Or you could use very stiff, wine-flavored applesauce.

Leftovers

The appetizer: Since the crab is already seasoned, I wouldn't try it in a hot dish, but it would make fine stuffing for hard-boiled eggs or delicious sandwiches.

The main dish: Duck scraps are good in soup, or in a pilaff, or sauced in cocktail puffs or patty shells with drinks. Paul and I like to make a cannibal lunch for ourselves, picking the carcass (which I've roasted 15 to 20 minutes after its bloody carving). Then it goes into the stockpot.

The vegetable course: If you passed the lemon and butter sauce separately, any remaining unseasoned broccoli would be nice in a salad, soup, or timbale.

The dessert: Since I make a rectangular rather than round cake, I save a bit of butter cream, then beat up the butter cream to soften it, refrost the cut end of the cake as described earlier, and serve it again.

Postscript

The keynote of this dinner is flavor, and the duck dominates. If you think about this menu, you'll see that every dish on it was carefully chosen to contrast, in taste and color, with the duck—except the parsnips, which are such a good accompaniment to the bird that the two flavors almost combine in the mouth. Duck deserves this sort of "feature presentation." Having devised a way of dealing with its eccentricities, I serve it much oftener now, as the centerpiece of a luxurious dinner—as well as the grand main course for a plain family dinner. Duck has so much natural flavor and succulence that it is really one of my favorite meat treats.

Post-Postscript: A birthday bonus recipe

The following recipe is totally different in flavor from the roast duck preceding, is very little trouble to do, and is quite good reheated. For a larger birthday party, say 10 to 12 people, I think this would be tidier to serve. I'd buy 3 ducks and increase all the recipe proportions to match. With it I'd serve broccoli flowerettes and baked baby tomatoes, and perhaps a purée of some sort (like the parsnips recipe above, or a purée of turnips or rutabagas, or the potato-and-turnip purée in *Mastering I),* or instead of a purée, a mixture of steamed rice sautéed with little mushroom *duxelles,* or plain mashed potatoes. You would never know how much garlic this lovely duck dish contains if the cook didn't tell you. I wouldn't even call this a "garlic sauce"—it's just a satiny, full-flavored nap for the duck meat.

Ragout of Duck with Twenty Cloves of Garlic

For 4 servings

A 4- to 5-pound (2- to 2¼-kg) duckling

1 head garlic, unpeeled, separated into cloves and roughly chopped

2 medium-size ripe tomatoes

1 Tb tomato sauce (if needed for taste and color)

Herbs and spices: 4 whole allspice berries, ½ tsp fennel seeds, ½ tsp thyme, 1 imported bay leaf

½ cup (1 dL) dry white French vermouth

1 cup (¼ L) brown duck stock or beef bouillon

Salt and pepper

Parsley sprigs

Preliminaries

Split the duck down the back on both sides of backbone and reserve backbone for duck stock, along with wing ends, which you sever at the elbows. Cut the peel off the gizzard and add to stock ingredients along with the neck. Cut the duck into 4 pieces, giving more breast meat to the wing portions than to the leg portions to even things out. Cut off and discard fatty skin pieces and any interior fat. If you wish to do so—and it makes the best sauce— prepare a duck stock by sautéing the backbone, wing, neck, and gizzard peel with ½ cup (1 dL) each chopped onions and carrots; when lightly browned, drain off fat, add water to cover, salt lightly, simmer for an hour, strain, and degrease.

Browning and simmering the duck

Prick the skin of the duck pieces all over at ½-inch (1½-cm) intervals and brown very slowly on all sides in a heavy chicken fryer or casserole, concentrating especially on the skin sides to render out as much fat as possible. Then drain out fat, add the unpeeled garlic cloves, tomatoes and optional tomato sauce, herbs, spices, vermouth, and stock to the pan, and season lightly with salt and pepper. Bring to the simmer, cover, and simmer slowly for about an hour, turning and basting occasionally, until duck leg and wing meat is just tender when pierced with a sharp-pronged fork. Remove from heat and let cool for 10 minutes or so, basting occasionally.

Remove duck pieces from pan, cut off the skin, and cut skin into strips. Sauté the strips slowly in a covered pan until they brown lightly, crisp, and render their fat; drain on paper towels and reserve. Meanwhile, thoroughly degrease the cooking liquid and strain it, pushing the garlic against the sieve to purée it into the liquid; boil down rapidly until sauce is lightly thickened. Return duck pieces to sauce and heat briefly, basting, to warm them. Carefully correct seasoning of sauce, and the duck is ready to serve.

🕐 May be done somewhat in advance, if you keep the duck pieces barely warm in their sauce, and reheat to the simmer just before serving.

Serving

Arrange duck on a platter and spoon the sauce over it. Decorate with parsley sprigs and sprinkle cracklings over the duck (you may wish to include the duck's liver, sautéed as the cracklings cook).

For unspecified numbers, at unpredictable hours, a festive but practical menu. One of its minor components is the Perfectly Peelable HB Egg, on which there is new news.

Holiday Lunch

Menu

Chicken Melon, or Poulet de Charente â la Melonaise
Rosie's Great Potato Salad
Mayonnaise in the Food Processor
Skewered Vegetable Salad
Boston or Butter Lettuce Salad

❧

Apple Turnover

❧

Suggested wines:
Beaujolais, Côtes du Rhône, Zinfandel, or a very good rosé

The thing is, we'd forgotten tomorrow was a holiday when we started asking people to lunch. Naturally it turned out they all were expecting houseguests, or children back from college with friends and about four sets of plans apiece. "See, Ma, if Johnny can get his clutch fixed he'll give us a ride back, but if he can't we'll have to take the two o'clock if you could just give us a lift over" kind of thing. Of course I said to the distracted ma's, "Well, come when you can, and bring whom you please," and thought no more about it until yesterday, when Paul pointed out that what we propose to do is feed lunch to anywhere from 6 to 20 guests, any time from noon until three.

It therefore follows, with cast-iron logic, that I am now doing funny things with chickens. Like most cooks, I tot up the limitations first, then look at the remaining possibilities. Six to 20 guests may mean huge leftovers; mustn't waste. We blew ourselves to veal on Monday, so we can't spend the moon today. We want to feel free tomorrow, so we cook now. We don't know all these friends-of-friends or their tastes: what does everybody like? And what is nobody allergic to? So far, a "made dish" (as opposed to a roast or sauté) of chicken looks a good answer. *But* it can't be hot, or it would dry out in three hours; and it can't be chilled, like an aspic, because the non-melting kind is rubbery. And we want the serving platter to stay attractive while under attack during a three-hour span.

However: the possibilities. Our friend Rosie the salad whiz is visiting us. We do have our faithful food processor, and Paul says he'll shell pistachio nuts and peel apples. Most of our friends' kids, home from cafeterialand, appreciate fancy food as never before.

So, our menu. Nothing could be more classical, or classier, than chicken boned to make *pâté* and roasted to a lovely color, and it feeds a lot of people. One could do it in the traditional *ballottine* shape, like a log; but you don't need calculus to see that the optimum form, with most volume to least surface, is a sphere. So a round, melon-shaped *pâté* it will be. I'll do three, keep one in reserve, put one, uncut, in the middle of my big round platter, then slice the third and make a wreath of perfect, even sections. No carving, no mess; and, if only half the people come, I'll have another party.

It won't take the three of us long to fix this festive meal, and right now the kitchen is a hive of industry. Rosie, with an artist's eye and a potter's deft hand, is preparing the makings of her three salads, each the last word of its kind: vegetable, lettuce, and potato. Perched on a high stool with a bowl in his lap, Paul is briskly popping pistachio shells for the tiny green kernels that look so pretty and crunch so nicely in a *pâté.* Every so often he darts a glance out the window: one of the resident

squirrels, extra lithe or extra smart, knows a way into the bird feeder. Sometimes we scold him, but mostly, I admit, we bribe him; and he loves pistachios. "Here, you rogue," and Paul flips one out.

I've boned and defleshed the chickens' skins and sewn each into a loose pouch. In goes the stuffing, nuts and all, while Paul starts peeling apples for the dessert. The chickens did look odd, bereft of shape; but now, tied in their cheesecloth corsets, they're firming up. Then the string: each loop, like a natural rib, reinforces the melon form. *Fathoms of string… can do most anything…* I find myself humming to "I Get a Kick Out of You," and realize suddenly that Cole Porter, as usual, got the tune right; but it took a cook to discover the real words. I have a Thing about String…

"So you have," says Rosie. "Why not decorate your turnover to look like a fat, well-tied parcel?"

Preparations

Recommended Equipment:
Knives and knife sharpening

To make Chicken Melon (see recipe), a sharp boning knife, white string, a trussing or mattress needle, and cheesecloth are essential. Especially important is the knife: if it won't cut like a razor, the boning and defleshing of a chicken are a horrendous if not impossible undertaking. You want a stout sharp-pointed knife, and I like a slightly curved 6-inch (15-cm) blade for this type of work. You should also have the proper sharpening equipment, since no knife, however fine its quality, will keep an edge—it will only take an edge. Get yourself, therefore, a proper butcher's steel, the kind with a foot-long (30-cm) rod of finely ridged steel set into a handle. To sharpen the knife, sweep its blade from its handle end to its tip down the length of the steel, holding the blade at a 20-degree angle—the movement is as though the steel were a long pencil that you were sharpening. Give a half-dozen swipes down one side, then down the other, and that should hone the blade to perfect cut-ability. For very dull knives, however, you should also have a carborundum oil stone, fine on one side and a little rougher on the other; use the same general technique first on the rough side, then on the smooth, and finish up on your butcher's steel.

Disagreement note

Some practitioners sharpen their knives in the other direction on the theory that this realigns the molecules in the steel. In my system you are pushing the steel back from the cutting edge to make it sharp. Both systems seem to work and if I have a particularly dull knife I sharpen it both ways, hoping for results.

Marketing and Storage:
Staples to have on hand
(Quantities for 6 people)

Salt
Black and white peppercorns (see Remarks, page 82)
Nutmeg
Fragrant dried tarragon
Optional: powdered cinnamon
Mustard (the strong Dijon type; see Remarks, page 5)
Cider vinegar and wine vinegar
Crisp dill pickles (1 small)
Canned pimiento
Chicken broth (½ cup or 1 dL)
Fresh olive, peanut, and/or salad oil ▼
Ingredients for a *vinaigrette* dressing ▼
Unsalted butter (12 ounces or 340 g)
Heavy cream (1 cup or ¼ L ; and more if desired to accompany dessert)
Eggs (12)
All-purpose flour (unbleached preferred)
Plain bleached cake flour
Granulated sugar

Lemons (1)
Onions (1)
Celery (1 stalk)
"Boiling" potatoes (3 pounds or 1½ kg)
Shallots or scallions
Curly parsley, chives, and/or other fresh herbs
Recommended: flat-leaf parsley
Cognac

Specific ingredients for this menu
(Quantities for 6 people)

Roasting chicken or capon (6 to 7 pounds or
    2¾ to 3¼ kg) ▼
Boned and skinned chicken breast (1, or
    possibly 2) ▼
Boiled ham (¼ pound or 115 g)
Pistachio nuts (4 ounces or 115 g)
Boston or butter lettuce (2 heads)
Cooking apples (4 or 5) ▼
For the skewered salad, select among the
    following:
Artichokes
Avocados
Cherry tomatoes
Cucumbers
Mushrooms
Onions (small white)
Peppers (bell type: green, red, or both)
Potatoes (small new)
Topinambours (Jerusalem artichokes or
    sunchokes)
Turnips
Zucchini

▶ *Remarks:*
Staples
Olive, peanut, and salad oils: These may be
used singly or in combination; just be sure
your oil is fresh and of best quality.
Homemade vinaigrette dressing: See page 205
for recipe.
Ingredients for this menu
Chicken: If you don't think yours is plump
enough to supply 4 cups (1 L) ground meat
after boning, buy an additional skinless,
boneless chicken breast. *Cooking apples:* See
recipe for varieties, and check page 40 for
background information.

Chicken Melon

*Boned and stuffed chicken formed, in its
own skin, into a pâté the shape of a
melon.*

You can perform this operation on a small
frying chicken, but it is far more impressive,
and serves far more people, when you find
yourself a large roaster or capon. In fact, there
is no reason why you could not use the same
system on a turkey—but heaven knows how
long a 20-pound (10-kilo) bird would take in
the oven. Not me! (My fanciful French title,
Poulet de Charente à la Melonaise, was
suggested by the small sweet spring melons
from the Charente district of France, plus a
corruption of *à la Milanaise,* a classical appel-
lation from the old school designating a cheesy
Italianesque concoction from the region of
Milan. Of course, this chicken contains neither
melon nor cheese, but it might describe to a
knowing gastronome some conception of the
dish. We have to have a little fun with this sort
of thing, I think!)

For 14 to 16 servings

A 6- to 7-pound (2¾- to 3¼-kg) roasting chicken or capon

For the stuffing
To make about 5 cups (1¼ liters)

4 cups (1 L) ground chicken meat—salvaged from the boned chicken, plus 1 or more skinless and boneless chicken-breast halves if needed

1 whole egg plus 1 egg white

1½ tsp salt

9 grinds of the pepper mill

2 Tb minced shallots or scallions

A big speck nutmeg

½ tsp fragrant dried tarragon

2 to 3 Tb Cognac

1 cup (¼ L) chilled heavy cream

Garniture for the stuffing

1 chicken breast, cut into ¼-inch (¾-cm) dice

⅔ cup (1½ dL) boiled ham, diced as above

5 Tb shelled pistachio nuts

Salt and pepper

1 Tb finely minced shallots or scallions

1 Tb Cognac

Pinch fragrant dried tarragon

Other ingredients

Salt and pepper

Drops of Cognac

Several Tb melted butter

Equipment

A very sharp boning knife; a large ball of plain white string (butcher's corned-beef twine); a trussing needle—a mattress or sail-makers needle; a square of washed cheesecloth about 20 inches (50 cm) to a side

Boning the chicken

Your object here is to remove the carcass from the chicken leaving the skin intact except at the openings at the back vent and the neck and along the backbone. The meat of the chicken will go into your stuffing, and the skin will be the container for the *pâté* mixture. Proceed as follows.

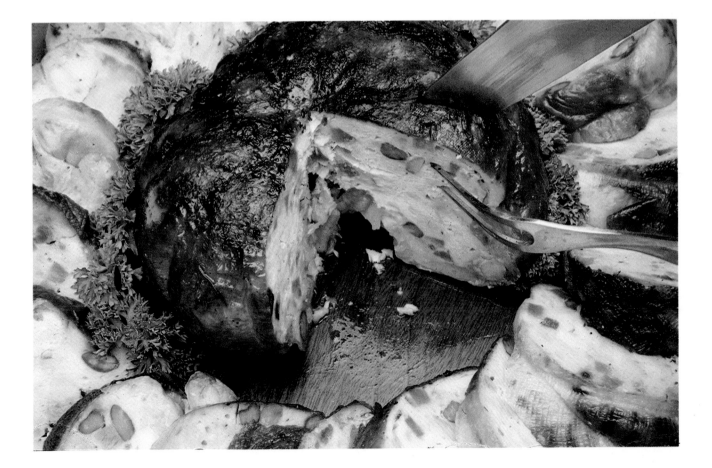

First, for easy removal of meat from skin after boning, slip your fingers between meat and skin at the neck opening, and loosen skin all around breast, thighs, and as far down the drumsticks as you can—being careful not to tear the skin.

Then turn the chicken on its side and make a slit down the backbone from neck end to tail end. One side at a time, scrape down backbone, severing ball joints of wings at shoulder and of thigh at small of back and continuing down rib cage and side of breastbone until you come near its edge, at top of breast. Stop! Skin is very thin over ridge of breastbone and easily pierced. Do the same on the other side. Finally lift carcass and scrape close under ridge of breastbone (not against skin) to free the carcass. To remove wing and leg bones easily, chop off wings above elbows and chop ball joints off ends of drumsticks. Then remove

wing, thigh, and drumstick bones from inside the chicken, poking their skin sleeves inside out onto flesh side of chicken. Carefully cut and pull as much of the meat as you can from the chicken skin without piercing it. Sprinkle inside of chicken skin with a little salt and drops of Cognac. Reserve bones and carcass for chicken stock. Dice one breast-meat half and reserve for stuffing garniture, using second breast half and rest of meat to grind up for stuffing.

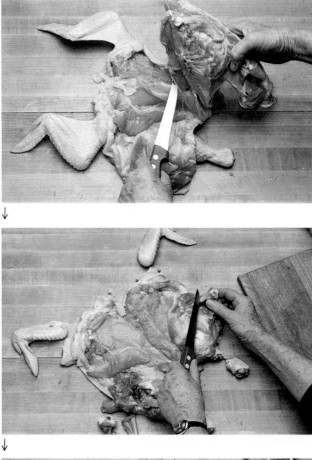

↓

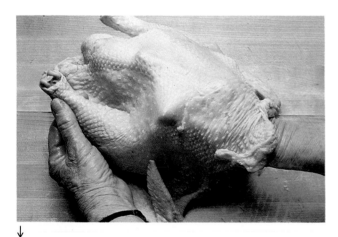

↓

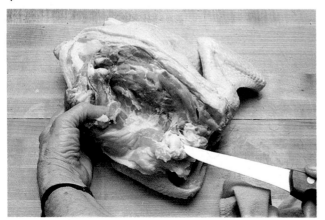

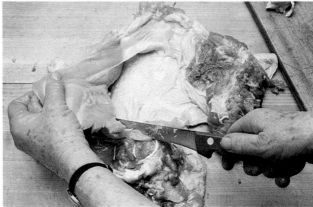

The stuffing
(If you do not have a food processor, grind up the meat, then beat in the rest of the ingredients.) Cut the meat into 1-inch (2½-cm) pieces and purée in the processor in 2 or 3 batches. Then return all to food processor, add the rest of the ingredients listed for the stuffing, and purée for a minute or so until finely ground. Sauté a spoonful in a small frying pan, taste, and add more seasoning if you think it necessary. Toss the garniture chicken, ham, pistachios, and seasonings in a bowl and let sit until you are ready to stuff the chicken, then fold into the stuffing.

Stuffing the chicken
Thread your trussing needle with a good 16 inches (40 cm) of string, and you are now ready to make a pouch, with drawstring, of the chicken skin. To do so, sew a loose basting stitch around the circumference of the chicken skin and draw up the two ends of the string slightly to make an open pouch. Fill the pouch with the stuffing (not too full), pull the string taut, and tie. Dip the cheesecloth square into melted butter, spread out on your work surface, and place the chicken, tie side up, in the middle. Tie the 2 opposite corners of cheesecloth together over the chicken, then the other 2 ends, to enclose the chicken in a ball shape. Cut off extra cheesecloth. Then, always from the central tie, wind successive rounds of string around the ball to make the melon pattern. (Hold one end of string taut as a guideline and twist free end about it to secure each loop as you wind it around the chicken.) Chicken is now ready to roast.

🕐 May be prepared a day in advance and refrigerated; may be frozen, but thaw before roasting.

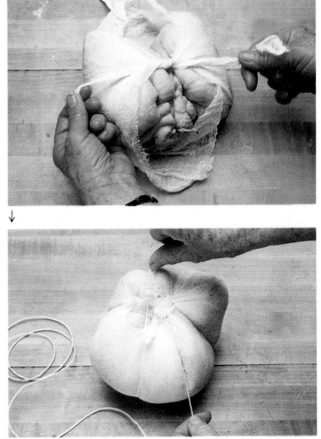

Roasting and serving

(So that chicken will brown nicely on the top as well as the bottom, but so that it will not lose its juices, start it tie side down and turn after 25 to 30 minutes, before any juices have managed to escape from that side.) Preheat oven to 350°F/180°C. Set chicken tie side down on a lightly buttered pie dish and roast in middle level of oven for 25 to 30 minutes to brown top nicely, then turn tie side up for the rest of the roasting. Baste occasionally with accumulated fat in dish. Chicken is done at a thermometer reading of 170°F/77°C. (Total cooking time is 1½ to 2 hours.) Remove and let rest 20 minutes, then carefully ease off the cheesecloth and string without tearing chicken skin.

Serve hot with pan juices and *béarnaise* sauce. Or let cool to room temperature, cover, and chill; serve as you would a *pâté*, as part of a cold lunch or as the first course for a dinner. To carve, cut into wedges, starting from the center, as though cutting a thick pie.

Rosie's Great Potato Salad

After Rosie had tried a number of off-beat combinations and additions, hoping that the best possible salad might be something unusual, she concluded that the thing to aim at was that old-fashioned taste where the potatoes dominate and where there is just enough onion, the right amount of celery for a bit of crunch, enough eggs for their subtle effect, plus a light but sufficient binding and melding with the best mayonnaise. Here is her recipe.

*For about 2 quarts (2 liters),
serving 6 to 8*

3 pounds (1½ kg) "boiling" potatoes, the type that will keep their shape when cooked and sliced—such as round red potatoes or new potatoes

½ cup (1 dL) chicken broth mixed with 2 to 3 Tb cider vinegar

Salt and pepper

1 medium-size to large mild onion, finely diced

1 medium-size stalk celery, finely diced

1 small crisp dill pickle, finely diced

3 hard-boiled eggs, diced

2 Tb minced fresh parsley, preferably the flat-leaf variety

1 canned pimiento, diced

½ to ¾ cup (1–1¾ dL) homemade mayonnaise (see next recipe)

For decoration

Strips of canned pimiento

Parsley and/or chives

Sliced or quartered hard-boiled eggs (see recipe at end of chapter)

Scrub the potatoes and boil in their jackets, in lightly salted water, just until tender (halve a potato and eat a slice to be sure). Then drain off water, cover pan, and let sit for 5 minutes to let them firm up and to make for easier slicing. Peel while still warm and cut into slices about 3/16 inch (¾ cm) thick. Toss the still-warm potatoes gently in a large mixing bowl with the broth and with salt and pepper to taste. Salt the diced onion lightly and add to the potatoes along with the celery, pickle, eggs, parsley, and pimiento. Toss and fold gently to blend flavors. Taste carefully and correct seasoning. When cool, fold in two-thirds of the mayonnaise, saving the rest for decoration.

🕐 May be made a day in advance; cover and refrigerate.

An hour or so before you are ready to serve, taste again for seasoning and turn the salad into a nice bowl; mask the top with the remaining mayonnaise and decorate with pimiento, herbs, and eggs.

Remarks:

Rosie suggests, when you are making larger quantities, that you toss the equivalent of the above ingredients in a mixing bowl (or several bowls), turn that into a larger bowl, and continue with the same amount, adding each batch as you do it to the larger bowl. This way you can easily manage the potatoes and the perfection of the seasoning without breaking the slices.

Mayonnaise in the Food Processor

Certainly the easiest way to make mayonnaise is in the food processor, where in 2 or 3 minutes you have 2 or 3 cups (or ½ liter). Regardless of method, the best mayonnaise is made from the freshest and best ingredients, since nothing can disguise a cheap-tasting oil, a harsh vinegar, or a fake lemon.

For about 2 ¼ cups (½ liter)

1 whole egg
2 egg yolks
1 tsp strong prepared mustard (Dijon type)
½ tsp or more salt
1 Tb or more fresh lemon juice or wine vinegar
2 cups best-quality light olive oil, salad oil, or fresh peanut oil—all one kind or a combination
White pepper

Using the metal blade (I never use the plastic one for anything), process the egg, yolks, mustard, and ½ teaspoon salt for 30 seconds. Then add 1 tablespoon lemon juice or vinegar and process half a minute more. Finally, in a very thin stream, pour in the oil. When all has gone in, remove cover, check consistency, and taste for seasoning: you will probably want to beat in a little more lemon juice or vinegar, and salt and white pepper, but you can also beat in driblets of cold water for a milder and lighter taste and texture.

Remarks:

The purpose of the whole egg here is to dilute the thickening capacity of the yolks, since if you have all yolks the mayonnaise stiffens so much in the machine you cannot add the full amount of oil. However, you can thin the sauce with droplets of water rather than egg white. The proportions I use are 3 yolks for every 2 cups or ½ liter of oil, and, in the processor, 1 egg white.

Turned, or thinned-out, mayonnaise: I am not always successful with the processor when I have a badly thinned-out mayonnaise. (This sometimes happens when the mayonnaise has been kept in too cold a refrigerator: the emulsion property of the egg yolks has broken down, and they release the oil from suspension.) To restore the mayonnaise it has to be reconstituted bit by bit, and because the processor can't manage a small enough quantity initially to begin the homogenizing and reconstituting process, I've had more luck bringing the sauce back by hand or in an electric blender. I suggest that you start with a half tablespoon of Dijon-type prepared mustard and a tablespoon of thinned-out mayonnaise and beat vigorously in a bowl or blender until the mixture has thickened; then beat in the thinned-out sauce by driblets—it is the very slow addition of the sauce, particularly at first, that brings it back to its thick emulsified state.

Freezing homemade mayonnaise: It often happens to me that I've a nice jar of homemade mayonnaise in my refrigerator and then we go off somewhere on a vacation. I've found that I can freeze it, let it defrost in the refrigerator, and then reconstitute it just as though it were the thinned-out mayonnaise in the preceding paragraph.

Using frozen egg yolks for mayonnaise: Thaw the egg yolks at room temperature or overnight in the refrigerator. Then whip them in an electric blender or food processor (if you have enough for the food processor—4 or 5 at least), adding a tablespoon of prepared mustard and another of lemon juice or vinegar, and proceed as usual.

Skewered Salad

Vegetable salad en brochettes

This attractive way to serve salad vegetables makes it easy for guests,who pick up a skewered collection and bear it off on their plates. Use any combination of cooked and raw vegetables that appeals to you and will skewer successfully. Be sure, however, to use skewers with flat sides or double prongs, or two skewers per serving; the vegetables must hang in there, and the skewer must be solid enough to stay rigid from platter to plate. I find it best to prepare each vegetable separately and then marinate it in dressing long enough for it to pick up the desired taste, but not so long as to wilt it. Green vegetables and tomatoes, for instance, can wilt, while potatoes and topinambours will thrive in a dressing. Skewer the vegetables half an hour or so before your guests arrive, arrange in a platter, cover, and refrigerate. Just before serving, spoon on a little more dressing and sprinkle on finely minced fresh herbs, such as parsley and chives, or whatever other herbal delight your garden offers, like fresh chervil, tarragon, or basil. Here are some vegetable choices that have been successfully skewered in our house. (See index for various dressings.)

Artichokes: hearts or bottoms, cooked in a *blanc* (as described on page 203) and halved or quartered, depending on size. Toss in the dressing half an hour or longer before skewering.

Avocados: skewered at the last minute. However, avocado chunks will hold quite nicely if you dip them first for a moment in a solution of cold water and lemon juice, in the proportions of 1 tablespoon of lemon juice for 8 of water.

Cherry tomatoes: either impaled whole, as is, or halved and tossed in dressing just before skewering.

Cucumbers: peeled, halved lengthwise, seeded, and cut into chunks. I always marinate them first for 20 minutes or longer in a little salt, a pinch of sugar, and droplets of wine vinegar (1/4 teaspoon salt, 1/8 teaspoon sugar, and 1/2 teaspoon vinegar per cucumber).

Mushrooms: use small caps or quartered large caps and drop for 1 minute in boiling water with lemon and salt to keep them fresh-looking. Toss in the dressing and leave for an hour, or more if you wish, before skewering.

Onions: the very small white ones. Drop into boiling water for 1/2 minute, then peel and simmer until just tender in lightly

salted water. Marinate for as long as you wish in the dressing.

Peppers: either green or red, halved, seeded, and cut into 1-inch (2½-cm) pieces. Drop them for 1 minute into boiling water just to soften slightly, then drain. Toss in dressing just before skewering.

Potatoes: small new ones. Boil in their skins in lightly salted water, just until tender. Peel or not, as you wish. Marinate while still warm in your dressing for as long as you like. (You wouldn't need potatoes when serving potato salad, of course, but they are good on skewers—be sure you have the waxy boiling kind or they will break up when pierced.)

Topinambours (Jerusalem artichokes or sunchokes): cook them in a *blanc* (as described on page 203) and toss while still warm in the dressing, letting them marinate for as long as you wish.

Turnips: white turnips or even the yellow rutabaga. Peel, cut into appropriate-size chunks, and boil in lightly salted water until just tender. Toss while still warm in the dressing, letting them marinate for as long as you wish.

Zucchini: scrub them, trim the two ends, but do not peel them. Boil whole in lightly salted water until barely tender. Cube them. Toss in dressing half an hour or so before serving.

Boston or Butter Lettuce Salad

Rosie very carefully separates each perfect leaf from the central stem, washes the leaves with care in a basin of water, drains them on a towel or in the dish drainer, then gently surrounds them with clean towels and a plastic bag, and refrigerates them. Half an hour or so before serving, she arranges them stem down and smallest leaves in the center in a big bowl, so that the salad looks like an enormous head of lettuce sitting there. She covers the bowl with plastic wrap and refrigerates it, and just before serving she dribbles a *vinaigrette* dressing, such as the one on page 205, all around and over the leaves. No tossing is necessary, and serving is easy since one picks up the leaves without disturbing the design—at least until near the end.

Apple Turnover

I am particularly fond of the free-form turn-over, since one can make it any size and shape, from mini to gargantua. Round is pretty, but either square or rectangular is more practical because it uses less dough and the leftovers are evenly shaped and therefore easily turned into decorations.

For 1 large turnover about 9 by 9 inches (23 x 23 cm), serving 6 to 8

Sweet pie dough
Pâte brisée fine, sucrée

1½ cups (215 g) all-purpose flour, unbleached preferred

½ cup (70 g) plain bleached cake flour

1½ sticks (6 ounces or 170 g) chilled unsalted butter and 2 Tb shortening

2 Tb sugar

¼ tsp salt

½ cup (1 dL), more or less, iced water

Other ingredients for the turnover

4 or 5 apples that will keep their shape in cooking, such as Golden Delicious, Rome Beauty, Newton, Monroe, Northern Spy

3 Tb or more sugar

½ tsp, more or less, powdered cinnamon (optional)

The grated rind and the juice of ½ lemon (optional)

1 Tb or more melted butter

Egg glaze (1 egg beaten in a cup with 1 tsp water)

Equipment

A food processor is dandy for making the dough; a rolling pin; a buttered pastry sheet; a pastry brush for glazing the tart

The dough

Of course you can make the dough by hand or in an electric mixer, but the food processor is sensationally fast and foolproof using these proportions. Proceed as follows: with metal blade in place, measure the flours into the bowl of the machine, cut the butter rapidly into pieces the size of your little-finger joint, and drop into the flour, along with the sugar, shortening, and salt. Using the on-off flick technique lasting ½ second, process 7 to 8 flicks, just to start breaking up the butter. Then, with water poised over opening of machine, turn it on and pour in all but 1 tablespoon of the iced water. Process in spurts, on and off, just until dough begins to mass together but is still rough with some unformed bits. Turn it out onto your work surface and mass together rapidly with the heel of one hand into a somewhat rough cake. (Dough should be pliable—neither dry and hard nor, on the other hand, sticky. Pat in sprinkles more of all-purpose flour if sticky; cut into pieces and sprinkle on droplets more water if dry and hard, then re-form into a cake.) Wrap in plastic and refrigerate for at least an hour, to congeal the butter in the dough so that it will roll easily, and to allow the flour particles to absorb the water so that it will handle nicely and bake properly.

🕐   May be made 2 or 3 days in advance and refrigerated—but if you have used unbleached flour it will gradually turn grayish; it can still be baked at that point if only mildly discolored since it will whiten in the oven. Or freeze the dough, which is the best plan when you want to have ready dough available; defrost at room temperature or overnight in the refrigerator— dough should be cold and firm for easy rolling.

The apples

Quarter, core, and peel the apples, then cut into thinnish lengthwise slices. Toss in a mixing bowl with sugar and optional cinnamon and lemon rind and juice. Cover with plastic wrap and let macerate for 20 minutes or longer, so that apples will exude their excess juices.

Forming the turnover
(Always work rapidly from here on to prevent the dough from softening; if it becomes difficult to handle, refrigerate it at once for 20 minutes or so, then continue.) Roll the chilled dough into a rectangle 20 inches long and 10 inches wide (50 x 25 cm) and trim off the edges with a pastry wheel or a knife—refrigerate trimmings for decorations later. Lightly flour surface of dough, fold in half end to end, and center on the buttered pastry sheet. Place a piece of wax paper at edge of fold, and unfold top of dough onto paper. Paint a border of cold water around the 3 edges of the bottom piece and pile the apples onto it, leaving a ¾-inch (2-cm) border free at the 3 edges. Sprinkle on more sugar, and a tablespoon or so of melted butter. Flip top of dough over onto the apples, and press edges firmly together, to seal. Turn up the 3 edges all around, then press a design into them (to seal further) with the tines of a table fork and, if you wish, press a decorative edging all around those sides with the back of a knife.

🕐   If you have time, it is a good idea at this point to refrigerate the turnover (covered lightly with plastic wrap) for half an hour (or for several hours); it will bake more evenly when the dough has had time to relax, and you, in turn, will have time to turn your leftover bits of dough into a mock puff pastry which will rise into a splendid design.

Mock puff pastry decorations
(For massed scraps about the size of a half tennis ball)
Knead leftover raw pastry scraps briefly into a cake, roll into a rectangle, and spread 1 teaspoon of butter down two-thirds of its length. Fold into 3 as though folding a business letter; repeat with another roll-out, buttering, and fold-up. Wrap and refrigerate for 20 to 30 minutes, then roll and fold (but omit butter) 2 more times. For the simple decorations I used on this turnover, roll out again into a rectangle about 10 inches (25 cm) long, and cut into 5 strips about ¼ inch (¾ cm) wide. Refrigerate, covered, until ready to use.

Decorating and baking the turnover

Preheat oven to 400°F/200°C. Paint top of turnover lightly with cold water. To simulate wrapping ribbon for your turnover "parcel," crisscross 2 strips of dough, laying them from corner to corner; lay 1 crosswise from top to bottom, and a final one horizontally, as shown. Loop the final strip into a loose knot and place on top. Pierce 2 steam holes 1/16 inch (¼ cm) in diameter in top of dough with the point of a knife, going down through the dough to the apples. Paint top of dough and decorations with a coating of egg glaze, wait a moment, and paint on another coat. (Egg glaze goes on just the moment before baking.) Make crosshatchings in the glaze with the back of a knife or the tines of a table fork—to give it a more interesting texture when baked.

Set turnover in the middle level of pre-heated oven and bake for 20 minutes, then check to see if it is browning too much. It bakes 35 to 40 minutes in all, and does best at high heat so the pastry will crisp; if it seems to be cooking too fast, turn oven down a little and/or cover top of turnover loosely with foil. It is done when bottom has browned nicely and when juices begin to bubble out of steam holes. Remove from oven and slide it out onto a rack. Serve hot, warm, or cold. You may wish to accompany the turnover with vanilla ice cream, fresh cream, lightly whipped and sweetened cream, or custard sauce.

Remarks:

Other sizes, other fillings. You can, of course, make turnovers any size and shape you wish, and you can use all sorts of fillings as long as they are not too juicy. Always macerate fresh fruit first with sugar and lemon to force out their excess juices, and a very juicy fruit should first be cooked. Canned fruits or jams bake well in turnovers, as do all sorts of dried nut and fruit mixtures.

Pie and Quiche Dough:

Use the same proportions of butter, flour, and water for meat pies, turnovers, and quiches but omit the sugar and increase the salt to ¾ teaspoon in all.

⏱ *Timing*

Wait till you hear the doorbell ring before drizzling dressing on the lettuce salad. Your only other last-minute job is the pleasant one of arranging beautiful platters and setting them out. Part of the skewered salad and the dressing can be prepared that morning, but the skewering itself, and the brief marination of mushrooms, cherry tomatoes, zucchini, and peppers, is done half an hour before guests are due.

Otherwise, all your preparations can be made the day before; and the turnover dough can be frozen. While the Chicken Melon roasts, you can cook the hard-boiled eggs, make mayonnaise, and prepare some of the salad vegetables: artichokes, onions, potatoes, topinambours, and turnips.

If you've never boned a chicken before, it's wise to make your first attempt at a leisurely pace, giving yourself time to stop frequently and take a fix on your location in the sometimes bewildering mass of flesh and bone. Once you've done it and understood it, this job is a breeze ever after, and takes little more time than, for example, carving a cooked bird.

Menu Variations

The Chicken Melon: You can bone, stuff, tie, and roast almost any bird, or bake it in a pastry crust (see *Mastering II*), or poach it instead of roasting it and finish with an aspic glaze. Or simply pack the *pâté* stuffing into a terrine and bake it that way, or bake it skinless in a pastry case. But if you have a crust here, you will not want one for dessert!

The salads: If you omit the potato salad, a loaf or two of French bread will provide starch. For the lettuce salad, when perfect leaf lettuce is unavailable, substitute one of the mixed salads in this book. The make-up of the skewered vegetable salad will be determined by the season anyway.

The Apple Turnover: You could make little individual turnovers by the same recipe— but baking time will be only 20 to 30 minutes. Or use the same dough to make a tart or tartlets: bake the shell or shells, waterproof the inside with a melted jelly glaze, arrange the fruit (cooked or not, depending on type), and glaze again (see *Mastering I* for a basic method).

An open-faced apple tart.

Leftovers

The Chicken Melon: You might plan to have a little extra of the stuffing mixture and save it for a special meal! Lightly formed into little cakes, dredged with flour, and sautéed, it is a charming luncheon or first-course dish, something between a *quenelle* or mousse and a chickenburger, and can be given extra savor by a creamy, full-flavored *béchamel* sauce (for which you'd save every drop of degreased roasting juice). You can freeze an uncooked *pâté* mixture or the raw chicken melon itself; but few *pâtés* take kindly to freezing after cooking. However, a cooked, finished "melon" will keep a week under refrigeration.

The salads: The potato salad will keep in the refrigerator for 3 or 4 days; but not if it has sat at room temperature for any length of time. That's because mayonnaise, like any egg mixture, is vulnerable to bacterial action. If you have marinated vegetables to spare, why not dice them, fold into a mayonnaise, and serve on lettuce next day as a *macédoine* salad?

The Apple Turnover: If you have extra dough, refrigerate it or freeze it (see recipe) and use again (see Menu Variations). Extra macerated fruit can always be cooked gently, then puréed and used as a sauce for custard or rice pudding. The cooked turnover itself will freeze and may be reheated in the oven.

HB Eggs

An unusual and successful way to boil and peel them

The perfect hard-boiled egg is one that is perfectly unblemished when peeled; its white is tender, its yolk is nicely centered and just set, and no dark line surrounds it. Excess heat toughens the egg, and excess heat also causes that dark line between yolk and white. To illustrate such a perfect estate, way back in the 1960s I did a whole television program on this earth-shaking subject, calling it "HB Eggs." No sooner was it aired than our French Chef office was flooded with suggestions, some of which were very useful indeed. As an example, one viewer suggested the use of an egg pricker, an instrument that pierces the shell at the large end to release the contents of its ever-present air pocket; if the air is allowed to remain it will expand when the egg heats, and that sometimes causes the shell to crack.

The most interesting idea came from the Georgia Egg Board, and the reason they got into the picture is that Georgia is a breeding ground not only for Presidents and peaches, but also for millions of eggs boiled and peeled by home cooks and especially by business enterprises. Because of the egg's commercial importance, scientists at the University of Georgia undertook a study involving over 800 of them and concluded that the best way of shrinking the egg body from the shell, to make for easy peeling, was to plunge the just-boiled eggs into iced water for one minute, meanwhile bringing the cooking water back to the boil, then to plunge the eggs into boiling water for ten seconds, and right after that to peel them. The iced water shrinks egg from shell, and the subsequent short boil expands shell from egg.

I tried out the Georgia method, found it good, and described it in my monthly column for *McCall's* magazine, thereby receiving even more new suggestions, including one from a testy 74-year-old asking if the U. of Georgia had nothing better to do! They should ask their grandmothers, said she who has been boiling eggs since she was a little girl: she boils them 12 to 15 minutes, plunges them into cold water, and has never had the slightest bit of trouble peeling them.

However, since an actual boil really does produce a tough egg, the Georgia people will just tolerate a simmer but prefer what I call "the 17-minute sit-in," where eggs are submerged in a pan of cold water, brought to the boil, then covered and removed from heat to remain for 17 minutes before their rapid cooling and peeling. I was therefore skeptical indeed when a letter came from the American Egg Board in Chicago outlining a series of experiments conducted by the Department of Poultry Science at the University of Wisconsin, using—of all things—the pressure cooker. How did they ever dream that up? I wonder. But it works very well indeed, and here is how to go about it.

HB eggs in the pressure cooker

1. Pour enough water into the pan of the cooker to cover the number of eggs you plan to cook—2 inches (5 cm) for 12 eggs is usually sufficient. Bring the water to the boil.

2. Meanwhile, wash the eggs in warm water with detergent to remove possible preserving spray from shells and to take the chill off the eggs. Rinse thoroughly. (Do not pierce them.)

3. Remove the pressure pan from heat, gently lower eggs into water, cover the pan, and bring rapidly to full (15 pounds) pressure. Immediately remove pan from heat and let sit under pressure for exactly five minutes.

4. At once release pressure, drain eggs, and cool them in cold water—or iced water.

5. Peel the eggs as soon as possible. I must admit that my first trial with this method gave me some qualms, but it worked— the eggs peeled beautifully. I kept at it, finding sometimes that the yolks were not entirely set at the very central point, but I never have had any trouble peeling. My last experiment was, I feel, pretty conclusive since I had managed to get some absolutely fresh eggs, laid by the young hens of a retired vicar on Cape Cod, each egg carefully dated on the large end. They were laid on a Sunday, boiled on a Monday,

and that's about as fresh a dozen eggs as I am ever likely to get. Here are the results:

1. Four eggs cooked by the coddle method (brought to the boil, removed from heat, covered, and let sit for 17 minutes). Two of these simply chilled in cold water—peeled with difficulty. Two of these chilled in iced water for 1 minute, plunged into boiling water for ten seconds, then chilled briefly and peeled —peeled with some difficulty but more easily than the first batch.

2. Four eggs done in the electric egg steamer/poacher. Peeled easily, but seemed a little tough. (And, by the way, mine poaches me a tough egg, too.)

3. Four eggs done in the pressure cooker. Peeled easily, and whites were tender.

Conclusion: The pressure cooker is great for HB eggs!

Peeling addendum

Two of my *McCall's* readers suggested a helpful peeling trick: after cracking the shells all over and peeling a circle of shell off the large end, slip an ordinary teaspoon between shell and egg and work it down the egg all around to the small end, manipulating the egg under a thin stream of cold water or in a bowl of water as you go.

The ugly dark line around the yolk on the left is due to excessive heat—the perfect HB egg is on the right.

*Don't try to fool a dieter's appetite. Excite it.
Beautiful, contrasting, full-flavored, this is
food, not fodder; and a little feels like a lot.*

Lo-Cal Banquet

Menu

Angosoda Cocktail

❧

Appetizer of Shrimp, Green Beans, and Sliced Mushrooms

❧

Chicken Bouillabaisse with Rouille, a Garlic and Pimiento Sauce

❧

Steamed Rice

❧

Caramel-crowned Steam-baked Apples

❧

Suggested wines: A hearty Pinot Blanc or white Châteauneuf-du-Pape

When you're on a diet, do you feel you "just can't give a dinner party"? Or does it depress you to plan a menu for dieting guests? I sympathize, because "diet food," as such, is dismal food: no fun to plan, no fun to fix. Pure labor in vain. Fake food—I mean those patented substances chemically flavored and mechanically bulked out to kill the appetite and deceive the gut—is unnatural, almost immoral, a bane to good eating and good cooking. I'd rather look at it this way: nothing, except conscious virtue, can mitigate the groaning intervals between a dieter's meals; but why should the meals, too, be a penance? On the contrary. Light food for sharp appetites should stimulate, then satisfy, with calories allotted to bulk and balance and a few strategically disposed—like crack troops—where they'll be most telling: for flavoring, for unctuous or crackling texture, for mouth-filling opulence. The relish of it! Dieters are the best audience a cook ever has, for they savor and remember every morsel.

Of course Paul and I have to diet every now and then. It helps to have happy, busy lives and to get some exercise. Believing in the healthy body's wisdom, that what you want is what you need, we seek variety and practice moderation, eat less and enjoy it more than when we were young string beans. But sometimes we have absentminded or greedy spells, and the day comes when we start planning and get out the old notebook. All right: 1200 calories each per diem. Breakfast, 150; lunch, 200; dinner, 800. Fifty calories are left out, you'll notice; it's our error factor—a small one, since we are faithful about recording every stray bite or sample while cooking. Authorities vary in the calorie amounts they give, so we take the highest we can find for each item. Better, we think, to deprive than to deceive ourselves; but we soften the deprivation by allotting 100 of our dinner calories to a glass of good wine. It never tastes better!

At parties, we eat a bit of everything, but we are glad of the growing fashion for lighter, more savory menus. More thoughtful planning, more scrupulous preparation, are the modern cook's response to the challenge: make every calorie count. Don't hesitate to invite nondieters to the meal I'm about to describe, or even the lean and hungry young. You can double quantities, add bread or extras like cookies or cakes for dessert for them, or otherwise supplement or vary the menu (see Menu Variations); but it's certainly not necessary. This meal is so delicious, they'll take big helpings and return for seconds; but a moderate portion of each dish, though you'd hardly believe it, adds up to a sensible 678 calories. There's no trick to it, and no secret—only a well-considered application of the simplest principles of sound gastronomy: contrast, balance, beauty, savor, and style.

A subtle appetizer of shrimp, fresh green beans, and thinly sliced raw mushrooms arranged on watercress; a bouillabaisse of chicken, robust and aromatic, heaped on steamed rice and richly enhanced with a Provençal *rouille;* and a fresh, fragrant dessert of apples, steam-baked with wine, lemon, and stick cinnamon, then webbed with glistening caramel—this meal has everything. Everything plus. The ingredients aren't expensive; most of the work can be done in advance; and, since the dishes are all cooked on top of the stove, you won't waste fuel. And finally, the leftovers: delicious, elegant, and infinitely transformable. Sometimes I buy and cook the whole works in double quantities. Why not have two meals for the effort of one?

A Note on Alcohol and Calories:

As opposed to wine, which is a food as well as something to lift your spirits, liquor is full of empty but horribly real calories that don't nourish you. Only the most serious dieters need omit wine altogether, but instead of a cocktail I suggest you try

The Angosoda Cocktail:

In a large, handsome stemmed glass, place several cubes of ice, dash on a few drops of Angostura Bitters, add a slice of lime, and fill up with sparkling water. The fizz, the rosy color, and the dot of green are attractive, and it tastes like a real drink.

On Wine in Cooking:

Calorie counters can use a lot, and I do. The alcohol, which carries the calories, evaporates away in a moment of cooking. The flavor, now a bit softer and subtler, remains to give your dish complexity and depth of taste that make it more satisfying as well as more delicious.

Preparations

Marketing and Storage:
Staples to have on hand

Salt
Peppercorns
Granulated sugar
Pure vanilla extract
Hot pepper sauce
Whole fennel seeds
Dried thyme
Dried oregano (if you can't get fresh basil) ▼
Bay leaves
Saffron threads ▼
Stick cinnamon
Dried orange peel ▼
Angostura Bitters
Plain canned tomato sauce
Long-grain untreated white Carolina rice ▼
Onions (ordinary white or yellow)
Garlic
Fresh bread crumbs (in the freezer;
    see page 6)
Lemons (1)
Eggs (1)
Canned pimiento
Dry white wine or dry white French
    vermouth
Soda water

Specific ingredients for this menu

Shrimp (24 "large medium") ▼
Chicken (two fryers, or 16 pieces of cut-up
    chicken) ▼
Green beans (½ pound or 225 g)
Mushrooms (12)
Watercress
Parsley
Leeks (about 4)
Tomatoes (about 12) ▼
Apples (6, Golden Delicious if possible) ▼

► *Remarks:*
Staples

Dried oregano: substituted for dried basil, because I don't think the latter has much flavor. *Fresh basil:* grow your own if you have a sunny spot; it's incomparable. *Saffron threads:* specified because powdered saffron may not be pure. The real saffron threads, which bear the pollen in a certain kind of crocus, are something of a luxury, but you use them sparingly. And you must, because too much saffron produces a medicinal taste which can't be corrected. *Dried orange peel:* to make your own, using a vegetable peeler take 2-inch-long (5-cm) strips of zest off an orange, let dry for a day or two on paper towels, then bottle—keeps indefinitely. *Long-grain untreated white Carolina rice* (see "Rice Talk," page 63): this is best

for steaming. The plump, nutty-flavored grains of Italian rice will too often degenerate into a gluey mass.

Ingredients for this menu

Shrimp: if you're lucky enough to live near the seacoast and to have a trustworthy market, you may be able to get them fresh and alive. Otherwise, your safest bet is to buy them raw in the shell, frozen solid in a block. Keep them that way until ready to cook; then thaw rapidly in lots of cold water and peel as soon as you can detach them from the frozen mass. Devein them: if you see a black line, it's the intestinal vein; you can usually pull it out from the large end without slitting the shrimp. (See "Fish Talk," page 111, for illustration.) *Chicken:* fryers are perfect for the fricassee method, which you employ in making this bouilla-baisse. It is easy to cut up your own.

But if you decide on ready-cut chicken, note that thighs are the best buy: they are cheaper than drumsticks and have more flesh and less bone. Before storing or cooking chicken, be on the safe side: rinse with warm water, inside and out, and dry before refrigerating. If you're going to keep it more than a day or two, refrigerate it in a plastic bag set in a bowl of ice cubes which you renew as needed. *Vegetables:* refrigerate unwashed beans in a plastic bag until ready to prepare; mushrooms and leeks ditto. Parsley and cress can be freshened by soaking several hours in cold water. Then drain; shake dry and roll up loosely in paper towels and refrigerate in plastic bags. Be sure your garlic is not dried out. Sniff your bottled herbs and spices for freshness—they should always be kept out of the light. *Tomatoes:* be sure you get in your tomatoes several days in advance to let them ripen properly. (See "Tomato Talk," page 159.) *Apples:* some of the most savory varieties turn into mush when steamed. Depending on where you live, try Golden Delicious, Rome Beauty, York Imperial, Greening, Newton, Monroe, or Northern Spy. The Golden Delicious, available in most regions, is always reliable, and its flavor will be enhanced by the spice and wine; its green-yellow skin is a nice pale topaz after cooking.

Appetizer of Shrimp, Green Beans, and Sliced Mushrooms

For 6 people
½ pound (225 g) green beans
12 large mushrooms
Fresh lemon juice
24 "large medium" shrimp
¾ cup (1 ¾ dL) dry white French vermouth or 1 cup (¼ L) dry white wine
1 Tb minced shallots or scallions
½ tsp salt
¼ tsp dried dill weed
Several grinds black pepper
Watercress or parsley
Garnish: lemon wedges; small pitcher olive oil

The beans

Several hours or the morning before serving, wash the fresh green beans. Snap off each end with your fingers, pulling down the bean's

scam to remove any lurking string. Plunge the beans into 3 to 4 quarts or liters of rapidly boiling salted water and boil uncovered 5 to 8 minutes (tasting frequently after 5 minutes) until beans are just cooked through. They are done when still a little crunchy and still bright green. (There has been a vogue for describing such beans as "crunchily underdone," but I do think such terms are used by those who have been brought up on frozen beans, which have no crunch, and little taste either, for that matter. Properly cooked beans are just cooked through; improperly cooked beans are either over- or underdone.) Once the beans are just cooked through, then, drain in a colander, run cold water into the kettle, and dump the beans back in to refresh them and stop the cooking—this also serves to retain their fresh texture and bright green color. Drain again, dry in a towel, and chill in a plastic bag.

The mushrooms

An hour before serving, trim the fresh large fine mushrooms, wash rapidly, and dry. Slice thinly and neatly, and toss in a little fresh lemon juice to prevent discoloration. Arrange on a dish, cover with plastic wrap, and chill.

The shrimp

Several hours or the morning before serving, simmer the raw peeled shrimp in the dry white French vermouth or dry white wine, minced shallots or scallions, salt, dried dill weed, and pepper. Toss and turn the shrimp in the liquid for 2 to 3 minutes, until shrimp curl and just become springy to the touch. Remove shrimp to a bowl, then rapidly boil down the cooking liquid to a syrupy consistency; pour it back over the shrimp, tossing several times. Chill.

To serve

An hour before serving, slice the shrimp in half horizontally—so they will look like more shrimp!—and arrange tastefully, either on individual plates or on a platter, with watercress or parsley, the beans, and the mushrooms. Cover with plastic wrap and chill until dinner time. Pass lemon wedges with the appetizer and a little pitcher of good olive oil for those who are permitted such luxury.

Chicken Bouillabaisse with Rouille

Fricassee of chicken with leeks, tomatoes, herbs, and wine, with a garlic and pimiento sauce on the side

For 6 people with ample leftovers

Two 3½-pound (1¼-kg) fryers, or 16 chicken pieces, such as thighs, drumsticks, breast halves
⅓ cup (¾ dL) olive oil
3 cups (¾ L) combination of thinly sliced white of leek and onions, or onions only
3 to 4 large cloves garlic
4 cups (1 L) fresh tomato pulp (about 2½ pounds or 1 kg tomatoes, peeled, seeded, juiced, sliced)
2 to 4 Tb plain tomato sauce, or as needed, for added flavor
½ tsp fennel seeds, 1 tsp thyme, large pinch saffron threads, two 2-inch (5-cm) strips dried orange peel, 2 imported bay leaves
Salt
2 cups (½ L) dry white French vermouth
Pepper
Fresh chopped parsley

Preliminary cooking of the chicken

If you are cutting up the chicken yourself, as I like to do, see illustrated directions in *J.C.'s Kitchen*, page 228. Dry the chicken pieces and place with the olive oil in a large skillet or casserole over moderate heat. Simmer about 10 minutes, turning the pieces several times in the hot oil until they stiffen slightly but do not brown. While the chicken is cooking, wash and slice the leeks, peel and slice the onion, and peel and chop the garlic.

When chicken has stiffened, remove it to a side dish, leaving oil in pan. Stir in the leeks, onions, and garlic; cook slowly 5 minutes or so, until fairly soft but not browned. Meanwhile, peel, seed, and juice the tomatoes (see "Tomato Talk," page 159); slice them roughly and fold into the leeks, onions and garlic along with the fennel, thyme, saffron, orange peel, and bay leaves. Taste, and if the tomatoes aren't flavorful enough, add a little tomato sauce as needed. Then salt the chicken on all sides. Arrange in the pan, basting with the vegetables. Cover and cook 5 minutes; turn, baste, cover, and cook 5 minutes more.

🕐   Recipe may be completed to this point several hours or even a day in advance. Let cool, then cover and refrigerate. Bring to the simmer again, covered, before proceeding.

Finishing the cooking
An hour before serving, pour in the wine, cover the pan, and simmer 15 to 20 minutes more, basting and turning the chicken several times just until the pieces are tender when pierced with a fork. Remove chicken to a side dish, tilt pan, and skim off all visible cooking fat; then rapidly boil down cooking liquid to thicken it. Taste very carefully for seasoning, adding salt and pepper to taste. Return chicken to pan, baste with the sauce, set cover askew, and keep warm (but well below the simmer) until serving time. When ready to bring to the table, arrange the chicken and sauce on a hot platter and decorate with parsley. Pass the special sauce (next recipe) separately.

Dieting Notes:
To cut down on calories, you can peel the skin off the chicken after it is cooked as described in the preceding paragraph and do a very thorough degreasing of the sauce before boiling it down—even pour it through a sieve, so that you can remove the fat more easily from the liquid. Then return contents of sieve and skimmed liquid to the cooking pan with the chicken.

Rouille

Garlic and pimiento sauce. To serve with a bouillabaisse, or with pasta, boiled potatoes or beans, boiled fish or chicken, and so forth

6 cloves garlic

1 tsp salt

12 large leaves fresh basil (or 1 tsp dried oregano)

⅓ cup (¾ dL) canned red pimiento

⅓ cup (¾ dL) lightly pressed down fresh white nonsweet bread crumbs

1 egg yolk

1 cup (¼ L) olive oil

Freshly ground pepper

Drops of hot pepper sauce

Equipment

A mortar and pestle are nice, but you can use the bottom of a ladle and a sturdy bowl, which, if not metal, should be set on a mat so it won't crack.

Purée the garlic cloves through a press into a mortar or bowl. Then pound the garlic with the salt into a smooth paste. Pound in the basil or oregano. When the mixture is smooth, add the pimiento and pound again; then add the crumbs, and finally pound in the egg yolk. Switch from pestle to wire whisk and, drop by drop at first, beat in the olive oil until mixture has thickened like mayonnaise, then beat in the oil a little faster to make a quite stiff sauce. Season highly with pepper and hot sauce.

🕐   May be made a day or two in advance. Refrigerate in a covered container; remove and let come to room temperature an hour before serving.

Remarks:

This redolent sauce, named for its rich rust color, is high in calories; but even a small dollop adds a voluptuous texture and hearty flavor to a serving of the bouillabaisse. I find it more satisfying to take one piece of chicken, rather than two, and enjoy it with the *rouille*.

Steamed Rice

For 4½ cups

1½ cups (3½ dL) plain raw white rice
2 tsp salt

In a large pot, bring 6 to 8 cups (1½ to 2 L) water to rolling boil, add rice and salt, and boil 7 to 8 minutes, or until *al dente.* Test by biting a grain. It should have a tiny hard core. Drain in a colander, and rinse under cold running water to remove all traces of starch—which would make the rice gummy.

🕐 Rice may be cooked ahead to this point even a day in advance, and its final cooking finished later.

About 15 minutes before serving, set colander of rice over a kettle of boiling water (bottom of colander should not rest in the water). Cover colander with a lid or a clean towel and steam just until rice is tender. Toss it once or twice to be sure it is steaming evenly. Do not overcook: ends of rice should remain rounded (splayed-out ends declare rice to be overdone).

Caramel-crowned Steam-baked Apples

1 cup (2 dL) white wine, or half wine or dry white vermouth and water, or water only
2 tsp pure vanilla extract
½ lemon
6 cooking apples (Golden Delicious or others that will keep their shape)
4 or more Tb sugar
Maraschino cherries
½ cup (1 dL) sugar
3 Tb water
Stick cinnamon
Equipment

Get a steaming rack, now available almost anywhere. It's perfect for most fruits and vegetables, though not for rice. The kind I like doesn't work for pudding, either, since it is lifted out of the pot by a vertical center handle. It's made of stainless steel and consists of a round perforated bottom dish standing on folding legs an inch or so high. Hinged around the circumference of the disk is a series of perforated flaps that fold inward for storage and outward, against the edge of the saucepan, when the steamer is in use.

Into a saucepan large enough to hold steamer and apples comfortably with a cover, put the liquid, vanilla, cinnamon, and several strips of

lemon peel, adding water if necessary so you have ½ inch (1½ cm) liquid in the pan for the steaming operation. Wash and core the apples, and peel half the way down from blossom (small) end, dropping peel into saucepan with steaming-liquid—to give added flavor and body to it for later. Place steamer in pan and the apples, peeled ends up, upon it. Squeeze the juice of the half lemon over the apples, and sprinkle on as much sugar as you think appropriate for the apples you are using. Bring to the simmer, cover the pan closely, and regulate heat so that liquid is barely simmering—too intense a steam will cause the apples to disintegrate—and keep checking on their progress. They should be done in 15 to 20 minutes when you can pierce them easily with a small knife.

❶   Apples may be cooked a day or more ahead and served cold.

Set the apples on a serving dish or on individual plates or bowls. Remove steamer from pan; boil down the cooking liquid rapidly until lightly syrupy, sweeten to taste, and strain over the apples. Decorate each with a maraschino cherry.

The caramel

Shortly before serving, prepare a caramel syrup. Bring ½ cup (1 dL) sugar and 3 table-spoons water to the boil in a small, heavy saucepan, then remove from heat and swirl pan until all sugar has dissolved and liquid is clear—an essential step in sugar-boiling operations, to prevent sugar from crystallizing. Then return to heat, bring again to the boil, cover, and boil rapidly for a minute or so until bubbles are large and thick, indicating that liquid has almost evaporated. Remove cover and boil, swirling pan gently by its handle but *never never* stirring, until syrup turns a nice, not-too-dark caramel brown. Immediately set bottom of pan in cold water and stir with a spoon for a few seconds until caramel cools slightly and begins to thicken. It should ooze off the spoon in lazy, thick strands. This is important, because if you put it on the apples too soon, when it's too hot or too thin, it'll just slide off onto the dish. Rapidly decorate the apples with strands of syrup dripped over them from tip of spoon, waving it over them in a circular spiral to make attractive patterns.

Remarks:

To clean the caramel pan and the spoon easily, simply fill pan with water and set to simmer for a few minutes to dissolve all traces of caramel.

⏱ *Timing*

This is an easy menu, and you can be leisurely getting most of it done ahead. If you want to do as much as possible in advance, start by deciding to serve the apples cold. Then look at the recipes for suggestions and for the point marked ⏱. For this menu, you can start as much as two days ahead of time.

There's only one last-minute job: as your guests sit down to their appetizer, turn on the heat under the rice for its final steaming.

Half an hour before serving the main course, finish simmering the chicken.

An hour before your guests arrive, take the *rouille* from the refrigerator, but don't give it a final stir until it has reached room temperature. Slice limes for your Angosoda Cocktail, and place in a covered dish.

About two hours before the party, arrange the appetizer on a large platter or individual plates, cover with plastic wrap, and refrigerate. Chill white wine if you're serving it.

Several hours—but not the day—before, accomplish the second stage of the bouillabaisse, that of boiling down the sauce, tasting and correcting the seasoning. Wash, blanch, drain, and dry green beans. Clean and slice mushrooms, toss in lemon juice to keep white, and chill. Prepare and chill shrimp. Make a caramel sauce, let cool a bit, and decorate the apples.

Still on the day of your party, start cooking chicken.

A day or so before, you can steam the apples and start the rice.

The bouilla-"base," the concentrate of vegetables, herbs, and wine, though better flavored if made with the chicken in it, can in fact be made well in advance. It doesn't hurt to cook the vegetables the day before you make the "base." Keep them covered and chilled.

The *rouille* actually tastes better if you make it a day before serving and let its flavors marry in the refrigerator.

Menu Variations

The *appetizer* could be varied by substituting asparagus tips for the beans, or fine small spinach leaves for the cress, or almost any shellfish for the shrimp. Raw bay or sea scallops may be marinated in fresh lime juice and seasonings, which delicately cook them—see the *seviche* on page 183. Green beans and mushrooms on cress, without shellfish, are delicious, perhaps with cherry tomatoes and a scattering of finely chopped chives or scallions.

The *bouillabaisse,* as you know, is most familiar as a hearty soup containing a mixture of fish. In this more condensed form, which of course you eat with a fork, you could exchange chicken for a firm-fleshed fish, for scallops, or for salt cod (but allow time to freshen it). It makes a grand main dish for vegetarians if you use chunks of presalted, sautéed eggplant instead of chicken; or else one of the bulkier pastas, like *rotini* and *rigatoni.* Only steamed rice is a proper complement to the bouillabaisse, so I have no alternative to suggest.

The *dessert* can be made with pears instead of apples. It can be lightened by omitting the caramel, or enriched by passing, separately, a bowl of custard sauce or lightly whipped cream.

*Rigatoni (left) and *rotini*.*

Leftovers

Rice: if you have extra, make a cold rice salad, or serve it in a soup, or use it to thicken a sauce *soubise.* As for the *bouillabaisse,* you can reheat it, and it will still be delicious. But I love it cold as a luncheon dish. If I plan on that, I usually pull the skin off all the chicken pieces (don't like cold chicken skin!), then arrange the chicken in a nice serving dish and spoon the sauce over. After chilling, the sauce jells; before serving, I remove any surface fat and sprinkle a bit of fresh chopped parsley over all. Delicious just as it is, or arranged on a bed of lettuce and decorated with black olives. The rice could even accompany the chicken again as a cold salad.

Here's another idea I developed after the television show, when I had quantities of chicken in bouillabaisse to play with. After reheating batches of it twice, serving it cold once, and still having more, I decided to purée the sauce in a food processor. It turned into a kind of horrid pudding, so I simmered it with a cup of chicken broth and tried to strain it, with no success. Then I thought of my trusty potato ricer. I lined it with a double thickness of washed cheesecloth, filled it with a ladleful of my rosy pudding, gave it a squeeze, and out came a savory, translucent, satiny rose liquid which I spooned over my chilled and peeled chicken and chilled again. A happy discovery.

The rouille will keep for a week or more and is delicious as a spaghetti sauce, with boiled or broiled fish or chicken, with boiled or baked potatoes, or stirred into a minestrone-type soup.

The apples are excellent cold, and will keep several days refrigerated in a covered dish. Or you may slice the flesh and serve with a fruit sauce (frozen raspberries, thawed, puréed and strained, are good, though rather high in sugar). To make more juice, simmer a fresh apple with a cinnamon stick, a slice of lemon, and an ounce or so of vermouth, then strain.

Postscript

Here's your calorie count. I put it last so as not to deter nondieters from trying this excellent meal—for the bald numbers are so shockingly low you may not believe, before tasting, that I have been talking about real food all this time.

Salad of shrimp, green beans, and sliced mushrooms	66
Chicken bouillabaisse (2 sauced pieces)	250
Rouille (1 tablespoon)	75
Steamed rice (½ cup)	100
1 apple with syrup and caramel crown	187

The ingredients
(calories per 3½ oz or 100 g):

Raw shrimp		91
Cooked green beans		25
Raw mushrooms		28
Watercress		19
Fryer, light meat with skin, without	120,	101
dark meat with skin, without	132,	112
Olive oil		884
Leeks		52
Onions		38
Raw tomatoes		22
Tomato sauce		39
Bread crumbs		392
Egg yolk		348
Cooked rice		109
Raw apple		117
Sugar		385
Wine, dry, sweet	85,	137
Gin, rum, vodka, whiskey (80 proof)		231
Beer		42

The calorie counts are those given in an excellent handbook by Bernice K. Watt and Annabel L. Merrill, *Composition of Foods: Raw, Processed, Prepared* (Agriculture Handbook No. 8, U.S. Department of Agriculture, Washington, D.C., revised December 1963). For sale from the Superintendent of Documents, U.S. Government Printing Office, Washington, D.C. 20402. Price: $2.35, domestic postpaid, or $2.00, GPO Bookstore.

Beautiful ingredients prepared with loving care but little effort: this simple menu is an example of the wisdom and sane good taste of civilized cookery.

Informal Dinner

Menu

Asparagus Tips in Puff Pastry, Lemon Butter Sauce

❦

Casserole Roast of Veal with Carrots and Celery Hearts
Wok Sauté of Grated Zucchini and Fresh Spinach

❦

Floating Island

❦

Suggested wines:
A light white wine with the first course, like a Chablis, Chardonnay, or dry Riesling; a red Bordeaux or Cabernet Sauvignon with the veal; a Champagne or sparkling white wine with the dessert

"Love and work," said Sigmund Freud when somebody asked him what he thought were the most important things in life. Not much work goes into cooking the ingredients for this simple, beautiful dinner. But in choosing them you acknowledge your guests' love of perfection and exercise your own.

You could spend half the money this menu demands and create a meal twice as impressive. There are several such menus in this book, and very good they are, too. But if your trusted butcher lets you know that he has been able to procure a veal roast of impeccable quality, wouldn't you plan to share it with friends who will appreciate its rarity? Wouldn't you go to market that morning for the freshest vegetables, imagining which ones would contribute to the flavor of the meat?

This serene, unpretentious perfection in dining is, indeed, the reward of love, expressed by care and respect for your guests and for the food you offer them. And if veal really is too expensive for you—or impossible to come by—try one of the less luxurious meats suggested in Menu Variations; the substitutes are perfectly suited to this kind of cooking method and will have a fine harmony of flavors.

A casserole is a very comfortable kind of informal cooking. You simply brown the meat, briefly blanch the vegetables, and put them all together with butter and seasonings. Then when you're ready to roast, you stick the casserole in the oven and let it cook quietly by itself, once in a while basting the meat and vegetables with their communal juices while you go about other things. The fresh, slightly crunchy spinach and zucchini, only lightly cooked at the last minute, will complete a pretty plateful and make a salad unnecessary.

What's a Chinese wok doing at this very traditional meal? Improving it, that's what, and
reminding us not to be pedantic…but you
could use a frying pan.

The main course doesn't include rice or
potatoes, but it doesn't need to if you serve a
loaf of French bread. And you may not even
need that because of the appetizer. These
crinkly little puff pastry "rafts" are all the rage
these days in France; but puff pastry was never
an everyday item there, any more than here,
until recently. With a new fast method (page
98), puff pastry dishes are almost effortless,
once you get the habit of making a batch of
dough at intervals and cutting some of it into
handy little rectangles to await your convenience in the freezer. Asparagus, formerly
such a luxury, is available here from February
through June at gradually decreasing prices.
You need only three or four spears per person.
Peel them, of course, or the dish is hardly

worth presenting. And, to round out the delicate contrast of texture and flavor, whisk up a
last-minute little sauce.

Be careful the butter doesn't overheat; be
careful the asparagus doesn't overcook; be
careful your oven thermostat is accurate.
Cooking, I do strongly feel, expresses love
more by fastidious everyday care than by fes-
tival bursts of effort. The effort, when you
come to the dessert, can be left to your heavy-
duty mixer. If you had to do this by hand, it
would indeed be heavy duty.

Floating island, as the French do it, is a
meringue soufflé about the size of Australia,
floating on a sea of pale gold custard sauce. I
like to serve it in archipelago form, cut into
Greenland-size chunks. Don't be daunted at
this point by the word "soufflé," in case you
aren't yet confident with them: this meringue is so foolproof you can unmold it any
time, or even put it in the freezer. The custard
sauce, too, can be made well in advance, and it
is very easy, provided you give it the few minutes' close attention (to prevent its curdling)
that this lovely satiny confection deserves.

"Make every meal an occasion" sounds
to me like "Live each day as though it were
your last"—just plain overwrought. People do
preach it, but does anyone practice? Not me!
But to love your art as well as your audience
does seem to make for pretty good living, day
by pleasant day.

Preparations

Recommended Equipment:
A wok is not essential for the zucchini and spinach dish, just an attractive option. But I would not tackle 12 egg whites without a big electric mixer and an appropriate bowl (see recipe).

Marketing and Storage:
Staples to have on hand
Salt

Black and white peppercorns

Cream of tartar

Pure vanilla extract

Fragrant dried tarragon

Light olive oil or fresh peanut oil ▼

Granulated sugar

Optional but recommended: superfine granulated sugar

Butter (¾ pound or 350 g)

Milk (1 pint or 2 cups or ½ L)

Eggs (13 or more, depending on size)

Onions (2)

Lemons (1)

Puff pastry (from the freezer)

Shallots or scallions

Dry white French vermouth

Optional: dark Jamaica rum or
    bourbon whiskey

Specific ingredients for this menu
Boneless roast of veal (3 pounds or 1¼ to
    1½ kg); please read the recipe
    before marketing

Fresh pork fat (or beef fat) ▼

Fresh asparagus (18 to 24 spears)

Fresh celery hearts (3 to 6 whole)

Fresh carrots (6 to 8 or more)

Zucchini (6 medium-size)

Fresh spinach (1½ to 2 pounds or ¾ to 1 kg)

Optional: heavy cream (2 to 4 Tb)

Optional: sprinkles for meringue (see recipe)

► *Remarks:*

Staples

Fresh peanut oil: Peanut oil can get rancid, so sniff yours before using.

Ingredients for this menu

Fresh pork fat: "Barding" fat, to cover a lean roast, is not always sold; so whenever I see some I buy it and freeze it. And I trim scraps of extra fat off pork roasts before cooking, and save them. If the strips you buy are too thick, place between sheets of wax paper and pound with a rubber hammer, rolling pin, or bottle to flatten them out. You can substitute fat trimmed from a beef loin or rib roast; it does the work, although not as neatly since it shrinks and tends to break as it cooks.

Asparagus Tips in Puff Pastry, Lemon Butter Sauce

Petites Feuilletées aux Asperges, Sauce Beurre au Citron

For 6 people as a first course

18 to 24 fresh asparagus spears (depending on size)

2 to 3 Tb butter and 1 Tb minced shallots or scallions

Salt and pepper

6 puff pastry rectangles about 2½ by 5 by ¼ inches or 6½ by 13 by ¾ cm (the recipe for French puff pastry is on page 98)

Egg glaze (1 egg beaten with 1 tsp water)

Lemon butter sauce

2 Tb fresh lemon juice

3 Tb dry white French vermouth

Salt and white pepper

1 stick (115 g) chilled butter cut into 12 fingertip-size pieces

The asparagus

Trim ends off asparagus spears and peel from butt to near tip to remove tough outer skin. Choose a deep skillet or oval flameproof casserole large enough to hold asparagus flat; fill with water and bring to the rolling boil, adding 1½ teaspoons salt per quart or liter of water. Lay in the asparagus, cover until boil is reached, then uncover and boil slowly just until asparagus is cooked through—5 to 8 minutes or so, depending on quality (eat a piece off the butt end of one to make sure). Immediately remove the asparagus and arrange in one layer on a clean towel to cool. Cut the tip ends of the spears into 5-inch (13-cm) lengths; save the butt ends for a salad.

🕐 May be cooked in advance. When cold, wrap and refrigerate.

Just before serving (and when the following pastry is baked and ready), melt 2 to 3 tablespoons butter in a frying pan large enough to hold the tips in one layer, add the shallots or scallions and cook for a moment, then add the asparagus tips, shaking pan by handle to roll them over and over to coat with butter; season lightly with salt and pepper and roll again.

The puff pastry rectangles

Preheat oven to 450°F/230°C. About 15 minutes before serving, arrange the pastries (still frozen, if you wish) on a baking sheet and paint the tops (not the sides) with egg glaze; in a moment, paint with a second coat, then make decorative knife cuts and crosshatchings in the surface. Immediately bake in middle level of oven for 12 to 15 minutes, until pastries have puffed up and browned and the sides have crisped.

🕐 May be baked somewhat ahead and left in turned-off oven, door ajar—but the sooner you serve them the more tenderly flakily buttery they will be.

To serve

While they are still hot, split the pastries in half horizontally, arrange 3 or 4 hot and buttery asparagus spears on the bottom half, their tips peeking out one of the ends, spoon a bit of the following sauce over the asparagus, cover loosely with the top, and serve at once.

Lemon butter sauce: an informal *beurre blanc* (which takes only 3 to 4 minutes to make; if you are not familiar with it, I suggest you do so just before serving since it is tricky to keep). Boil the lemon juice, vermouth, and ¼ teaspoon salt slowly in a small saucepan until liquid has reduced to about 1 tablespoon. Then, a piece or two at a time, start beating in the chilled pieces of butter, adding another piece or two just as the previous pieces have almost melted—the object here is to force its milk solids to hold in creamy suspension as the butter warms and softens, so that the sauce remains ivory colored rather than looking like melted butter. Season to taste with salt and pepper.

🕐 Sauce can be held over the faint heat of a pilot light or anywhere it is warm enough to keep the butter from congealing, but not so warm as to turn the sauce into melted butter. However, if this happens you can often bring it back by beating over cold water until it begins to congeal and cream again.

Remarks:

Jacques Pépin, the able French chef and teacher based in Connecticut, has another version of the sauce where you bring 2 tablespoons each of lemon juice and water to the rolling boil and rapidly beat in 1 stick (115 g) of soft butter in pieces; bring the sauce to the rolling boil again for a few seconds, turn into a sauce boat, and serve at once. It produces the same effect of a warm creamy liaison of butter, rather than melted butter.

Puff pastry rectangle before and after baking.

Casserole Roast of Veal with Carrots and Celery Hearts

Rôti de Veau Poêlé à la Nivernaise

A fine roast of veal of top quality has no pronounced flavor of its own and no natural fat to keep it moist while it is cooking. I therefore like to tie my veal roast with strips of fat and to roast it slowly in a covered casserole with herbs and aromatic vegetables. As it cooks, the aroma of its savory companions seeps into the meat and the meat itself flavors the vegetables, both exuding a modicum of fragrant juices which combine to make a spontaneous sauce.

For 6 to 8 people

A 3-pound (1¼–1½ kg) boneless roast of veal, of the finest quality and palest pink (see notes on veal at end of recipe)

Strips of fresh pork fat (or beef fat) to tie around roast (about ⅛ inch or ½ cm thick and enough to cover half of the roast)

Light olive oil or fresh peanut oil, for browning meat

3 to 6 celery hearts

6 to 8 or more carrots

1 medium-size onion, sliced

Salt and pepper

1 tsp fragrant dried tarragon

2 Tb melted butter

Equipment

White butcher's string; a heavy covered casserole or roaster just large enough to hold meat and vegetables comfortably; a bulb baster; a meat thermometer

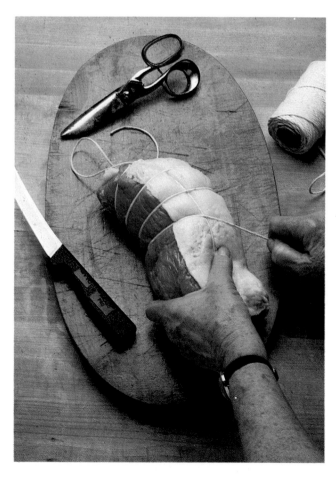

Preliminaries to roasting

Dry the veal in paper towels and tie the fat in place over it so you have strips on both top and bottom of veal. Film a frying pan or bottom of casserole with oil and brown the meat slowly over moderately high heat. Meanwhile cut the celery hearts into 5-inch (13-cm) lengths and reserve tops for another recipe. Trim celery roots, being careful not to detach ribs from them and trim any bruised spots off ribs. Cut into halves or thirds lengthwise and wash under cold water, spreading ribs carefully apart to force sand and dirt out from around root end. Set aside. Peel the carrots and cut into thickish bias slices about 2½ inches (6½ cm) long. Drop both celery and carrots into a large pan of boiling salted water and blanch (boil) for 1 minute; drain.

Arranging the casserole

If you have browned the meat in the casserole, remove it and discard browning fat. Strew the onion slices in the bottom of the casserole, season the veal with a good sprinkling of salt and pepper, and place in casserole, a fat-stripped side up. Sprinkle on half the tarragon, and arrange the celery hearts on either side of roast. Sprinkle hearts with salt and a pinch of tarragon, then strew the carrots on top, seasoning them also. Baste with the melted butter.

🕐 Casserole may be arranged several hours before roasting.

Roasting the meat

Roasting time: 1¼ to 1½ hours

Preheat oven to 350°F/180°C. About 2 hours before you wish to serve (reheat casserole on top of the stove if you have arranged it ahead), set casserole in lower-middle level of preheated oven. Roast for 20 minutes, then rapidly baste meat and vegetables with accumulated juices (a bulb baster is best for this) and turn thermostat down to 325°F/170°C. Baste every 20 minutes, and when an hour is up begin checking meat temperature. Meat is done at 165–170°F/75–77°C.

🕐   May be roasted somewhat ahead but should be kept warm; set cover slightly askew and keep in turned-off oven with door ajar, or over almost simmering water, or at a temperature of 120°F/50°C.

Serving

Slice the veal into thin, even pieces and arrange down the center of a hot platter, with the carrots bordering the meat and the celery hearts ringing them. Baste meat and vegetables with a little of the casserole juices. Spoon accumulated fat off remaining juices, correct seasoning, and strain into a hot sauce bowl.

Notes on Veal:

Veal is the meat of a young calf, and the best or Prime quality comes from an animal 10 to 12 weeks old that has been fed on milk or milk by-products. It is of the palest pink in color and has both texture and flavor—although the flavor of veal is never robust, like that of lamb or beef. Such veal is very expensive indeed but produces beautiful boneless cuts of solid meat from the leg (such as the top round) and from the loin and rib. Younger and less expensive veal, which should also be of the palest pink in color, is usually too small to furnish top or bottom round cuts, so one should take the whole leg and either roast it as is or have it boned and tied.

Wok Sauté of Grated Zucchini and Fresh Spinach

Sauté de Courgettes, Viroflay

In this attractive combination, the fresh spinach gives character to the zucchini, and the zucchini tenderizes the bite of the spinach, while a little onion lends its subtle depth. Although you can cook it all in a frying pan, the wok is especially successful here.

For 6 people

6 medium-size zucchini
Salt
1½ to 2 pounds (¾–1 kg) fresh spinach

2 to 3 Tb light olive oil or fresh peanut oil

3 to 4 Tb butter

1 medium-size onion, sliced

Pepper

Equipment

A food processor (optional) for grating the zucchini—or the coarse side of a hand grater; a wok (also optional), preferably with stainless-steel or nonstick interior so that spinach will not pick up a metallic taste

Trim off the ends and scrub the zucchini under cold water, but do not peel them. Grate either in a processor or through a hand grater and place in a sieve set over a bowl; toss with a teaspoon of salt and let drain while you trim the spinach.

Pull the stems off the spinach and pump leaves up and down in a basin of cold water, draining and repeating process if necessary to be sure spinach contains no sand or dirt. Drain in a colander.

🕐 May be prepared several hours in advance; refrigerate if you are not proceeding with recipe.

When you are ready to sauté, heat 1 tablespoon of oil and 1½ tablespoons butter in the wok (or frying pan). When butter has melted, add the spinach (if spinach is dry, add also 2 to 3 tablespoons water). Toss and turn for 5 minutes or so, until spinach is wilted and just cooked through, then remove it to a side dish. While spinach is cooking, by handfuls squeeze the juices out of the zucchini and set on a plate. When spinach is done and out of the wok, add more oil and butter and the sliced onion. Toss and cook for a minute or two, then add the zucchini, tossing and turning it for several minutes until just tender. Press any accumulated liquid out of spinach, and toss spinach with

zucchini, tossing and turning for a minute or two to blend and heat the two vegetables together. Taste carefully for seasoning, adding salt and pepper as needed, and you are ready to serve.

🕐 Most of the cooking may be done in advance, but in this case cook the spinach and set aside, then cook the zucchini until almost tender; finish the cooking just before serving, then add the spinach, tossing and turning for a moment or two.

Remarks:

You could add several tablespoons of heavy cream near the end of the cooking, or enrich the vegetables with more butter at the end of the cooking. Alternatively, you can cook with oil only, or use less of the amounts of both butter and oil specified in the recipe—that is the versatility of cooking in a well-designed wok.

Pulling the stems off spinach leaves.

Squeezing the juices out of grated raw zucchini.

Floating Island

Ile Flottante—A giant meringue soufflé floating on a custard sea

Here is a dramatic yet light and lovely cold dessert that is simplicity itself to make when you have a well-designed electric mixer that will keep the whole mass of your egg whites in motion at once, so that you get the lightness and volume egg whites should produce.

For 6 to 8 people
1⅔ cups (3¾ dL) egg whites (about 12)
½ tsp cream of tartar and 1/16 tsp salt
1½ cups (3½ dL) sugar (preferably the very finely granulated or instant kind)
2 tsp pure vanilla extract
3 cups (¾ L) Custard Sauce (see notes at end of recipe)
4 to 5 Tb decorative sprinkles for top of meringue, as suggested in Serving paragraph below (optional)
Equipment
(Besides the mixer): a 4- to 5-quart (4- to 4¾-L) straight-sided baking dish or casserole, interior heavily buttered and dusted with sugar; a round flat platter for unmolding

Cautionary remarks

Be sure that your egg-beating bowl and beater blades are absolutely clean and dry, since any oil or grease on them will prevent the egg whites from mounting. Also, because you are separating so many eggs, it is a good idea to break the whites, one at a time, into a small clean bowl and add each as you do it to the beating bowl; then if you break a yolk, it will ruin only one egg white, not the whole batch (since specks of egg yolk can prevent the whites from rising). Finally, chilled egg whites will not mount properly; stir them in the mixing bowl over hot water until the chill is off and they are about the temperature of your finger.

The meringue mixture

Preheat oven to 250°F/130°C. Start beating the egg whites at moderately slow speed until they are foamy. Beat in the cream of tartar and salt and gradually increase speed to fast. When the egg whites form soft peaks, sprinkle in the sugar (decreasing speed if necessary) by 4-spoonful dollops until all is added, then beat at high speed for several minutes until egg whites form stiff shining peaks. Beat in the vanilla. Scoop the meringue into the prepared baking dish, which should be almost filled (but do not worry if dish is only three-quarters full—it makes no difference).

Baking the meringue

Immediately set the dish in the lower-middle level of your preheated oven and bake 35 to 40 minutes, or until the meringue has souffléed (or risen) 2 to 3 inches (5 to 8 cm) and a skewer plunged through the side of the puff down to the bottom of the dish comes out clean. If necessary, bake 4 to 5 minutes or so more—a very little too much is better than too little. Remove from oven and set at room temperature for 30 minutes or until cool; it will sink down to somewhat less than its original volume, and will eventually shrink from sides of dish. When cool, cover and refrigerate.

❶   May be baked several hours or even a day or two in advance; may even be frozen.

Serving

(You may unmold it onto a round platter, pour your custard sauce around, and serve as is, or use the following system.) Run a thin knife around edge of dish to detach meringue, then push the whole meringue gently with a rubber spatula all around to make sure bottom is not sticking. Turn a flat round dish, like a pizza pan, upside down over baking dish and reverse the two, giving a slap and a downward jerk to dislodge meringue onto round dish. Pour a good layer of custard sauce into a round platter, cut large wedges out of the meringue with a pie server, and arrange in the custard. Just before serving, sprinkle the meringue wedges, if you wish, with pulverized nut brittle, crumbled macaroons, toasted ground nuts, or something like the baked meringue-nut layers of a Los Gatos Gâteau Cake (page 11).

Custard Sauce:

You will need about 3 cups (¾ L), using the general outline of the recipe on page 73, with 6 egg yolks, ⅔ cup (1½ dL) sugar, 1½ cups (3½ dL) milk, 1½ tablespoons pure vanilla extract, plus an addition I like with this dessert—3 to 4 tablespoons dark Jamaica rum or bourbon whiskey—and 3 to 4 tablespoons unsalted butter beaten in at the end.

⏱ *Timing*

When we're "just family," or have invited guests to dine informally, we often eat in the kitchen so that last-minute jobs don't interrupt the conversation. With this menu, which does involve some final touches, we'd surely eat there. Before sitting down, one must turn the asparagus in butter; and, since the little sauce is tricky to keep warm, it's a good idea to make it at the last minute. And the spinach and zucchini dish is at its best if you finish its cooking, a matter of moments, just before eating it. The veal and vegetable platter takes only a minute to arrange, so do it on the spot.

The puff pastry is best when just baked, which takes no more than 15 minutes. I'd remove mine from the freezer and slip it into the preheated oven just about halfway through our apéritifs or cocktails.

Otherwise, this meal puts only slight demands on your time. Two hours before dinner, start cooking your casserole. You can arrange it in the morning; and that's when, ideally, you'd shop for the freshest asparagus, spinach, and zucchini. You can boil the asparagus then and precook the wok vegetables.

Both the custard sauce and the meringue, though the latter looks so ethereal, can be made and refrigerated a day or so ahead, and the puff pastry dough, any time at all.

Menu Variations

The appetizer: Inside a hot split piece of puff pastry, you can place a creamed shellfish mixture, sauced wild mushrooms or chicken livers, or—using the butter sauce—substitute peeled broccoli flowerets for the asparagus, or spears of peeled and seeded cucumber cooked in butter with chopped shallots and herbs. Instead of pastry, you can use hard-toasted bread (*croûtes*), and a nice way to make them crisp and rich is to butter sliced crustless bread on both sides and bake till golden in a moderate oven. Or hollow out two-finger-thick rectangles of unsliced white bread, butter tops, sides, and insides, and brown in the oven for *croustades.*

The casserole roast: A boned loin of pork roast works beautifully in this recipe, as does a boneless half turkey breast. Though the slices will be inelegant, you can keep that lovely veal flavor by using a cheaper cut, boned and rolled. Or substitute a boneless cut of beef; but use only meat of roasting quality, like *filet*, sirloin strip, or extra-fine rump.

For aromatic vegetables which will hold their shape and color, think of such roots as onions, turnips, rutabaga, celery root, or oyster plant to combine with the likes of fennel, leeks, or endive. These flavors are strong, so adjust your herbs accordingly.

The wok sauté: For something leafy and green combined with something soft and succulent, one could substitute very young beet or turnip greens, young dandelion leaves, kale, or stemmed chard for the spinach; and for the zucchini, summer or pattypan squash, pumpkin, cucumber, or slivers of white turnip, which are remarkably good with spinach.

The dessert: The American form of floating island has little islets of meringue poached in milk afloat on a custard sauce flavored with vanilla only. I wouldn't use any custard-and-meringue variant involving cake or pastry, since it would be a little heavy, considering the pastry appetizer; but that still leaves a vast range, from the elegant sabayons (of which Zabaione Batardo Veneziano on page 205 is a

cousin on the Bavarian cream side). There are mousses and flans and unmolded custards, simple cup custards baked or boiled; and you could even bake a meringue case with a custard filling and decorate it with fruit. You can make a charming fruit soufflé by adding a thick purée of fruit like prunes or apricots to the meringue mixture, in the proportion of 1 cup (¼ L) purée to 5 egg whites; this, of course, you serve hot. And there are many delicious cold "soufflés."

Leftovers

The casserole: The leftover vegetables, and all the juice, will be good additions to a soup. Cold sliced veal is excellent with a piquant sauce; add any scraps to a creamed dish.

The wok sauté: One delicious by-product is the bright green juice extracted from the zucchini by the grater. If you add it to a soup, be careful with salt, as it contains a lot. Any leftover cooked zucchini and spinach would also be good in a soup; or use it as filling for omelets or quiche.

The dessert: You can refrigerate any leftovers and serve again the next day. Extra custard sauce can be frozen and is wonderful on all kinds of puddings, particularly Indian (see page 72). Or you can stir in any leftover sprinklings, add chopped nuts and chopped candied fruit, and freeze, for a sort of biscuit tortoni. Extra baked meringue is pleasant with a fruit sauce—raspberry, for instance.

Wok sauté of spinach with turnips.

Postscript

The French are given to classifying everything, usually on a scale of grandeur. In ascending degrees, cooking is divided into *la cuisine bonne femme* (goodwife), sometimes also termed *paysanne* or peasant; next step up, plain family cooking, or *la cuisine de famille;* then *la cuisine bourgeoise,* or fancy family cooking; and, finally, great, or high-class, cooking, *la grande* or *la haute cuisine.* The differences are not easy to define.

Perhaps some examples will help. If you have had dinner at midday and now make your supper on a hearty potato-and-leek soup taken with chunks of bread and a local wine and followed by a bowl of cherries, you are eating goodwife or peasant style—which I love to do. If your idea of a Sunday lunch is a starter of sliced tomatoes *vinaigrette,* then roast garlicky leg of lamb with green beans cooked in lard, then cheese, then perhaps an apple tart from the baker's, that's family cooking. Bourgeois cooking—a bit more sophisticated and expensive, but not showy and never eccentric—is exemplified by the menu in this chapter. Grand, or classy, cuisine really means the cooking of great chefs and grand restaurants: with its hierarchy of foundation stocks and sauces and flavored butters, its complexity, and, occasionally, its emphasis on display or on rare ingredients.

In her scholarly *Great Cooks and Their Recipes: From Taillevent to Escoffier* (New York: McGraw-Hill Book Company, 1977), Anne Willan cites Escoffier's turn-of-the-century recipe for Tournedos Chasseur as "a good example of the step-by-step preparation of *haute cuisine,* resulting here in a deceptively simple steak with wine sauce. The recipe requires four basic preparations—stock, demi-glace sauce, meat glaze...and tomato sauce—for the final sauce." *Demi-glace* and meat glaze, as she reminds us, are themselves cooked for hours and are composed of other, still more basic preparations. Nonetheless, the dish is "one of Escoffier's easier recipes for tournedos, with no elaborate garnish."

Cooking of such complexity will rarely be practical at home, though none of the four basic preparations is technically difficult; but other formerly *haute, grande,* and indeed formidable dishes are now perfectly manageable, thanks to the processor, the freezer, etc.

"In reality," wrote Escoffier, "practice dictates fixed and regular quantities, and from these one cannot diverge." He was writing about sauces, of which, in his *Guide Culinaire,* he described 136, not counting dessert sauces. The great codifier put enormous emphasis on correctness, hence predictability. In Escoffier's case, as in politics, his creativity and revolutionary work were succeeded by a long period of gradual rigidification; thirty years after his death in 1935, great chefs were following his dictates everywhere. If you ordered a dish in any great restaurant, you knew by its name precisely what you were getting. If, for instance, your *coulibiac* failed to contain *vesiga,* or a sturgeon's spinal marrow (a minor and almost unobtainable ingredient), then it wasn't *coulibiac* at all, and the chef had scandalously flouted the proprieties.

In the seventies, cooking was released from this straitjacket by the joyously anarchic *nouvelle cuisine,* whose most familiar exponent—to Americans—is Michel Guérard. Best known here for the ingenious diet recipes of *la cuisine minceur*—which is only one aspect of his work—Guérard is a classically trained chef of great sensitivity. His unprecedented combinations and piquant menus have inspired some bizarre travesties; but cooking has been liberated by his daring and original genius. Several of the recipes in this book are *nouvelles* in a restrained way, like the little composed salads which serve as appetizers, or the Choulibiac and the Chicken Melon, both of which, though classical in flavor, are untraditional assemblages.

A natural rightness rather than a pedantic correctness is my goal in cooking. And in composing a menu—or a dish—nobody's codes or classifications have any bearing whatever, so far as I'm concerned. One turns with relief from words to realities.

Essay

Four basic types of rice: (clockwise from upper left) Carolina long-grain, Italian Arborio, short-grain, and converted rice.

Rice Talk

Opening my Rice file is like entering the Tower of Babel. So many kinds of rice, so many recipes, so many cooking methods—and so many disagreements, including, as I experiment over the years, those between J.C. Past and J.C. Present. There is universal agreement, though, on the desired end result for general cooking: perfect rice is dry and fluffy, with every grain separate, and feels very slightly resistant to the tooth. If you encounter a tiny hard core, like a grain of sand, when you bite into a kernel, cook your rice a moment longer. If the kernels appear splayed out at each end, the rice has been cooked too long. Better luck next time.

Rice is so widely cultivated on this earth (we eat more of it even than wheat) that a great many types and cooking methods have evolved, adapted to different climates and cultures. But all rice cookery is based on the fact that rice can absorb at least twice its volume of liquid. It may do this before cooking, as in the Persian *chelo* (pronounced like "hello") with its lovely golden crust: the rice is first soaked for hours, then cooked in butter, without water, in a thick-walled pot. Or the rice may be boiled in a great quantity of liquid; it may be simmered in "just its size" of liquid until all is absorbed; or it may be braised—that is, warmed in oil or butter and then simmered; it may be steamed over (but not *in*) water; or it may be cooked in a combination of liquid and liquiferous substances, like fruits or vegetables.

As it is packaged in America nowadays, rice does not need the preliminary washing always called for in old recipes. This was intended to remove the coating of starch left on the grain after husking, since the starch, combined with moisture, turned into the equivalent of flour paste and made the grains stick gummily together. Brown rice doesn't need washing either: this is rice whose outer hull has been husked, but whose bran coating remains. It is cooked like white long-grain rice but takes twice as long to become tender. I like it, but its pronounced nutty flavor argues with the more delicate sauces. You may have to resort to a health-food store for brown rice, or to a gourmet-type shop for wild rice (which isn't real rice at all, but a grass).

For rice used as an accompaniment to a sauced dish, or rice which I want to serve cold in a salad, or in fact for 90 percent of the rice that we eat in our family, we buy the easily available white long-grain type grown in the Carolinas. You will find our favorite cooking method on page 44. For rice used as a main dish, as in the Italian risottos and the Eastern Mediterranean pilafs, I like a more absorbent rice and choose a shorter grain when I can get it, though the long-grain type will do. Long-grain is so much the easiest type to get here that most Italian cookbooks published in this country prescribe it. For Italian ways with rice, originally adapted to the delicious plump Arborio grain of the Po river valley, I refer you to Marcella Hazan's *The Classic Italian Cook Book* (New York: Alfred A. Knopf, 1976) or to Giuliano Bugialli, *The Art of Fine Italian Cooking* (New York: Quadrangle/The New York Times Book Company, 1977).

But for one especially pleasing main dish, the Spanish paella, you really can't use long-

Brown rice and wild rice.

grain rice. If you can't find the short-grained Spanish sort, or the fat Arborio, look for the patented packaged rice which is clearly labeled "parboiled enriched long-grain rice." The following recipe suggests an international medley of ingredients and equipment; though you don't have to use an electric wok, it does work nicely, and I'm all for being eclectic. Since a paella is essentially a peasanty family dish—although it is wonderful for a party—you can put into it anything you want as long as you have rice, saffron, garlic, and paprika as your base. The following features shrimp, chicken, sausages, and other easily found ingredients, but it could include rabbit, fish, lobsters, snails, mussels, and even squid.

An American Paella in a Chinese-Style Electric Wok

For 8 people

Adapted from *The French Chef Cookbook* and *From Julia Child's Kitchen.* Copyright ©1976 by Alfred A. Knopf, Inc. All rights reserved.

1 pound (450 g) fresh chorizos or Italian sausages, or fresh pork breakfast sausage

2 Tb olive oil

1 cup (¼ L) each sliced onions and green or red bell peppers

8 or more chicken thighs or drumsticks

½ cup (1 dL) dry white wine or dry white vermouth

3 cloves garlic, minced

4½ cups (1 L) chicken broth

½ tsp saffron threads

1 tsp paprika

¼ tsp ground coriander

1 bay leaf

2 cups (½ L) Italian Arborio rice, short-grain rice, or packaged parboiled rice

16 to 24 raw shrimp in the shell

3 medium-size ripe red firm tomatoes peeled, seeded, juiced, and roughly chopped

2 cups (½ L) fresh shelled green peas or diced fresh green beans blanched (boiled) for 5 minutes in a large pan of water, drained, and refreshed in cold water

1 cup (¼ L) chick peas (garbanzos), fresh cooked or canned

½ cup (1 dL) black olives

2 lemons, quartered

Parsley sprigs

Equipment

An electric wok or an electric frying pan, a chicken-fryer skillet, or even a paella pan

Preliminaries with sausages and chicken
Prick sausages in several places with a pin and place in the wok (or whatever you are using) with ¼ inch (¾ cm) water; cover and simmer slowly for 5 minutes and then drain, discarding liquid. Cut sausages into ½-inch (1½-cm) pieces and sauté in pan with the oil until lightly browned; stir in the onions and peppers. Cover and cook slowly until they are tender. Remove with a slotted spoon, leaving fat in pan. Dry chicken pieces with paper towels, heat fat in pan, and brown chicken on all sides. Drain fat out of pan; add the sausages, onions and peppers, and then the wine or vermouth, garlic, chicken broth, saffron, paprika, coriander, and bay leaf. Cover and simmer slowly 15 minutes —chicken will be half to two-thirds cooked and will finish later, with the rice.

🕐 May be cooked in advance; bring to the boil before proceeding.

Finishing the paella
About half an hour before serving, bring chicken-sausage mixture to the rapid boil. Sprinkle in the rice, mixing it down into the liquid with a spoon. Boil rapidly 5 or 6 minutes, uncovered—do not stir the rice. When it has swollen and begun to rise to the surface, rapidly push the shrimp tail-end down into the rice, strew on the tomatoes, peas or beans, chick peas, and olives. Again do not stir; simply push these ingredients down into the rice with a spoon. Carefully correct seasoning. Reduce heat and let paella simmer for another 8 or 10 minutes, or more, always uncovered, until rice is just tender—slightly *al dente*. (It is best not to cover pan, but if you feel rice is not cooking properly, cover for a few minutes, sprinkling on a few tablespoons or so of stock or water if rice seems dry; then uncover to finish the cooking).

At the end of the cooking, the rice will have absorbed the liquid. Serve the paella from its cooking pan, and decorate with the lemon quarters and parsley.

Paella for sharing
Like the dishes on pages 210–225, paella is a fine contribution to a friend's party. Although it may be fully cooked and reheated, it is infinitely better when freshly cooked. I would therefore suggest that you bring the paella to the party with the chicken-sausage mixture done, then add the rice, and finish with the rest of the cooking and the garnish there at the party—and with an electric wok, you can do all of this in public rather than being buried in the kitchen.

"Love in a cold climate" is the phrase for these hearty, comforting dishes from Down East. Great food when a gale is howling outside.

New England Potluck Supper

You would think every northern region of the world would have a version of New England chowder: salt pork and potatoes and onions are everywhere, to combine with whatever fresh or salt fish—or even vegetables—might be handy. But it isn't so: chowder is as typical of New England as the Down East accent which pronounces it to rhyme with "howdah." Equally typical is Indian pudding, so called because it is based on "Indian Meal," the ground dried corn which the early settlers obtained from the Indians of the Bay Colony.

Born a Californian, I first tasted Indian pudding as an adult. It was made by—of all people—an Armenian chef in a restaurant in Lexington, Massachusetts. I loved that first Indian pudding. It was hearty and rich and elemental, deep in flavor, in texture almost like caramel, and I felt it was born out of a harsh climate and an economy of scarcity. I can't taste Indian pudding without thinking of it simmering all of an iron-hard January afternoon, slowly releasing its comfortable spicy scent into a cold dark little cabin. It must have hit the spot for frozen weary people who'd been hacking all day at the endless forest. Chowder, on the other hand, has a summery quality to me, perhaps because I associate it with July and August in Maine, with salty sun-baked granite around me and the sea crinkling below—and with the knowledge that a pail of wild berries is waiting in a cool purple cranny in the rocks. But it's a great dish any time, and a hearty one.

The name comes from *chaudière,* French for the big iron cauldron which was an all-purpose cooking vessel in early times. It could be hung from a fireplace crane, or, if of the footed type, be stood in the warm embers. We borrowed a beautiful old one from the ancient Wayside Inn at Sudbury, Massachusetts, for our television show on chowder, as well as showing forth some machines for grinding your own Indian pudding corn. Of course you can make chowder in any old pot, and of course you can buy cornmeal anywhere; it doesn't make much difference. But I wanted to make a point of the earthy, primal simplicity of these great American dishes. There are loads of recipes around for both fish chowder and Indian pudding, and many cooks insist their particular recipes are the only authentic versions; but the ones I'm giving here are the ones I like, so for me they're the best, the most gen-

uine, indeed the only recipes worth cooking. I like my chowder with untraditional trimmings: croutons instead of pilot biscuits, and sour cream and parsley instead of a final blob of butter. My Indian pudding version is severely plain—unusual, though, in that it contains grated apple; but in fact it's a very old version.

It is adapted from the recipe of Lydia Maria Child (no relation to me), an early feminist of stern and rockbound character, who never, I suspect, threw away a scrap of paper or string and whose mission in life was to teach us all how to live sparely. Her book *The American Frugal Housewife* was first published in 1829, and went through many editions. (A facsimile of the twelfth, published in 1971, is available through the Office of Educational Services, Ohio State University Libraries, Columbus, Ohio 43210.) Mrs. Child's recipe for pudding involves long slow baking and two applications of milk, stirred in the first time, floated on top the second. The result is rich, redolent, and guaranteed to stick to your ribs. There are versions with eggs, or versions cooked quickly; but they don't have that primeval New England Puritan quality that I find so appealing in Lydia Maria Child.

In their journals and in letters home, the settlers gave touchingly fervent thanks for the variety of fish, game, and wild berries they found in New England; but they hadn't much choice of ingredients that kept well. Maybe, if put to it, some good wives occasionally had to use salt pork, onions, and molasses twice in the same meal. Mercifully, we don't, so my excellent recipe for authentic-tasting baked beans, adapted to modern methods, is not suggested for this menu, but placed at a discreet distance, as a bonus.

Lydia Maria Child.

Preparations

Marketing and Storage:
Staples to have on hand

Salt, regular and coarse or kosher (which is
   optional)
Peppercorns
Herbs and spices: sage or thyme; imported bay
   leaves; caraway or cumin seed;
   powdered ginger ▼

Wine vinegar
Mustard (the strong Dijon type; see Remarks,
   page 6)
Flour
Sugar
Butter
Milk
Eggs
Lemons
Celery, carrots, scallions, purple onion, green
   pepper
Fresh parsley

Specific ingredients for this menu

Fish: Several fish frames, if available, for fish
   stock, or bottled or canned clam
   juice (16 ounces or ½ L)
Fresh fish (2½ pounds or 1¼ kg), or see recipe
   for details ▼
Dark unsulphured molasses (½ cup or 1 dL)
Pure vanilla extract
Cornmeal (¼ cup or ½ dL), preferably stone
   ground ▼
Nonsweet white bread, for croutons
Milk (2 quarts or 2 L)
Sour cream (1 pint or ½ L) for chowder and
   cole slaw
Homemade mayonnaise (⅓ to ½ cup or 1 dL),
   optional for cole slaw
Fat-and-lean salt pork (6 ounces or 180 g) ▼
"Boiling" potatoes (4 pounds or 1¾ kg)
Onions (1½ pounds or 675 g or 6 medium-
   size)
Cabbage (1 small-medium)
Vanilla ice cream
Heavy cream
Tart apples (2 medium-size)

▶ *Remarks:*

Staples

Powdered ginger: you can season Indian pudding with a variety of spices, including cinnamon, nutmeg, allspice—alone or in combination—all of which the Puritans could get from the Caribbean Islands along with their molasses and their rum. But I like ginger alone, mostly for its taste but also for its eighteenth-century association with blue and white jars and the tall ships of the China trade.

Specific ingredients for this menu

Cornmeal: can be yellow or white, and I prefer it to be stone ground or home ground, although when it is cooked so long and with such strong flavors the regular supermarket kind is permissible. *Salt pork:* since this is an essential chowder ingredient it should be of top quality; I either use my own (page 250), or look and feel around in the supermarket display until I find a nice softish piece, meaning it is quite freshly salted. The blanching of the pork, in the recipe, not only removes excess salt but freshens the taste. *Fish:* certainly the beauty of a chowder resides in the quality of its fish, which must smell and taste as fresh as possible; see discussion in "Fish Talk," page 111. The clam-juice substitute for your own fresh fish stock is acceptable, although it cannot compare in beauty of taste to the real thing.

New England Fresh Fish Chowder

For 6 people, as a main course

Either—2 or more large meaty fish frames (head and bone structure of freshly filleted fish) from cod, hake, haddock, sea bass, or other lean fish (to provide fish meat and fish stock)

Or—2½ pounds (1¼ kg) fresh cod, hake, haddock, or other lean fish fillets, all one kind or a mixture, plus either 4 cups (1 L) fish stock, or 2 cups (½ L) bottled or canned clam juice and 2 cups (½ L) water

6 ounces (180 g) fat-and-lean salt pork (rind off), diced into ⅜-inch (1-cm) pieces and blanched (boiled 5 minutes in 2 quarts or liters water and drained)

About 4½ cups (1 L) sliced onions

3 Tb flour (optional, but I like a light liaison here)

About 5 cups (1¼ L) sliced "boiling" potatoes

½ tsp sage or thyme

2 imported bay leaves

¼ tsp peppercorns, roughly crushed

Salt (coarse or kosher preferred) and pepper

Fish stock, milk, or water as necessary

½ cup (1 dL), or more, sour cream

⅓ cup (¾ dL) roughly chopped parsley

2 cups (½ L) toasted croutons tossed in butter, salt, and pepper

Equipment

A pressure cooker, optional

Fish stock from fish frames

If you are using fish frames, remove gills (the feathery red tissue) from head and whack fish into pieces that will fit into a kettle; cover with cold water, salt lightly, and boil 3 to 4 minutes or until meat is just cooked on bones. Scrape meat from bones and reserve; return remains to kettle and boil 20 minutes, then strain, discarding bones; this liquid is your fish stock.

The chowder base

Sauté the blanched salt pork several minutes in a 3-quart (3-L) saucepan (or bottom of pressure cooker), to brown very lightly and render fat. Stir in onions and cook 8 to 10 minutes, stirring frequently, until tender and lightly browned (or pressure-cook 2 minutes and release pressure). Drain out fat. Stir in optional flour, adding a little rendered pork fat if too dry, and cook slowly, stirring, for 2 minutes; remove from heat. Bring fish stock or clam juice and water to the simmer, then vigorously beat 4 cups (1 L) into the onions and pork; add the potatoes, herbs, and peppercorns, but no salt until potatoes are tender (or pressure-cook 2 minutes, release pressure, then simmer slowly 5 minutes to bring out flavors). Correct seasoning; you wait until now to add salt because salt pork may still be a bit salty, and store-bought clam juice, if you used it, is bound to be.

🕐 May be completed in advance to this point; refrigerate, and cover when chilled. Will keep 2 days.

Finishing the chowder

Shortly before you are ready to serve, bring chowder base to the simmer. If you are using fresh fish, cut into 2-inch (5-cm) chunks and add to the chowder base along with additional stock, or milk, to cover ingredients; simmer about 5 minutes or until fish is just cooked—opaque rather than translucent and lightly springy. Do not overcook. If you are using cooked fish-frame meat, simply add it when chowder is at the simmer, along with more stock or milk, if you wish; it needs only warming through. Taste carefully and correct seasoning.

🕐 May be completed, chilled, then brought to a simmer again just before serving. Or you may keep the chowder warm for 20 minutes or so, loosely covered and set on an electric hot plate.

To serve

Ladle into wide soup plates, top with a dollop of sour cream, a sprinkling of parsley, and a handful of croutons.

Cole Slaw

For a low-calorie version, simply omit the mayonnaise and/or the sour cream (the liquid from the vegetables makes a natural dressing). Or, as a compromise, include the sour cream but pass a bowl of mayonnaise separately.

4 cups (1 L) thinly shredded cabbage

½ cup (1 dL) each diced green pepper, diced celery, grated carrot, minced scallions or purple onion

1 small apple, grated

3 Tb fresh minced parsley

2 Tb each wine vinegar and fresh lemon juice

1 Tb Dijon-type prepared mustard

1½ tsp each salt and sugar

2 pulverized imported bay leaves

½ tsp caraway or cumin seed

⅓ to ½ cup (¾ to 1 dL) homemade mayonnaise, or sour cream, or a mixture (optional)

Toss together the cabbage, vegetables, apple, and parsley. Combine the other ingredients to make dressing; toss with the cabbage mixture, taste carefully, correct seasoning, and toss again. Taste again; cover and refrigerate for several hours.

Indian Pudding

For about 6 cups, serving 6 to 8 people
Cooking time: 5 to 6 hours

¼ cup (½ dL) cornmeal, stone ground recommended

2 cups (½ L) cold milk, regular or low-fat

2 to 3 Tb butter or chopped fresh beef suet

1 tsp salt

2 tsp fragrant powdered ginger

Scant ½ cup (1 dL) excellent dark unsulphured molasses

1 tart apple, peeled, cored, and coarsely grated (scant 1 cup or ¼ L)

1 cup (¼ L) additional milk

To serve with the pudding: vanilla ice cream, or lightly whipped and sweetened cream, or Custard Sauce (see recipe), or heavy cream and sugar

Equipment

Corn grinder (see right)

Place the cornmeal in a heavy-bottomed 2-quart (2-L) saucepan and with a wire whip gradually beat in the milk. (Old recipes say to sprinkle cornmeal into boiling milk; do it this way if you prefer, but I find no need for it.) Set over moderately high heat and add the butter, salt, ginger, and molasses. Bring to the boil, stirring and beating with a wire whip to be sure all is smooth, then add grated apple. Boil 10 to 15 minutes, stirring frequently, until you have a thick, porridgelike mixture. Meanwhile, preheat oven to 350°F/180°C.

🕐 This preliminary cooking may be done ahead; set aside or refrigerate, and bring to the boil again before proceeding.

Turn the hot pudding mixture into a buttered 2-quart (2-L) baking dish and set uncovered in the middle level of the preheated oven for 20 minutes, or until bubbling. Stir up the pudding, blend in ½ cup (1 dL) additional milk, clean sides of dish with a rubber spatula, and turn oven down to 250°F/130°C. Bake 1½ to 2 hours longer.

Stir up again as before, and pour over surface of the pudding the remaining ½ cup (1 dL) milk, letting it float on top. Continue baking uncovered another 3 to 4 hours; the top will glaze over.

🕐 If you are not ready to serve by that time, cover the pudding and keep it warm, but not too hot or it will dry out.

Serve the pudding (which will look like a very thick caramel-brown sauce) warm, with the ice cream, whipped cream, the following sauce, or cream and sugar passed separately.

Custard Sauce (optional):
For 2 cups or ½ liter

Gradually beat 5 Tb sugar into 4 egg yolks and continue beating until mixture is pale yellow and forms the ribbon. By dribbles beat in 1 cup (¼ L) boiling milk. Set over moderately low heat and stir slowly with a wooden spoon, reaching all over bottom of pan and watching carefully as mixture slowly thickens: at first bubbles will appear on surface, and as they begin to disappear custard is about to thicken; a wisp of steam rising from the surface is another indication. Stir more rapidly, and as soon as custard lies in a creamy layer on the back of the spoon, it is done. Immediately remove from heat, stirring vigorously to cool. Beat in a tablespoon of unsalted butter and tablespoon of pure vanilla extract. Serve hot, warm, or cool.

🕐 May be made a day or two in advance and reheated carefully by stirring over hot water. May be frozen.

🕐 *Timing*

There is only one last-minute job in this menu: adding the fish to the chowder 5 minutes before you serve it. That's for A-Plus results. But there are alternatives, none of which gets less than A-Minus. You can keep chowder warm; you can reheat it; you can make the "base" 2 days in advance. Note—start early if you are using the salt fish suggested in the following variations: 2 or 3 days to soak a whole fish, depending on its size; 24 hours or more for packaged salt cod; a few hours for chopped or shredded salt cod.

Cole slaw must, of course, be made and chilled in advance: anywhere between a few hours to 2 days.

Indian pudding is prepared half a day before serving, since its cooking time is 5 or 6 hours. It can, of course, be made in advance and reheated over hot water; but then you will probably lose the glazed crust because you will need to stir it as it warms.

Menu Variations

The chowder: Using the traditional chowder base of salt pork, onions, and potatoes, you can vary the recipe in a number of ways. You might like to use frozen fish or soaked salt codfish instead of fresh fish, with a fish stock. Vegetarians could make a hearty main course of corn chowder, using butter for salt pork and fresh cream-style grated corn (see "Dinner for the Boss," page 127). I wouldn't use such delicate, expensive shellfish as lobster or crab; but you could have scallops or mussels, and certainly clams. For mussels or steamer clams, because they can be terribly salty I always soak them an hour or more in several changes of cold water. Then steam them open with ½ inch (1½ cm) water in a covered kettle; the steaming liquid becomes the chowder stock, and the shellfish meat, now fully cooked, goes into the finished chowder. Since hard-shelled clams can be tough, I steam them open, chop the meat, and cook it until tender with the pork and onions. As to other chowder systems, some cooks thicken their chowders by running one-quarter of the cooked potatoes through the blender with a little stock and returning them to the pot before the fish goes in. Some garnish chowder with extra bits of fried salt pork, chips of onions fried till dry and brown, or chopped chives. It's all good, and, providing you stick to the traditional base, it's all chowder.

Cole slaw: This splendid stuff has almost as many variations as it does aficionados, as a tour through the basic cookbooks amply illustrates. There's another good cole slaw, based on my friend Avis DeVoto's version, in *J.C.'s Kitchen.*

Indian pudding: "Maybe it's sacrilege," says Anthony Athanas of the Boston waterfront restaurant Anthony's Pier Four, "but we use raisins." For a light, eggy Indian pudding, you couldn't do better than his: ½ cup (1 dL) light cream is brought to the simmer in a double boiler with 2½ cups (6 dL) whole milk; you then add 3½ tablespoons cornmeal and 4 tablespoons granulated sugar, whisking as you go, and let simmer while you beat together 3 "extra-large" eggs, 2½ tablespoons brown sugar, 4 tablespoons molasses, a good pinch each cinnamon and ginger, a pinch nutmeg, and a small pinch salt. Add the heated milk and cream, blend completely, and stir in 5 tablespoons raisins; then pour into a baking dish, set in a pan containing 1 inch (2½ cm) boiling water, and bake for 2 hours at 400°F/200°C.

Leftovers, or:
Use it up, wear it out,
make it do,
or do without

Fish chowder: A completed chowder is good reheated and maybe frozen (once). In some thrifty New England households, part of the liquid is drained off and the solids are topped with buttered crumbs and baked until golden brown. The "base," with the stock added or not, is versatile indeed (see Menu Variations) and may be frozen. Extra fish stock, well strained and frozen, is a kitchen staple for sauces and soups. A very Yankee way of using extra cooked fish is to moisten it with cream or with a "cream" sauce (as they call it although it's usually creamless; the French would call it

Fish cakes and baked beans with English muffins.

béchamel if the liquid is milk, or *velouté* if it is stock) and bake it topped with crumbs or pastry; "fish pie" is a Sunday-night staple Down East, and very good if you add a bit of crab or lobster, dry Madeira, and a speck of nutmeg. Leftover salt cod and potatoes make deep-fried fish cakes (eaten with baked beans on Sunday morning), or, mixed with thick white sauce and crumbed, it becomes fish croquettes. If you made your chowder with smoked fish, it's not far to finnan haddie for a second round. If you used clams, and have a few too many, steam extra raw soft-shelled ones and eat with melted butter; or steam open the hard-shelled type, chop the meat and mix with crumbs, season highly, stuff in the shells, and bake. Or save the soft-shelled type, which, raw and unopened, keep for 3 days in the refrigerator, and use them in the paella on page 64. (Steamer clams have rubbery black necks, which make them unappealing raw.) I really don't see much future (except reheating) for the remains of a corn chowder; but extra raw cream-style corn (see "Dinner for the Boss," page 133) is a treasure not to be wasted.

Cole slaw: A completed cole slaw will keep for several days, though you will want to drain its accumulated juices after a while. You wouldn't want to shred extra cabbage unless you planned to use it soon, because the cut edges wilt, though iced water helps. Cabbage wedges, however, are integral to a New England boiled dinner. Quickly boiled, shredded cabbage is nice with butter and a few caraway or poppy seeds. Braised, with chestnuts or apples, or with sausage and salt meat (as in a *choucroute garnie*), it is delicious. You can bake it with tomato sauce, or with cream or cheese or bits of ham or bacon; you can stuff a strudel with it; or, perhaps best of all, you can combine it with leeks and potatoes for a hearty peasant soup. Or you can save a few outside leaves and stuff them (see *Mastering I*).

Indian pudding: It can be eaten cold or it can be reheated—best done in a double boiler.

Postscript: Another way to bake beans

A few summers ago a friend of ours on the coast of Maine dug a deep hole in his back yard and lined it with big round rocks. Then, one early morning, he built a fire in it and let it smoulder for several hours, raked coals out from the center, and put in a big iron pot filled with pork and beans. He raked the coals back over the pot, piled seaweed on top, and covered that with a canvas tarpaulin which he anchored in place with more big round rocks. In a few hours we could smell those beans cooking, and at 7 o'clock in the evening he unloosed the tarp, raked the seaweed and coal ash from around the pot, and lifted it out, its hoop-shaped handle grasped by a hook-and-pulley contraption he had constructed over the bean hole. We sat out on the grass, in a circle, while he lifted the lid to release the aroma of those slow-cooked beans with the flavor of onions, molasses, and pork baked right into them. They were almost crusty although surrounded by thick juices, and we ate them with great helpings of cole slaw and homemade rye bread.

I thought to myself at the time that I loved the idea of the bean hole, and I loved the beans that came out of it, but why wouldn't an electric Crock-Pot give the same effect? While not quite the same, as I found from experiment, it does produce an easy-cooking meal of pork and beans, and to make things even more untraditional I precooked the beans in a pressure cooker. Anyway, as with a fish chowder, there is no set recipe for baked beans, from Fannie Farmer, Mrs. Rorer, Lydia Maria Child, and on up to the old Boston restaurant of Durgin Park. All the recipes have beans and pork, of course, but in differing quantities; some have molasses, or brown sugar, or even honey or maple syrup. Others include mustard, and vinegar, and tomato, while some have no onion at all, and so forth. I have therefore seasoned my beans to my own taste, which means more onions than usual, a little garlic, herbs, molasses, tomato, and mustard.

Manufacturing Notes:

The Crock-Pot, I find, is slow on cooking raw vegetables; thus I recommend precooking the onions separately with the pork before adding them to the beans. The beans themselves need precooking before they go in, and if they are not quite soft enough beforehand they may remain a little too crunchy even after several hours of crockery. As to the pork, I prefer to blanch it before cooking, to get rid of its salt; otherwise it can oversalt the beans. And whether or not to leave the pork whole or sliced is up to you; I like it cut into strips so that it distributes its considerable charms throughout the beans. Finally, if you don't have a Crock-Pot, just cook the beans in a casserole or bean pot in a 275°F/140°C oven, and if you've no pressure pan for the precooking, simmer the soaked beans in an open pot.

Baked Beans or Boston Baked Beans or Pork and Beans

For about 2 quarts baked beans, serving 6 people

1 pound (450 g) small white beans
6 cups (1½ L) water (more if needed)
8 ounces (225 g) fat-and-lean salt pork (rind included)
2 cups (½ L) diced onions (2 medium-size onions)
2 large cloves garlic, minced or puréed
¼ cup (½ dL) each: dark molasses, plain tomato sauce or purée, and Dijon-type prepared mustard
1 Tb minced fresh ginger (optional)
1 imported bay leaf
½ tsp dried thyme, or mixed herbs such as Italian or Provençal blend
1½ tsp salt

Quick soaking and precooking of the beans

Toss the beans in a sieve and pick over carefully to remove any tiny stones (I found 14 in a box of beans the other day!), rinse under cold water, and place in pressure pan (or saucepan) with the 6 cups (1½ L) water. Bring rapidly to the boil and boil uncovered exactly 2 minutes; remove from heat, cover pan, and let sit exactly 1 hour. Then cover with lid and pressure valve and bring rapidly to full pressure for exactly 1 minute; set aside for 10 minutes, then release pressure (or simmer an hour or so in partially covered saucepan until beans are almost tender when you eat several as a test).

The pork, onions, and other ingredients

Meanwhile cut the salt pork into slices (including rind) ⅜ inch (1 cm) thick and, if you wish, cut the slices into sticks; drop into 2 quarts (2L) cold water and simmer 10 minutes, then drain. Sauté for several minutes in a heavy-bottomed 10-inch (25-cm) frying pan until they start rendering some fat, then fold in the onions. Cover and cook over moderately low heat for 10 minutes or so, stirring up several times, until onions are quite tender but not browned. While onions are cooking, measure out the rest of the ingredients into the Crock-Pot (or a 3-quart or 3-L casserole).

Assembling and baking the beans

When the beans are done, drain them in a colander set over a bowl, and turn them into the Crock-Pot (or casserole), folding them together with the pork and onions and other ingredients. Pour in bean-cooking juices just to level of beans, adding additional water if you need more liquid. Cover Crock-Pot and set at "high" until contents are bubbling, usually 30 minutes, then cook at "low" for 6 to 8 hours, or until you feel the beans are done. (Or set casserole of beans in a 350°F/180°C oven for ½ hour or until bubbling, then turn oven down to 275°F/140°C and bake for 6 to 8 hours.) As they cook, the beans turn a brownish red—a more pronounced color in the oven than in the Crock-Pot—and the various flavors meld themselves into the beans while the juices thicken; their point of doneness is up to you.

🕐   May be baked several days in advance; let cool uncovered, then cover and chill. Reheat to bubbling either in Crock-Pot or in a casserole in a 325°F/170°C oven, and if they seem dry, add spoonfuls of water.

An exquisite and fanciful luncheon menu for your most sophisticated acquaintances, under the Sign of the Smiling Fish.

VIP Lunch

Menu

Apéritif: Kir au Champagne—Champagne with black currant or raspberry liqueur

❧

Choulibiac—Fillets of sole and mushrooms baked in choux pastry

❧

Watercress Salad with Endive and Cucumbers Melba Toast or Toasted Pita Bread Triangles

❧

Sorbet aux Poires—Fresh pear sherbet

❧

*Suggested wines:
A fine white Burgundy or Pinot Chardonnay*

This luncheon menu is elegant but not fussy, unusual but not eccentric, and eminently suitable for those occasions when you want to offer a charming surprise either to distinguished guests, or to friends well-versed in cookery who enjoy innovative food and good wine. The main course, the Choulibiac, is so spectacular a dish in both its composition and its presentation that it needs nothing accompanying it. I follow it with a bit of greenery, and then end the meal with fresh pear sherbet —a delight of the purest and most refreshing kind. Therefore I serve no first course, and offer only a glass of chilled Champagne before the meal. To give a stylish and colorful touch, Paul adds a few drops of black currant or raspberry liqueur to each glass.

Such a creation as the Choulibiac was unthinkable in all but the grandest houses and greatest restaurants until a few years ago, when the invention of the food processor brought such culinary fantasies right to the ordinary kitchen's doorstep. Almost anyone now may produce with ease many a classical preparation of the *haute cuisine* (such as a velvety, airy mousse of fish, which once took hours of labor with mortar and pestle, then beating over constantly renewed bowls of ice, then forcing the mixture through hair-fine sieves). In addition, the basic elements are easily available. So the modern cook's imagination is freed to devise original and fanciful assemblages like the Choulibiac.

In its rococo style, it is almost a playful dish. Even its name is a pun on the Russian *coulibiac,* an envelope of brioche pastry stuffed with salmon, mushrooms, and *kasha*...and a very good dish, too, though a heavy one in comparison to this. The Choulibiac is so much lighter because it rests on a giant crêpe rather than on a layer of brioche dough, and it is encased in the thinnest possible cloak of *choux* or cream puff pastry—just enough to protect its overall inside covering of fish mousse, under which rest layers of the freshest of sole fillets interspersed with wine-flavored minced mushrooms.

What you present to your guests as the finished dish is a plump golden-brown pillow topped with a fat flirtatious fish, wearing such a broad smile that one knows he is proud to have become a Choulibiac. When sliced it is dark brown, white, and daffodil yellow—the layering of mushroom *duxelles,* fish fillets, and fish mousse. Each serving is surrounded with a beautifully buttery yellow sauce.

After the salad, the silver-white pear sherbet seems to capture with icy intensity the flavor and perfume of a ripe pear at its fleeting peak. You can't always count on having perfect pears ready for a given day, and, if you do find some, you can't keep them. But this simple, artful recipe does seem to preserve their indescribable taste intact. You may discreetly enhance it with a touch of Williams pear brandy, which is sold by a few knowing shops to connoisseurs. (It comes with a plump pear lolling about in the bottle. When the pear tree buds, the bottle is slipped over a choice twig and acts as a little private greenhouse for the fruit which ripens inside it, and which will flavor the spirit.)

It seems a bit pedestrian, perhaps, for me to remind you that most of the elements of this meal—except for the final assemblage and baking—can be prepared long in advance, that it requires no novel or difficult techniques, and that it is not particularly expensive. Like so many delightful examples of the rococo, it is simply a happy combination of tried-and-true basic components; and, like them, it is sound and practical. It just happens to be great fun, too.

Preparations

Choulibiac is not a recipe I would attempt at all without a food processor. One could do it, of course, spending several hours mincing acres of mushrooms, grinding the fish, beating over ice—but not me! I'd pick another recipe, and I have made suggestions for variations and alternatives in Menu Variations later in the chapter. And you do need an ice-cream maker with dasher for the sherbet.

Marketing and Storage:
Staples to have on hand

Salt
White peppercorns ▼
Nutmeg
Mustard, the strong Dijon type (see Remarks, page 6)
Olive oil and cooking oil
Optional: semisweet chocolate (4 ounces or 115 g); unsweetened chocolate (1 ounce or 30 g)
Sugar (instant superfine useful but not essential)
Instant-blending flour (⅓ cup or ¾ dL), useful but not essential ▼
All-purpose flour
Milk
Heavy cream (1 to 2 cups or ¼ to ½ L)
Butter (½ to 1 pound or 225 to 450 g), depending on the way you make the sauce for the Choulibiac)
Eggs (8 "large")
Lemons (4)
Shallots and/or scallions
Onion, carrot, celery stalk, and imported bay leaf—for fish stock
Wines and liqueurs: dry white French vermouth and Cognac

Specific ingredients for this menu

Coarse salt (2 pounds or 1 kg) for freezing sherbet
Sole fillets (about 2 pounds or 900 g, 16 skinless and boneless pieces about 9 by 2 inches or 23 x 5 cm) ▼
Halibut fillets or additional sole (½ pound or 225 g) ▼
Fresh fish trimmings (enough to make about 2 cups or ½ L), for fish stock ▼
Fresh mushrooms (1 quart or 10 ounces or 285 g)
Cucumbers (2)
Watercress (2 or 3 bunches)
Belgian endive (3 or 4 heads)
Fresh parsley (1 bunch)
Optional: fresh dill weed (a stalk or two; see Remarks, page 96)
Optional: cherry tomatoes (about 1½ dozen), for salad
Melba toast (page 124) or toasted pita bread triangles (page 203)
Pears (5 or 6 ripe, full-of-flavor) ▼
Pear liqueur (Eau-de-Vie de Poire Williams recommended)
Champagne (1 bottle)
Crème de cassis or liqueur de framboise (¼ bottle black currant or raspberry liqueur)

▶ *Remarks:*

Staples

White peppercorns: not always to be found on supermarket shelves, these can be had bottled at specialty shops. White pepper, used in most fish dishes or white sauces, is the mature pepper berry with its husk rubbed off; black is the dried immature berry. *Instant-blending flour:* the patented granular type, which is so useful for crêpes; if you can't find it, use regular flour in the recipe, as indicated.

Ingredients for this menu

Fish: see "Fish Talk," page 111, for details. *Fish stock:* to make the sauce for the Choulibiac; or use a hollandaise sauce, as described on page 171 (but you will probably want to omit the *béchamel* stabilizer needed for that Breakfast Party holding operation). *Pears:* most pears as you buy them are not fully ripe, but some, if they were picked when immature, will never ripen. Therefore, look for firm flesh that has just begun to soften. The best pears for your sherbet are full-flavored varieties like Bartlett (buy when turning yellowish or rosy), or Anjou or Comice (buy yellow-green). Be careful there is no weakening of the flesh near the stem (an indication the pear is immature); avoid wilting or shriveling flesh, dull skin with no gloss, and spots on the sides or at the blossom (large) end of the fruit. Ripen for a few days at room temperature in a closed paper bag or a ripening device (the purpose of either is to trap the harmless—indeed benign—ethylene gas exuded by ripening fruit). A nearly ripe apple or tomato, enclosed with your pears, will hasten the work. When perfectly ripe, the skin color is yellower or rosier and the pear is very fragrant. At this point, chill if you can't use at once; but don't wait long.

Choulibiac

Fillets of sole baked with mushrooms and fish mousse in a choux pastry crust

This free-form rectangular structure built upon a giant crêpe is an elegant creation and definitely *grande cuisine*, but parts of it may be assembled bit by bit, as you have time—and as you will see from the following recipe.

For a rectangular Choulibiac about 12 by 5 by 2½ inches (30 x 13 x 6½ cm), serving 6 to 8 people

Batter for Giant Crêpe
Baked in an 11-by-17-inch (27-x-42-cm) jelly roll pan, nonstick if possible

⅓ cup (¾ dL) Wondra or instant-blending flour, or all-purpose flour
½ cup (1 dL) milk
1 "large" egg
1 Tb cooking oil
½ tsp salt

Pâte à choux
About 3 cups (¾ L), for fish mousse and for encasing Choulibiac

1½ cups (3½ dL) water in a heavy-bottomed 2½-quart (2½-L) saucepan
6 ounces (1½ sticks or 180 g) butter, cut into ½-inch (1½-cm) pieces
1½ tsp salt
1 cup (¼ L) flour (measure by scooping dry-measure cup into flour and sweeping off excess)
6 "large" eggs

Filling ingredients

16 skinless and boneless sole fillets (each about 9 x 2 inches, or 23 x 5 cm), or about 2 pounds (900 g)

½ pound (225 g) skinless and boneless halibut, or more sole fillets

1 cup (¼ L) heavy cream, chilled

1 quart (10 ounces or 285 g) fresh mushrooms

Miscellaneous

Several shallots and/or scallions

A little Cognac and 3 Tb dry Port or Sercial Madeira

Salt, freshly ground white pepper, ground nutmeg

4 or more Tb butter (for greasing pans, sautéing, etc.)

4 funnels made of aluminum foil (twisted around a pencil), ⅓ inch (¾ cm) in diameter and 1 inch (2½ cm) long

Egg glaze (1 egg beaten with 1 tsp water in a small bowl)

3 cups (¾ L) white wine sauce (next recipe) or hollandaise, page 171, to serve with the Choulibiac

Equipment

You need a sturdy, level jelly roll pan, preferably with a nonstick surface. An old battered pan is going to produce an uneven crêpe since the batter is spread so thin—there may even be areas that are not covered, while other areas, where the batter settles, will be too thick. Also, your oven must be absolutely level. If you don't have reliable equipment, make two large, thin crêpes in your biggest frying pan, then piece them together to obtain approximately the dimensions called for in the final assembling.

The giant crêpe

Place the flour in a mixing bowl and beat in the milk, egg, oil, and salt; let rest for 10 minutes. Meanwhile preheat oven to 400°F/200°C, smear jelly roll pan with a tablespoon of soft butter, roll flour in it, and knock out excess. Pour crêpe batter into pan to a depth of about ⅛ inch (½ cm), and set in lower level of oven for 4 to 5 minutes, until batter has set. Then place pan 4 to 5 inches (10 to 13 cm) under a medium-hot broiler element to brown top of crêpe slowly and lightly—it will seethe and bubble a bit as it browns but do not let it overcook and stiffen. Remove from oven and with a flexible-blade spatula carefully loosen crêpe all around from edges to center of pan. If it sticks, it has not cooked quite long enough; return to lower level of oven 2 to 3 minutes more. Slide crêpe off onto a cake rack.

🕐 You may roll crêpe, when cool, between two sheets of wax paper and refrigerate, or wrap airtight and freeze.

Seasoning the fish fillets

Mince enough shallots or scallions to make 3 tablespoons and set aside in a small bowl, reserving half for the mushrooms later. Choose a rectangular or oval dish 10 to 12 inches (25 to 30 cm) long, sprinkle 1 teaspoon shallots on the bottom, and arrange over them a layer of overlapping sole fillets; season lightly with salt and pepper, a sprinkling of minced shallots or scallions, a few drops of Cognac, and continue with the rest of the fillets, making probably three layers in all. Cover with plastic wrap and refrigerate. (Set over ice if wait is more than a few hours.)

The pâte à choux

Bring the 1½ cups (3½ dL) water rather slowly to the boil with the cut-up butter and the salt. As soon as butter has melted, remove from heat and immediately dump in all of the cup (¼ L) of flour at once, beating vigorously with a portable mixer and/or wooden spoon. When smooth, set over moderately high heat and beat for several minutes until mixture begins to film the bottom of the pan—indicating excess moisture has boiled off.

When using a food processor, scrape hot paste into machine, activate it, and break in 5 eggs rapidly, one after the other, then stop the machine. (Do the same if you have a table model mixer, beating just until each egg is absorbed before adding the next. By hand,

make a well in center of hot paste in saucepan, then beat in 5 eggs one by one with either a portable mixer or a wooden spoon. Break sixth egg into a bowl, blend yolk and white with a fork, and how much to add to the paste depends on its thickness—it should just hold its shape in a spoon. Beat in as much of the final egg by droplets as you judge safe, remembering the more egg the more the pastry puffs, but you don't want the batter to thin out too much.)

Remove ½ cup (1 dL) of the *choux* pastry to a medium-size metal mixing bowl and reserve for fish mousse, next step. For the food processor, scrape paste back into the saucepan, and do not wash out processor; simply replace blade; cover pastry with plastic wrap, set in a pan of warm but not too hot water, and hold for final assembly.

The fish mousse

Set the reserved bowl of *choux* pastry in a larger bowl with a tray of ice cubes and water to cover them, and stir several minutes with a wooden spoon to chill; leave over ice. For the food processor, cut the halibut and one of the sole fillets into ½-inch (1½-cm) pieces and place in the processor with the cold *choux* paste, ¾ cup (1¾ dL) chilled cream, ½ teaspoon salt, several grinds white pepper, and a big pinch nutmeg; activate the processor for about a minute, until the fish is ground into a fine paste. If still stiff, beat in more cream by dribbles—mousse must be just firm enough to hold its shape for spreading; scrape out of food processor into *choux*-paste bowl; do not wash processor; simply replace blade and use for mushrooms, next step. (Lacking a processor, put fish twice through finest blade of meat grinder and beat resulting purée into the *choux* paste over ice; then, with a portable mixer, beat in the seasonings and, by driblets, as much of the cream as the mixture will take and still hold its shape.)

Cover bowl with plastic wrap and, still over ice, refrigerate.

⏱ Or cover airtight and freeze if wait is longer than 12 hours.

The mushroom duxelles

Trim the mushrooms, wash rapidly, and if you are using a food processor, chop by hand into ½-inch (1½-cm) pieces, then mince 1 cup (¼ L) at a time in the processor—flipping it on and off every second just until mushrooms are cut into ⅛-inch (½-cm) pieces; otherwise mince by hand with a big knife. To extract juices, either squeeze in a potato ricer or twist by handfuls in the corner of a towel. Sauté in a frying pan, in 2 tablespoons hot butter and 1 tablespoon minced shallots or scallions until mushroom pieces begin to separate from each other—4 to 5 minutes over moderately high heat, stirring. Season lightly with salt and pepper, pour in 3 tablespoons Port or Madeira, and boil down rapidly to evaporate liquid. Scrape the *duxelles* into a bowl and reserve.

⏱ If done in advance, cool, cover, and either refrigerate for up to 4 or 5 days, or freeze.

Assembling the Choulibiac

Spread the giant crêpe, browned side down, on a buttered baking sheet (nonstick if possible)

and trim off any stiff edges with scissors. Spread ⅓ of the fish mousse in a rectangle about 12 inches (30 cm) long and 5 inches (13 cm) wide down the center, and over it arrange ½ of the fish fillets, slightly overlapping. On top of that spread ½ of the mushroom *duxelles*, then the rest of the fish fillets and remaining *duxelles*. Beat any fish-seasoning juices into reserved mousse, spread mousse over top and sides of fish structure, then bring the ends and sides of the crêpe (cutting out the corners) up over the fish. Trim off excess crêpe, leaving a side edging on top of only 1 inch (2½ cm). Reserve ½ cup (1 dL) or so of pastry for final decorations; then, using a flexible-blade spatula dipped in cold water, spread ⅛ inch (½ cm) *choux* pastry evenly over top and sides, masking the structure completely. Poke holes ⅛ inch (½ cm) across and ½ inch (1½ cm) deep, angled toward center of structure, in the lower part of each of the four corners, and insert buttered foil funnels (to drain out any juices during baking).

⏱ Refrigerate the Choulibiac if you are not continuing—but plan to bake it within a few hours.

Final decorations and baking

Baking time: about 45 minutes
Preheat oven to 425°F/220°C and set rack in lower-middle level. If *choux* pastry has cooled and stiffened, beat over hot water to soften and warm to tepid only; spoon it into a pastry bag with ½-inch (1½-cm) cannelated tube. Paint Choulibiac with a coating of egg glaze, then pipe *choux* pastry decorations onto it—such as the fanciful outline of a fish with mouth, eyes, fins; or a zigzag border all around the edges and a number of rosettes on top. Glaze the decorations, and the rest of the pastry, with two coatings of egg.

Immediately set in oven and bake for 15 to 20 minutes at 425°F/220°C, or until the pastry top has begun to brown and to puff slightly; turn thermostat down to 375°F/190°C and continue baking another 20 min-

utes or so. Choulibiac is done when you begin to smell a delicious odor of pastry, fish, and mushrooms, and, finally, when juices start to exude onto baking sheet. (Pastry will not puff a great deal, just slightly.)

Plan to serve as soon as possible, although the Choulibiac will stay warm in turned-off oven, door ajar, for 20 to 30 minutes—the longer it sits the more of its vital fish juices will exude. Loosen bottom of Choulibiac carefully from pastry sheet, using a flexible-blade spatula, and slide it onto a hot platter or a serving board.

To serve, cut into crosswise pieces from one of the short sides and surround each portion with sauce—either the following, which can be made well ahead, or hollandaise (see page 171).

Sauce Vin Blanc:
White wine velouté sauce

For about 2½ cups

If you plan on this sauce for the Choulibiac, save out 5 to 6 tablespoons of the *choux* pastry (scrapings from the pastry bag, for instance), and the sauce is practically made, except for the white-wine fish stock. Here's how to go about it, in a rather free-form way.

2 cups (½ L) fresh fish trimmings (or extra sole or halibut)

1 small onion, chopped

½ carrot, chopped

1 small celery stalk, sliced

8 to 10 parsley stems (not leaves)

1 imported bay leaf

1 cup (¼ L) dry white French vermouth

1 cup (¼ L) water

½ tsp salt (and more as needed)

5 to 6 Tb ready-made *choux* pastry in a bowl

About 1 cup (¼ L) milk

About ½ cup (1 dL) heavy cream

White pepper

Drops of fresh lemon juice

Softened unsalted butter, as your conscience permits

Simmer the fish trimmings or fish with the vegetables, herbs, wine, water, and ½ teaspoon salt for 20 to 30 minutes; strain, then boil down rapidly to 1 cup. Gradually blend into the *choux* pastry, pour into saucepan and simmer, thinning out as necessary with spoonfuls of milk and cream. Sauce should coat a spoon lightly; season carefully with additional salt, pepper, and drops of lemon juice.

🕐 If made in advance, clean sauce off sides of pan and float a spoonful of cream over surface to prevent a skin from forming. Bring to the simmer before proceeding.

Just before serving, taste again carefully for seasoning, then remove from heat and beat in softened butter by spoonfuls. (Just a spoonful or two will enrich the sauce nicely, but you may beat in as many more, almost, as you wish, as though you were making a hollandaise.)

Watercress Salad with Endive and Cucumbers

The salad should really be served after the Choulibiac, but this depends on your table and service arrangements. Whether to serve it on a platter or in a big bowl, or arrange each serving individually—which can be very attractive—is also a matter of your choice and facilities. Pass the Melba toast or pita separately. For recipes, see page 124 for Melba toast and page 203 for homemade pita.

For 6 people

2 or 3 bunches watercress, depending on size
2 cucumbers
3 or 4 heads Belgian endive
1 tsp Dijon-type prepared mustard
1 Tb fresh lemon juice
4 to 5 Tb best-quality light olive oil or salad oil
Salt and pepper
Fresh minced dill weed or parsley, halved cherry tomatoes (optional)

Trim off tough stems from watercress, wash the cress, spin dry, and wrap loosely in a clean towel; refrigerate in a plastic bag. Peel the cucumbers, slice thin, and refrigerate in a bowl of salted water; drain thoroughly and dry in a towel before serving. Separate the leaves from the central stems of the endive and refrigerate in a damp towel and plastic bag. Place the mustard, lemon juice, and oil in a screw-topped jar, season with salt and pepper, shake to blend, taste, and correct seasoning.

At serving time, toss each ingredient separately in a little of the dressing (well shaken first), correct seasoning for each, and make your arrangement. One I like is to place the endives first, like the spokes of a wheel, then make a bed of cress, and a topping of cucumber slices. (You may also like a sprinkling of fresh minced dill or parsley tossed with your cucumbers, and a few halved cherry tomatoes placed around for color.)

Cocktail Party

Cocktail parties aren't what they used to be, and that's all right with me. Goodbye to boozing and starving and crowding and screaming, to five-to-seven and six-to-eight, to the sudden exodus, to the ruined parlor; and goodbye, above all, to that day-after-Christmas feeling, when you realize you never had a minute with the people you most wanted to see. And welcome, with three loud cheers, to easy evenings of good wine and good food and good friends.

We like to give our guests a *spread.* I hate it when people get hungry after a couple of drinks and charge out somewhere to supper before I even get to see them. So Paul and I set out plates and forks and napkins as a hint to stay; and I serve a great big puffy something I baked specially, and something fishy and fresh, and lots of good hearty treats on the side: chicken wings and oysters and clams and stuffed eggs, and meatballs and rabbit food. And peanuts too. Of course we serve the usual drinks—including at least one of Paul's special inventions—but our friends mostly prefer wine for a long evening, so we have plenty of that.

In line with the good new custom of more cheer for fewer people, we give our parties in the kitchen, right in the heart of the house. People can't come into a kitchen and not relax. And we've gotten bored anyway with "Queen Anne in front and Mary Anne behind": the parlor gussied up with coasters and teeny napkins while frenzy reigns out back. Yes, there's some mess. Puff pastry means crumbs and shellfish mean shells. We just line a couple of wastebins with plastic bags which we replace as they fill up and hoist out the back door.

Paul had the thought of making a big wood frame lined with heavy plastic (with a drain for drips) for the cold things. We heap it with ice and set it right on the stove top, where it looks bounteous. We flank it with hot dishes on an electric tray, and use cutting boards to serve a couple of ham Pithiviers tarts, high as hassocks and light as clouds. They're not much work, if you make your puff pastry in advance and do it the fast new way. Puff pastry can be your best friend too, and if you've not yet mastered it, bear in mind three great truths. Don't be afraid of it. Keep it cold. And finally, don't fight it: rest it often, just as you would a fussy baby.

That big slab of fish on the ice mound is *gravlaks,* salmon rubbed with salt, bedded on dill (and spruce twigs if you have them), anointed with Cognac, weighted down, and macerated in the refrigerator for three or four days at least. It's an exquisite preparation, fresher and more delicate than smoked salmon but not raw-tasting (for the salt "cooks" it). I first sampled *gravlaks* in Oslo when Paul was Cultural Attaché at the American Embassy. The salmon was served with scrambled eggs and creamed potatoes as a main course. Delicious! But I also like it for cocktails served with buttered pumpernickel.

Spicy things are nice with cocktails, too, and I always like something hot, so we make minimeatballs of ground beef mixed with a bit of pork sausage for richness, as well as a delightful, vaguely Oriental preparation of chicken wings. Radish roses with little topknots of sweet butter, stuffed eggs flavored with lemon and anchovy and topped with enormous capers the size of fat peas, and peanuts, of course. Without peanuts, it isn't a cocktail party.

Preparations

Recommended Equipment:
You'll want plenty of beer can openers, oyster knives, and paring knives for the shellfish, and something you can make a bed of ice in: a giant bowl, a washtub, or a deep tray. Or, if you have two sinks, use one for the purpose, as we do our vegetable sink.

A proper rolling pin is essential for puff pastry, one at least 16 inches (40 cm) long. If yours is too short, you're better off with a broomstick. (See the recipe for details and illustrations.) A pastry marble, cut to fit your refrigerator shelf, is most desirable if you are going in for any serious pastry making. (Look in the Yellow Pages under Marble or Tombstones; the seller will cut one to size for you.) A heavy-duty electric mixer is the way to lightning-fast puff pastry; but, if you do it by hand, don't use a pastry blender for the new method. It cuts the butter too fine. Pleasant but nonessential aids are a roller-pricker and a large ravioli cutting wheel.

A pastry bag with two cannelated (toothed) tubes, one medium sized for the eggs, one tiny for the radishes, will prettify them.

An electric warming tray and a couple of portable cutting boards are a great help in serving, as are two or three wastebins with plastic trash bag liners for the debris.

Marketing and Storage:
Staples to have on hand

Salt
Peppercorns
Granulated sugar
Orange bitters
Bottled sweetened lime juice
Hot pepper sauce, soy sauce, Worcestershire
    sauce
Capers
Orange marmalade
Oregano or thyme
Italian seasoning (an herb blend)
Mustard, the strong Dijon type (see page 6)
Tomato purée or sauce, canned

Olive oil or fresh new peanut oil (see page 52)
Garlic; shallots or scallions
Beef stock or bouillon, frozen or canned
Fresh bread crumbs (in the freezer; see
    page 6)
Wines and liqueurs: dry white French
    vermouth, Cognac, orange liqueur

Specific ingredients for this menu

Boiled ham (6 ounces or 180 g per Pithiviers)
Center-cut fresh salmon and/or other fresh
    fish (5 pounds or 2½ kg per recipe
    gravlaks) ▼
Fresh pork sausage meat (4 ounces or 115 g
    per recipe meatballs)
Lean ground beef (1 pound or 450 g per recipe
    meatballs)
Chicken wings (24 per recipe)
Small amounts (optional): fermented dry black
    Chinese beans; dark sesame oil; dried
    Chinese mushrooms; fresh or pickled
    ginger—for chicken wings ▼
Mayonnaise, anchovy paste, curry powder,
    and/or other items for stuffing hard-
    boiled eggs
Pumpernickel bread
Peanuts and/or various nuts, to serve with
    drinks
Heavy cream (4 Tb per Pithiviers)

Eggs (3 per Pithiviers, 1 for the meatballs, plus
    however many you wish for stuffed egg
    recipe)
Cheese for grating—Cheddar, Swiss, Parmesan
    or a combination of all three (1 pound or
    450 g at least; to be used for cheese
    appetizers and 6 ounces or 180 g per
    Pithiviers) ▼
Unsalted butter (2½ pounds or 1125 g for puff
    pastry, plus butter for pumpernickel
    bread, radishes, and other purposes)
Cake flour, plain bleached (1 cup or 140 g per
    puff pastry recipe)
All-purpose flour, unbleached (3 cups or 420 g
    per puff pastry recipe) ▼
Lemons (4 per chicken wing recipe, plus those
    needed for serving oysters and clams,
    drinks, etc.)
Limes, for drinks
Oranges (1 per apéritif recipe for 6 people)
Parsley and/or watercress, for decoration
Fresh or fragrant dried dill weed and, if
    available, spruce branches for *gravlaks* ▼
Radishes
Oysters and clams ▼
Ice cubes for drinks, and crushed ice for shellfish
Red wines, white wines, and dark Jamaica rum
Other drinks for your usual bar set-up

▶ *Remarks:*

Fresh fish: be sure to buy the fish for your *gravlaks* well enough ahead—see recipe for details. *Fermented dry black Chinese beans and dark sesame oil:* obtainable in Chinese and Japanese grocery stores and many fancy food stores; good items to know because they add a very special flavor to all kinds of dishes, not only chicken, but shrimp, fish, and so forth. No reason to confine them to Oriental cooking. *Dried Chinese mushrooms:* you need only 2 or 3 of these pungent mushrooms to give a fine mushroom flavor to many a dish; soak them in warm water until they have softened, and if the stems remain tough, cut them off and discard them. Then slice or chop the mushrooms and use like fresh mushrooms. *Ginger:* fresh gingerroot is to be had in many supermarkets these days. You can freeze it and grate or slice it—still frozen—into whatever you are cooking, using just what you need and storing the rest in the freezer. Pickled ginger, put up in brine and usually vinegar, keeps for months in the refrigerator; you can normally find it in Japanese and Chinese grocery stores. *Cheese for grating:* I find it a very good idea to grate up leftover hard cheeses like Cheddar, Swiss, and Parmesan and to package them together in a plastic bag or container in my freezer; I always have cheese on hand, then, and none is wasted. *Unbleached all-purpose flour:* essential, in my experience, for puff pastry, since bleached flour makes a tough pastry and is also hard to roll out; if your market doesn't carry unbleached flour, look for it in health food stores. *Dill weed:* fresh dill is always preferable to dried when you can find it, and you can store it in your freezer: stem it, wash and dry it thoroughly, then chop it fine and pack it in small parcels for freezing. This works with chives too. The secret is to exclude all moisture and air before freezing. Sometimes you can find fragrant dried bottled dill weed; smell it before using to be sure it is full of flavor and aroma. *Oysters and clams:* see "Fish Talk," page 111, for details, including a clever way to open oysters.

A Preamble to French Puff Pastry— made a new fast way

The most marvelous of all doughs, to my mind, is French puff pastry, the pastry of a thousand leaves that puffs up in the oven as it bakes because it is made of many many layers of paper thin dough interspersed with many many layers of butter. It is light as air, flaky, tender, buttery, and so good to eat just of itself that it hardly needs an accompaniment. It not only makes *vol-au-vent* pastry cases and patty shells, but all manner of tarts and cookies, cheese and ham concoctions, dessert cakes, and so forth. For a cocktail party it is practically a must, and, since you can prepare it months and months ahead, you could even consider it a staple ingredient to have on hand in your freezer. Once made, it can quickly be turned into a spectacular, like the ham Pithiviers to serve at this party—shown below just out of the oven.

I must admit to having spent years and years on puff pastry, starting out in Paris way back in the early 1950s. I learned to make it in the classical way, where you start with a flour-water dough that you spread out into a thick pancake and fold around an almost equal amount of butter. Next, you roll that out into

a long rectangle and the butter follows along inside the dough. Then you fold that into three, like a business letter, and roll it out again. All the time the butter is extending itself in layers inside the dough, and every time you fold it those layers triple in number until by the sixth roll-and-fold you have 729 layers of butter between 730 layers of dough.

All this manipulation gives the dough a heavy workout, which is fine when you have flour with a low gluten content, like French flour. But when you are working with regular American all-purpose flour, which has a relatively high gluten content, the dough becomes rubbery, refuses to be rolled out, and you have to let it rest and relax until you can continue. My French colleague Simone Beck and I almost gave up on *pâte feuilletée with* American flour until I happened to be doing a television show on entertaining at the White House, and their then pastry chef, Ferdinand Louvat, produced some splendid *vol-au-vent* structures. He used all-purpose flour, he told me, but for every 3 parts all-purpose flour he put in 1 part cake flour; the cake flour lowered the gluten content and made the dough easy to handle.

That was our first breakthrough, and the recipe for classic puff pastry using that formula is in Volume II of *Mastering*. The second breakthrough is an entirely new way of making the pastry, suggested by a reading of *La Cuisine de Denis* (ed. Robert Laffont, Paris, 1975). Instead of forming the dough into a package encasing a mass of butter, you break the butter up into large pieces the size of lima beans and mix them with the flour, salt, and water; then you form this messy-looking mass into a long rectangle, patting and rolling it out. You fold it into three, roll it out, fold it again, and it begins to look like dough. After 2 additional turns it is smooth and fine; you then rest it 40 minutes and it is ready for its final 2 rolls and folds and its forming and baking. Now puff pastry can be made in an hour, rather than the 3 or 4 hours usually necessary for the classical method using all-purpose flour.

Because the butter is in large lumps, they form themselves into the required layers as you proceed to roll and fold the dough. You can see from the illustrations that the puff pastry rises dramatically as it should—just as much if not more so than the classical puff pastry. In fact, since experimenting with this new system I've not gone back to the old method at all.

Puff pastry proportions
Proportions for the new fast puff pastry are 5 parts butter to 4 parts flour—the large amount of butter necessary because you have to flour the dough more as you roll it than in the old method. These amounts easily translate into metrics as 125 grams butter for every 100 grams flour. In cups and spoons they approximate:

1 cup (5 ounces or 140 g) flour as follows: ¾ cup (3½ ounces or 105 g) unbleached all-purpose flour, and ¼ cup (1¼ ounces or 35 g) plain bleached cake flour
1½ sticks plus 1 Tb (6½ ounces or 185 g) chilled unsalted butter
Scant ½ tsp salt
¼ cup (½ dL) iced water

Hand versus machine
I like to make my pastry in a heavy-duty electric mixer with flat beater, using 4 cups of flour and ending up with a goodly amount of dough. It does not work well in a food processor, because the butter becomes too much broken up and the pastry does not puff dramatically. Mixing by hand works out nicely, but be sure not to soften the butter too much; cut it into ½-inch dice, then rub it with the flour between the balls of your fingers until it is broken into thickish disks, like fat cornflakes. The water goes in after the butter and flour have been mixed together, making a very rough, barely cohesive mass.

Fast French Puff Pastry

Pâte Feuilletée Exprès

For one 9-inch Pithiviers and 36 or more cheese appetizers; or for a rectangle of dough some 36 by 12 by ¼ inches (90 x 30 x ¾ cm)

Note: Measure flour by dipping dry-measure cups into container, then sweeping off excess even with lip of cup; no sifting necessary.

3 cups (420 g) unbleached all-purpose flour
1 cup (140 g) plain bleached cake flour
6½ sticks (26 ounces or 735 g) chilled unsalted butter
1½ tsp salt
1 cup (¼ L) iced water
Equipment
A heavy-duty electric mixer with flat beater (useful); a 1½-by-2-foot (45-x-60-cm) work surface, preferably of marble; a rolling pin at least 16 inches (40 cm) long; a pastry sheet (for lifting and turning dough) about 10 inches (25 cm) wide; a pastry scraper or wide spatula; plastic wrap

Mixing the dough

Place the flour in your mixing bowl. Rapidly cut the sticks of chilled butter into lengthwise quarters, then into ½-inch (1½-cm) dice; * add to the flour—if you have taken too long to cut the butter and if it has softened, refrigerate bowl to chill butter before proceeding. Add the salt. Blend flour and butter together rapidly, if by hand to make large flakes about an inch in size. By machine the butter should be roughly broken up but stay in lumps the size of large lima beans. Blend in the water, mixing just enough so that dough masses roughly together but butter pieces remain about the same size.

The first 4 turns

Turn dough out onto a lightly floured work surface, as illustrated in the first picture on the right. Rapidly push and pat and roll it out into a rectangle in front of you—12 to 14 inches for 2 cups of flour, about 18 for 4 cups (30 to 35 cm and 40 to 45 cm). It will look an awful mess! Lightly flour top of dough and, with pastry sheet to help you, flip bottom of rectangle up over the middle, and then flip the top down to cover it, as though folding a business letter. Lift dough off work surface with pastry sheet; scrape work surface clean, flour the surface lightly, and return dough to it, settling it down in front of you so that the top flap is at your right. Lightly flour top of dough, and pat, push, and roll it out again into a rectangle; it will look a little less messy. Fold again into three as before—each of these roll-and-fold operations is called a "turn." Roll out and fold 2 more times, making 4 turns in all, and by the last one the pastry should actually look like dough. You should see large flakes of butter scattered under the surface of the dough, which is just as it should be. With the balls of your fingers (not your fingernails) make 4

If you have bought the kind of butter that seems soft and sweats water when you cut it, that means it is inferior quality and will not make this puff pastry rise as it should. In this case you eliminate the extra moisture by first kneading it in ice water and then squeezing in a damp towel to remove excess water. Then chill.

depressions in the dough to indicate the 4 turns, as I've done in the final picture below— just in case you go off and forget what you've done.

Finishing the dough—the 2 final turns
Wrap the dough in plastic, place in a plastic bag, and refrigerate for 40 minutes (or longer) to firm the butter and relax the gluten in the dough. Give the dough 2 more turns, beating it back and forth and up and down first if chilled and hard. Let dough rest another 30 minutes if it seems rubbery and hard to roll; then it is ready for forming and baking.

🕐 Dough may be frozen after the first 4 turns, although it is easier to complete the 6 of them before freezing. It will keep, wrapped airtight, for months. Defrost overnight in the refrigerator, or at room temperature.

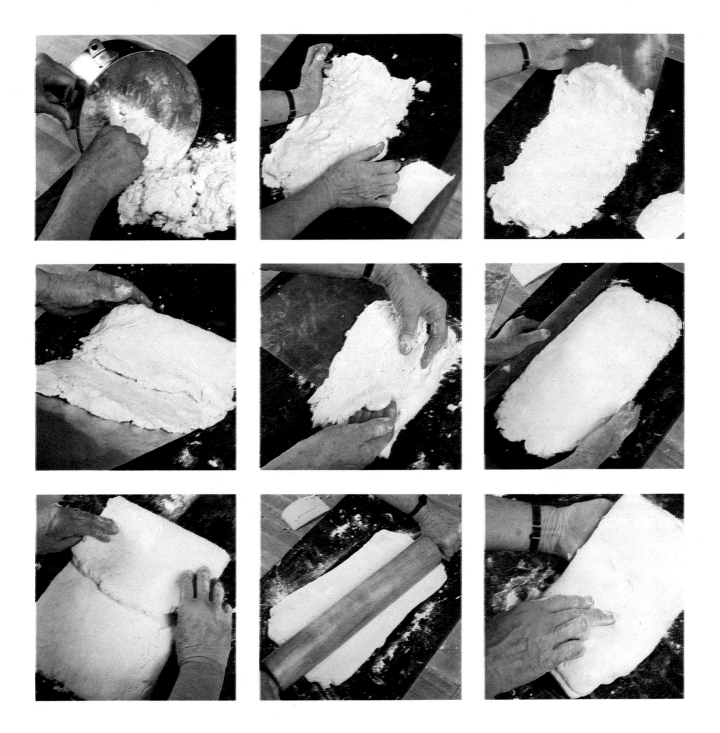

Ham Pithiviers

Puff pastry tart with ham filling

For a 9½-inch (24 cm) tart serving 8 to 10 generously, or 20 cocktail bites

⅔ previous puff pastry (cut after rolling out, as described in this recipe)

6 ounces (180 g) best-quality boiled ham

2 Tb butter

2 Tb minced shallots or scallions

2 egg yolks

¼ cup (½ dL) heavy cream

Drops of Worcestershire sauce

Drops of hot pepper sauce

Freshly ground pepper

6 Tb freshly grated Parmesan, Swiss, and/or Cheddar cheese

Egg glaze (1 egg beaten with 1 tsp water)

Equipment

(In addition to items suggested for puff pastry recipe above): a baking sheet, round nonstick pizza tray recommended; a roller-pricker, or two table forks; a pastry brush

The ham filling

Cut the ham into thin irregular slices about 1 by 1 by ⅛ inches (2½ x 2½ x ½ cm) and sauté briefly in the butter with the shallots or scallions, just to warm through thoroughly. Remove from heat. In a small bowl, beat the egg yolks with the cream; stir this mixture into the ham along with drops of Worcestershire and pepper sauce and freshly ground pepper to taste. Warm over low heat, folding the ham into the sauce, until it thickens but does not boil. Set aside to cool and thicken even more. It should be cold when it goes into the Pithiviers.

🕐   Filling may be prepared in advance and refrigerated.

Forming the dough

Roll the dough (the whole of the recipe) out into a rectangle about 18 by 9 inches (45 x 20 cm) and cut into thirds crosswise; refrigerate 2 pieces, wrapping and storing one of them for another use. Roll remaining piece, which will be the bottom of the tart, into a square 12 inches (30 cm) to a side; using a pie plate or cake pan to guide you, cut a 9½-inch (24-cm) disk out of the center of the dough. Remove surrounding dough and set on a bake sheet for reconstituting later. Lightly fold disk in half

and set upside down on dampened baking surface. Roll out second piece of dough to a thickness of slightly more than ¼ inch (¾ cm)—it must be this thickness to puff dramatically—and cut it into a disk the same size as the first. Refrigerate it along with the surrounding dough pieces from both disks.

🕐 Dough disks may be formed and stored in the freezer.

Assembling the Pithiviers

With the balls of your fingers, push and pat bottom disk of dough out onto its baking surface to make an even circle slightly larger than your cutting guide. With a roller-pricker or two forks, prick dough all over at ½-inch (1½-cm) intervals, going down through dough to pastry sheet to keep this bottom layer from rising too much. Form the ham into a round cake, about 4½ to 5 inches (12 to 13 cm) across—layers of ham interspersed with sprinklings of cheese— and place in the center of the dough. It is important to leave a 2-inch (5-cm) border of clear dough all around the ham to prevent leakage of filling during baking. Paint border of dough with cold water, and immediately center top layer in place, stretching gently as necessary. With a sharp-pointed knife, make a little hole ⅛ inch (½ cm) wide in the center of the dough, going down into the filling, to allow for escaping steam during baking. Then, with the ball of your first three fingers, firmly press the two pieces of dough in place all around. (Dough should probably be chilled at this point, but if it is still firm, proceed to the scalloped edging described in next step, then chill it.)

🕐 May be wrapped airtight and frozen at this point, or after its scalloped edging. May then be decorated and baked, still in its frozen state.

Decorating the Pithiviers

Preheat oven to 450° F/230°C, and set rack in lower-middle level. Make a scalloped edging around the Pithiviers as follows: set an upturned bowl slightly smaller than the Pithiviers over it, and use it as a guide in cutting 2-inch-wide (5-cm) scallops all around the circumference; decorate their edges all around by pressing upright lines against them with the back of a knife. Just before putting it in the oven, and after making sure top of dough is chilled and firm, paint the top with a film of egg glaze; then wait a moment and paint with a second film of glaze. Finally, with the point of a small knife, cut decorative lines 1/16 inch (¼ cm) deep in the top of the dough. A typical pattern is curving lines from center to edge, like the spokes of a wheel; or trace 4 long ovals from center to edge with straight line down the center and shallow crosshatch marks in between.

Baking, holding, serving

Baking time: 45 to 60 minutes
Immediately set the Pithiviers in the preheated oven and bake for about 20 minutes, until it has puffed and is beginning to brown nicely—it should rise dramatically, to a height of at least 2 inches (5 cm). Turn oven down to 400°F/200°C and bake 20 to 30 minutes more, watching it does not brown too much—cover loosely with foil if it does, and turn thermostat a little lower if you think it necessary. Baking takes longer than you might think, since all the pastry layers should cook and crisp. The Pithiviers should be done when the sides feel quite firm; to be sure, turn oven off and leave the Pithiviers in for another 10 to 15 minutes. You may keep it in a warming oven or on an electric hot tray for an hour or more, but the sooner you serve it the more tenderly flaky and delicious it will be. To serve, with a serrated knife simply cut into wedges like a pie.

Puffed Cheese Appetizers

Reconstituted leftover puff pastry dough
You can easily turn the fresh leftovers of your unused dough back into first-class puff pastry as follows: keep the bits and pieces all in one flat layer and glue them together by wetting the edge of one piece with cold water, laying the edge of another piece on top, and so on until you have made a patchwork mat of dough. Roll it with your pin, and give it 2 turns (rollings and foldings into three). If you want to use it plain, give it 2 more turns, but to transform it into cheese appetizers, roll it out into a rectangle, and for a piece 12 by 14 inches (30 x 35 cm), spread about 4 tablespoons grated cheese across the middle. Flip bottom of dough over to cover it, spread more cheese on that upturned portion, and flip the top third of the dough over to cover it. Repeat with another roll-out and cheese fold-up, then roll out the dough into a rectangle slightly thicker than ¼ inch (¾ cm). Cut into strips 2 inches (5 cm) wide—if too narrow the appetizers will topple

over as they rise in the oven. Then cut into lengths 3 inches (8 cm) long and set on a bake sheet.
🕐   May be wrapped and frozen at this point.

Just before baking, preheat oven to 450°F/230°C, paint tops of pieces with egg glaze, and sprinkle on a layer of grated cheese. Bake about 15 minutes, until appetizers have puffed and browned. Best kept warm until serving time, but they can be frozen and reheated, still frozen.

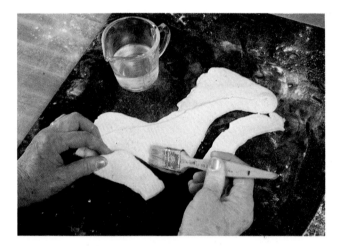

Gravlaks

Dilled fresh salmon (or sea bass)

For a 5-pound center cut of fish, boned (thus in two large halves or fillets), with skin intact

Spruce branches (if available)

2½ Tb salt and 1¼ Tb sugar mixed in a small bowl

Large bunch fresh dill weed, or 1½ Tb fragrant dried dill weed

4 to 5 Tb Cognac

Equipment

A porcelain, enamel, or glass dish, just large enough to hold fish comfortably; wax paper or plastic wrap; a plate or board that will just fit inside dish; a 5-pound (2-kg) weight

Rub fingers over the flesh to locate any bones that may still remain; salmon fillets often have small bones running slantwise from top to bottom of the thick side of the flesh. Remove with pliers.

If you have fresh spruce, cut enough twigs to cover the bottom of the dish and arrange a layer of fresh dill on top. Lay one fillet of fish skin side down in the dish and the other skin side down on your work surface. Rub the flesh sides of each fillet with the salt-and-sugar mixture and the dried dill if you are not using fresh. Sprinkle on the Cognac. (If you are using fresh dill, arrange a layer over the fish in the dish.) Place second fillet over first, flesh to flesh, but reversing its direction so that the thick or backbone part of the second fillet is resting against the thin or belly part of the first. Cover with more fresh dill and spruce twigs if you have them. Spread paper or plastic over the fish and the plate or board, and weight. Refrigerate for 2 days, basting with liquid in dish two or three times. After 2 days, taste by slicing a bit of fish off; add a teaspoon or so more salt if you feel it is not salty enough, and perhaps a sprinkling of Cognac. Reverse the fish so bottom fillet will be on top and return to refrigerator with board and weight for another 2 to 3 days, making 4 to 5 days in all. Taste carefully; the fish should now be ready to eat.

To serve

Set a fillet skin side down on a board and with a very sharp, long knife, start 4 to 5 inches (10 to 13 cm) from larger end of fillet and make paper-thin slices toward the tail, with your knife almost parallel to the board.

Remarks:

For a quicker cure, 3 to 4 days at most, you may slice your fish before curing and arrange in slightly overlapping layers, lightly salted and dilled, until the dish is full. Cover, weight, and refrigerate as before.

🕐 Dilled fish will keep for 10 days to 2 weeks under refrigeration.

Minimeatballs

For 40 to 50 meatballs about 1 inch (2½ cm) in diameter

½ cup (4 ounces or 115 g) pork sausage meat

2 cups (1 pound or 450 g) lean ground beef

1 egg

⅔ cup (1½ dL) fresh nonsweet white bread crumbs soaked in 5 Tb dry white French vermouth

2 cloves garlic, puréed

8 drops hot pepper sauce

2 tsp soy sauce

1 tsp salt

8 grinds black pepper

½ tsp oregano or thyme

Flour (for dredging)

    Serving sauce

1 cup (¼ L) beef stock or bouillon

1 tsp soy sauce

2 Tb Dijon-type strong prepared mustard beaten to blend with ½ cup (1 dL) dry white French vermouth

Salt, pepper, and oregano or thyme

2 Tb tomato purée or sauce (optional)

Beat meat, egg, crumbs and seasonings together, using a food processor if you want a very smooth mixture. Roll gobs into balls 1 inch (2½ cm) in diameter; roll lightly in flour, and arrange in one layer in a lightly oiled baking dish or jelly roll pan. Bake in a preheated 450°F/230°C oven in upper-middle level, 7 to 8 minutes, turning once or twice, to brown nicely and just to stiffen. Drain in a sieve or a colander. Boil down the ingredients for the sauce until lightly thickened, carefully correct seasoning, and fold in the minimeatballs.

At serving time, reheat and place in a casserole on an electric warming device, or in an electric frying pan on lowest heat. Have a jar of toothpicks close by.

Peking Wings

Sautéed chicken wings with Oriental overtones

24 chicken wings, folded akimbo
4 lemons
4 thin slices fresh or pickled ginger (optional)
2 Tb soy sauce
½ cup (½ dL) olive oil or fresh peanut oil
1 tsp dark sesame oil (optional)
1 tsp thyme or Italian seasoning
4 large cloves fresh garlic, puréed
½ tsp cracked peppercorns
Salt and pepper
Fresh minced parsley (optional)
Optional Oriental touches, to be added to pan after chicken has browned
2 Tb fermented dry black Chinese beans
Handful of dried Chinese mushrooms, softened in warm water, stemmed, and sliced

Marinating the chicken

Dry off the chicken in paper towels and place in a stainless steel bowl. Zest 2 lemons (remove yellow part of peel with a vegetable peeler), and cut zest into julienne (matchstick) strips along with the optional ginger. Add both to the chicken as well as strained juice of 2 lemons, the soy sauce, 4 tablespoons oil, the optional sesame oil, the thyme or Italian seasoning, the garlic, and the peppercorns. Turn and baste the chicken. Marinate for 2 hours or longer in the refrigerator, turning and basting several times. Just before cooking, scrape marinade off chicken and back into bowl. Pat chicken dry in paper towels.

Cooking the chicken

(The wings are first browned, then simmered in their marinade liquid.) Film a large frying pan with oil and heat to very hot but not smoking; then brown on all sides as many chicken wings as will fit easily in one layer, remove, and brown the rest. When all chicken wings are browned, lower heat and return them to pan with the marinade ingredients and optional black beans and mushrooms; cover, and simmer. Meanwhile slice remaining lemons thin; carefully remove seeds. After 10 minutes, turn the chicken and baste with the accumulated juices; spread the lemon slices over the chicken.

🕐 You may complete the recipe to this point, uncover the chicken, and set aside until 10 minutes or so before you wish to serve.

Continue cooking the chicken slowly 8 to 10 minutes longer, or until tender when pierced with a small knife; baste several times during this final cooking. Correct seasoning; if you wish, sprinkle parsley over the chicken, and the wings are ready to serve. Transfer to an electric heating device (or an electric frying pan) along with the cooking juices and keep over low heat.

Oysters and Clams:

See illustrated directions for opening them, as well as directions for buying and storing them, in "Fish Talk," page 111.

Stuffed Eggs:

Directions for hard-boiling and painless peeling are on page 34. For a party like this I like a quite simple filling made of sieved yolks flavored with salt, pepper, homemade mayonnaise, and a little anchovy paste, lemon, capers, or curry powder, and no recipe is needed for this. However, I do think eggs look most attractive and professional when filled with a pastry bag and cannelated tube.

Buttered Radishes:

Combining the bland and peppery flavors of butter and radishes is very French. A pretty way is to cut radish roses, let them spread out overnight in a bowl of iced water, hollow the white tops a bit with a knife point, and pipe in a little squirt of beaten unsalted butter. Chill again in iced water and serve in plenty of crushed ice to keep the topknots stiff.

A la Recherche de l'Orange Perdue

Paul Child's rum and orange cocktail

For 6 cocktail-size drinks, using jigger measurement of 1 ½ ounces

2 jiggers (6 Tb) dark Jamaica rum
½ jigger (2 tsp) bottled sweetened lime juice
Juice of 1 lime
½ jigger (2 tsp) orange liqueur
1 Tb orange marmalade
3 jiggers (9 Tb) dry white French vermouth
1 whole orange, quartered
5 shakes orange bitters
6 ice cubes

Place all ingredients in jar of electric blender and blend 20 seconds. Strain through a sieve into a pitcher. Cover and refrigerate until serving time. Stir before serving, and pour into chilled cocktail glasses.

◑ Timing

There are no last-minute jobs for this party, since you open the oysters and clams as you serve them. We find, too, that people enjoy doing their own, by the surefire method described on pages 112-4.

Cook the chicken wings that afternoon for best flavor; but if you do want to do it earlier, peel off as much skin as you can right after cooking—that's where the reheated flavor seems to lodge. It's so difficult to keep the stuffed eggs from darkening and drying that I usually pipe in the stuffing (prepared earlier and covered closely) just before the party; but you could do it that morning and sprinkle the tops with finely minced chives, parsley, or ham.

Puff pastry is at its glorious best served fresh from the oven, but you can make, shape, and freeze the dough months in advance, make and refrigerate the ham filling a day early, and assemble the pastries in the morning. Keep chilled until you bake them.

Cut the radish roses the night before, refrigerate them in iced water, stuff them in the morning, and put them back in more iced water.

Oysters and clams keep very well properly packed and refrigerated; buy them a day or two beforehand and store unopened.

Gravlaks, if you're doing it in two pieces, must be started almost a week beforehand and tasted after two days to see how it's doing. If you slice it before salting, three or four days should suffice.

Menu Variations

Puff pastry: The possibilities are limitless—see *Mastering II* and *J.C.'s Kitchen* for many good ideas.

Gravlaks: Salmon is always very expensive and sometimes unobtainable, and (though *laks* means salmon) I find the method for *gravlaks* works beautifully for sea bass and bluefish, and often, as in this menu, I like to serve two kinds. A warning: sole (perhaps because it is so lean) is, I think, less successful in taste and texture.

Peking wings: Using the same general cooking techniques, you could substitute small drumsticks for chicken wings, or pieces of boned chicken breast served on toothpicks.

Oysters and clams: If you don't like your shellfish raw, you can make a noble presentation by boiling a monster lobster, cooling it, and serving the meat, cut in chunks, in the shell. It is simply an old wives' tale that large lobsters are tough. They're delicious.

These are Cotuit oysters from Cape Cod.

Leftovers

Puff pastry: The Pithiviers and the cheese appetizers can be frozen and reheated. Although they will never have quite their glorious original taste, they will still make very good eating.

Gravlaks: Will keep for ten days or so under refrigeration. As to using it hot, I find it very salty if baked or broiled—a good illustration that you oversalt cold dishes slightly, and should exercise restraint with hot ones. However, I have used it in a creamy fish soup, as part of a quiche mixture, with creamed potatoes, and as part of a fish stuffing, since in these cases the surrounding ingredients draw the salt out of the salmon. One has to be careful, of course, not to salt anything else because of the salmon's salt.

Minimeatballs: These can be reheated, or served cold with sliced onions, tomatoes, cucumbers, and so forth. Or you can chop them and add to a hearty soup.

Peking wings: These are delicious cold, but if you want to reheat them, skin them first. The meat is good in a salad, sandwich, or soup.

Oysters and clams: These will keep unopened in the refrigerator for a week or more. They are delicious broiled on the half shell, or in a stew or chowder.

Postscript

I can't leave this cocktail party without again extolling the virtues of French puff pastry. It is now, with this fast method, so easy to make and is so infinitely versatile that I always have a hefty package of it on hand in my freezer. After one television bout some years ago, I kept several batches of it for two years! It thawed, rolled out, and baked just as beautifully as anyone could wish when I finally exhumed it. If you enjoy pastry making, this is a very satisfying dough, all neat and squared when you get the turns going, and it lends elegance to any menu. It even sounds nice when you break or bite into it—something between a crackle, a crunch, and a rustle, like a fire as it kindles.

Essay

An assortment of New England fish and shellfish.

Fish Talk

The average American consumes only eleven pounds of fish a year, which argues that he doesn't like it much…"it" meaning not the whole marvelous universe of fish, but the frozen packaged fillets which are his staple purchase. Habit, I think, is why many of us buy fish that way, habit and caution. Freezing *seems* a safeguard when everybody knows that fish deteriorates from the moment it leaves the sea (unlike meat, which has to be hung for an interval to become tender). And it's true that a good fish which is gutted, filleted, and flash-frozen (in immaculate conditions, and as soon as caught) and which arrives on your stove in no more than three months—having been maintained throughout that time at a temperature of $-5\,°F/-20.5\,°C$—is very fine eating indeed. You will not often find such fish, and only rarely from mass packagers: remember, the majority of them get most of their fish from abroad and cannot control shipboard conditions. I think it's safer to find a dealer you can trust, a specialist in fish who knows his suppliers.

Anyway, if you do buy frozen packaged fillets (and I'd certainly rather have them than no fish at all), open the package in the store and inspect it with a jaundiced eye and alert nostrils. Complain to the manager (who will pass it on and maybe improve his stock) *if:* the cut edges look dry; or the flesh has whitish patches; or there is any discoloration, especially a yellowish or even rusty streak down the center of the fillet's darker side. The same goes for frozen fillets bought by the piece. Frozen whole fish should be completely encased in a glaze of ice, and shrimp should be frozen in their shells in a solid block. Thawed fish should be treated like fresh: bedded on ice in the dealer's case.

If you buy any thawed or fresh fish, remember that fish has no odor when just caught; in the store it should have at most a mild, faint, fresh scent, which I find very appetizing. Insist on the sniff test; and check the thermometer in the freezer compartment: $1\,°F$, no higher—and preferably lower.

Away from the coast, you really can't expect to find the very perishable shellfish, like shrimp and scallops, sold fresh; twenty years ago, any fresh seafood—and all but local fresh-water fish, like the beautiful Idaho trout and upper Great Lakes whitefish—was hard to find anywhere inland. But nowadays, with our air-freight network so well developed, with the Bureau of Fisheries' careful policing, and with modern techniques of aquaculture, we could, if we insisted on it, have fresh-caught fish available daily all over the country, at least in cities and towns. Once one has tasted it, little else will do; it's like a sunny day compared to a smoggy one.

It is not difficult to identify fresh-caught fish. The skin color is intense and bright, the gills are bright red inside, the eyes are bright and bulging. After two days, the eyes begin to flatten; don't buy a fish whose eyes are flush with its skin. Another test, especially if you are buying fresh fish by the piece, is to press the flesh with a fingertip; the imprint should quickly disappear. You can soon become expert; but you still need a good dealer. The Japanese Americans, who use only the most

perfect fish in raw dishes like sushi and sashimi, are the people to follow. If you are lucky, like me, in having a local Japanese-American population, find out where they buy fish.

Fresh fish will stay fresh longest when it is kept at a temperature of 30.5°F/−1°C, which you achieve by packing in ice. Incidentally, fish does not freeze at this temperature—water does. The best way to keep fish when you get home is to unwrap it, place it in a plastic bag, and set it in the refrigerator in a bowl of ice sprinkled with a little coarse salt; pour off the water as it accumulates and renew the ice twice a day. Very fresh fish will keep even two or three days when handled this way.

Shellfish must be alive until eaten or cooked. When you buy bivalves (oysters, clams, mussels, scallops, etc.), they should be tightly closed. If the shells are slightly ajar, rap them sharply; they should close at once. If any bivalve feels unduly light, it means the occupant is dead. If unduly heavy (especially in the case of clams or mussels), the shell may be full of seabed sand or mud. Don't use any with chipped or broken shells.

The general rule for storing bivalves is to take them home promptly, scrub the shells thoroughly with a stiff brush, and refrigerate.

Cover oysters with dampened paper towels and foil, and be sure to store them with the larger, more convex side down so the oyster may bathe, and live, in its juices.

Now that the sturgeon are returning to a few of our refreshed rivers, it may not be long before we're all preparing a cheap and nutritious household staple: our own caviar. Meanwhile, since we have relearned the 2000-year-old art of oyster culture, oyster prices are on the decline. Where I live, a dozen great succulent Cotuits, so fresh they twitch under a squirt of lemon juice, cost less than a good delicatessen sandwich. I hope they (or another good variety) are available where you live; and there's no reason they shouldn't be. Refrigerated properly, they keep an amazing four weeks after harvesting; certainly you are safe in storing them at least a week after buying

them. In the 1880s, my own grandmother in rural Illinois would have oysters shipped from the East during the winter months and always kept a barrel of them in her cellar.

Always open oysters *as*, not before, you eat them; savor the flesh and every drop of the liquor, and you will have tasted the very essence of the living, fertile sea. In our family we eat them with spoons rather than the conventional forks, and drink the liquor from the shell.

Except—perhaps—at breakfast (a fine time for them), oysters are best accompanied by quartered lemons, a pepper grinder, buttered dark bread, and a dry white wine. They aren't that hard to open—after all, some Stone Age peoples managed—but since, unlike those of the other bivalves, oysters' shells seal tightly shut and, moreover, overlap, it's difficult to find the seal itself. Oysters can be obdurate, and I am afraid many of us give up and buy them already shucked by a professional. His method is to use a strong, long-bladed knife, both for levering the shells apart and for scraping the inside of each shell in order to detach the firm adductor muscle which binds shell to flesh. I've learned something new since I described this method in detail (in *J.C.'s Kit-*

chen). The oyster's hinge is not as strong as its muscle, and you can lever the shells apart by using an ordinary beer can opener: place the oyster curved side down, hinge toward you; poke around the hinge for an opening into which you can plunge the point of the opener— its curved side down—thrust it in, pry open the hinge, and you'll hear it pop. Once the shells part slightly, use an oyster knife, or even a paring knife, to sever the muscle under the top shell, northeast-by-east side. Protect the oyster-holding hand with a pot holder, and don't jab or shove.

For the occasional diehard, try the conventional method of opening at the side, using an oyster knife. If that doesn't work, the fol-

lowing two methods are inelegant but sure-fire. You can "bill" oysters by knocking off a bit of the lip with a hammer, producing a crevice for your knife tip. Or you can heat them quickly in a 450°F/230°C oven or over a burner, just till the shells part. The flesh will still be cold.

Other bivalves aren't so firmly sealed, which makes them easier to open and harder to keep. Unlike oysters, they should be stored uncovered in circulating air; and, if you ice them, be sure to pour off the melt frequently. The illustration below shows a clam-opening procedure.

To open scallops, the easiest of the lot, just feel with your knife for a vulnerable spot in the seam between the shells, starting about one-third of the way outward from the hinge, and simply lever open. Actually, it's most un-likely you'll be able to buy scallops in their beautiful fluted shells (since these take too much room in the scallop boats' holds). But if you do get some, don't throw away the deli-cious red or golden tongue-shaped roe, which constitutes one-third of the scallop. Eat it raw or in a *seviche* (see "Chafing-Dish Dinner," page 183), or cooked—just as you would the white portion, which is the scallop's muscle and the only part you can usually buy in fish stores. And when you buy them, keep them iced and eat them soon; they don't keep longer than a day or so.

Crustaceans are arthropods, meaning creatures with jointed feet: shrimp, lobsters, various kinds of crab, and crayfish. The best way to buy shrimp, since only one percent of the catch is sold fresh, is frozen: in their shells, in a solid block. (See Remarks in "Lo-Cal Ban-quet," page 40, for details.) Incidentally, when you see the word "scampi" on a restaurant menu, it undoubtedly means shrimp, since *scampi* is Italian for the rare "Dublin Bay" prawns or langoustine, small lobsterlike sea creatures.

The best-known crabs of the Atlantic are the blue crabs, which when molting are known as soft-shell crabs and are cooked and eaten almost whole; when their shells are hard, you boil them, as you do all other kinds of crab. Unless you live in Alaska, you are not likely to acquire a king crab fresh, and if you did, you might find it an alarming guest: one enormous leg can make a couple of servings. Generally,

These are Eastern bay scallops, the female has an orange roe, the male gray roe. The fluted shell belongs to the European scallop. (Below) Pulling out the black intestinal vein from a shrimp.

To open clams, insert knife one-third of the way down from the hinge; press, using the fingers of your other hand for leverage; and pry open.

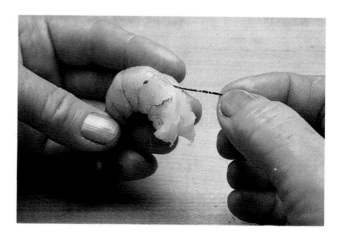

king crabs are sold boiled and frozen in the shell, in segments. Two other well-known varieties are the large delicious Dungeness crab of the Pacific and the stone crab of Florida.

The thing to remember about frozen crabmeat, which is what most of us buy—or really about any frozen flesh—is to thaw it slowly, in the refrigerator, so that lingering ice crystals don't pierce the thawing flesh, making it mushy. An excellent alternative to frozen crabmeat is canned pasteurized crab, which will keep for months in the refrigerator.

There's not space here—or anywhere!—to say all I want to about fish and shellfish: their thousands of fascinating species, their variety of life cycles, their value and their vulnerability, their beauty and their excellence. Though overfishing, careless fishing, and pollution have badly depleted our supply, we can take heart—provided we and our elected representatives remain vigilant. New regulations and treaties, and new techniques of water management and of sea farming (as well as

pond and river farming) are gradually changing all that. Thank goodness, for fish is a good source of protein and trace minerals, has about one-quarter the calories of meat, is more easily digested, cooks many times faster (saving energy), and uses Earth's resources better. An acre of sea can produce 23 tons of oyster meat, for example—150 times the weight of beef produced by an acre of pasture.

The best specific information you can get, and the most up to date (for their research is unending), is from the U.S. Bureau of Fisheries. Its devoted, diligent, and cooperative public servants will share their expertise and enthusiasm with you for the price of a telephone call. For the moment I have to content myself with summarizing my advice in four maxims whose initials—with a wrench or two—spell FISH. Buy fish and shellfish *fresh* whenever you can; buy from an *immaculately* clean place; *store* it on ice; and eat it in a *hurry*.

These lovely crabs are (clockwise from left) the Alaskan king crab, stone crab claws, Dungeness, blue crabs (female with roe), and soft shell crabs.

An impressive dinner for guests who like their food conservative and luxurious; and a dissertation on choosing, trimming, and roasting fine beef.

Dinner for the Boss

Menu

Consommé Brunoise
Melba Toast

❧

Standing Rib Roast of Beef
Timbale of Fresh Corn
Brussels Sprouts Tossed in Butter

❧

Macédoine of Fruits in Champagne
Bourbon-soaked Chocolate Truffles

❧

Suggested wines:
A fine full-bodied Burgundy or Pinot Noir;
Champagne with dessert

What I mean at the moment by "boss," you might mean by the Queen of England or the Chairman of the Membership Committee: a formidable personage (a) whom you want to impress and (b) whose taste in food runs to the conservative, the expensive, and the simple. For somebody like that, I think automatically of roast beef. Like the "Blue Danube," it may be square, but it's wonderful and everybody loves it. Before spending all that money, though, we ought to know a few things about the choosing and roasting of beef. However, roast beef isn't the only possible choice for the boss, so in case it is too expensive for you, I have listed a number of other ideas in Menu Variations, farther on.

Speaking of menus, I all but fell into an elementary planning error myself when I did this meal. I wanted to end it with a knockout blow, like a soufflé, and was mooning over the extravagances of Escoffier: Soufflé à la Régence? à la Reine? Rothschild? Sans-Souci? Vésuvienne? But, running an imaginary tongue over the succession of dishes, I tasted an over-richness, an imbalance... anyway, something wrong. The soufflé on top of the timbale was the trouble, I realized: eggs twice. It wrecks a menu to repeat ingredients, so I eliminated the soufflé.

As for the timbale, I never even used to consider recipes that called for grated fresh corn. It was just too much work to run a knife point down every single row on the ear and then to scrape out the milk and pulp with the back of the blade. Then my brother-in-law gave me a wooden corn scraper one Christmas, and, mad to use it, I discovered that fresh corn was available almost all year round. I confess I had never looked at it before—dismissing it as inedible out of the summer season. But I found it delicious when scraped off the cob with my new grater and turned into cream-style dishes. I also discovered that there are a number of scraper gadgets on the market, mostly available through mail-order catalogues for country-store type places.

Then, given the warm colors and flavors of the beef and the corn, I wanted a strong-tasting, unstarchy green vegetable with some crunch—so, Brussels sprouts. Green, I say; and crunchy, I insist. Overcooking has given the cabbage family a bad odor and a bad name. Apropos, I remember a story about my old *maître*, Chef Max Bugnard, who did one stage of his classic apprenticeship at a station hotel in London where, he related, cabbage was boiled for several hours, drained, piled into a round platter, and formed into a solid cake by jamming it hard against the kitchen wall. Then this cabbage cake was placed in a steamer and sliced into wedges on demand. Chef said it was years before he could bear boiled cabbage again, or any member of the cabbage family,

for that matter. I thought of him in our TV studio when our director wanted a boiling pot on the stove; we didn't think to change the water after lifting out our Brussels sprouts, and pretty soon a dismal reek, familiar from bad old days and bad old hotels, began to overwhelm the fresh aromas of corn and beef. The smell bore no relation to the briefly boiled emerald green sprouts awaiting their final toss in hot butter; it simply proved once again that overboiling the cabbage family produces nauseating results.

Green, red, and gold on the plate, the sprouts, beef, and corn demand a pretty dessert. Something cool and delicate, too, not puddingy after the timbale, but something inviting to the tooth. So, I thought, fruit—with a splash of Champagne for tingle. The sparkling macédoine's name, incidentally, means any kind of a combination of fruits—or vegetables—from Alexander of Macedon, whose vast empire included so many disparate populations.

The consommé, though it comes first, was my last decision. Something light before beef, something classic to please the boss, something hot and savory to kindle a good appetite. The brunoise garnish of minced vegetables looks like a scattering of jewels and adds a fresh flavor to the strong winy broth. A pleasantly crisp accompaniment when you don't want anything buttery like cheese straws is homemade Melba toast. The only difficulty with that, however, is finding a loaf of plain nonsweet white sandwich bread that is unsliced. The last time I traipsed all over town to find unsliced bread, I realized I would have saved myself time and energy had I made my own!

The truffles (so called because they look vaguely like the rare underground fungus sniffed out by special dogs—sometimes pigs—in the oak groves of Périgord and sold like diamonds to bosses and their ilk) were not a decision but a fantasy. They are fun to make and unctuous to the tongue: a luxurious final touch.

Preparations

Recommended Equipment:

A corn scraper, as previously mentioned, is virtually essential for the timbale recipe.

Marketing and Storage:
Staples to have on hand

Salt
Peppercorns
Hot pepper sauce or Cayenne pepper
Grated cheese (in the freezer; see page 6)
Fresh bread crumbs (in the freezer; see page 6)
Unsalted butter (½ pound or 225 g)
Eggs (6)
Heavy cream (½ pint or ¼ L)
Onions (6)
Carrots (6)
Garlic
Fresh parsley and/or other fresh herbs
Bay leaves
Dried thyme
Wines and liqueurs: Port, Madeira, or sherry; dry white wine or dry white French vermouth; bourbon whiskey or dark Jamaica rum

Specific ingredients for this menu

Prime roast of beef, fully trimmed (3 to 5 ribs)
Consommé (2 quarts or liters)
Unsliced nonsweet white sandwich bread, 1 day old (1 loaf)
Gingersnaps, best-quality (6 ounces or 180 g)
Semisweet baking chocolate (7 ounces or 200 g)
Unsweetened baking chocolate (1 ounce or 30 g)
Unsweetened cocoa powder (½ cup or 2 ounces, or 60 g)
Instant coffee (¼ cup or 1 ounce, or 30 g)
Celery (2 stalks)
Leeks (2)
White turnips (2)
Fresh green beans (¼ pound or 115 g)
Fresh corn (12 to 14 ears)
Fresh fine Brussels sprouts (two to three 10-ounce or 285-g packages)
Fruits for the dessert (see recipe)
Ripe tomatoes (1)
Champagne for dessert (2 bottles)

How to Buy and Trim a Rib Roast of Beef

A rib roast comes from one side of the steer's back and includes the ribs from the primal (wholesaler's) "rib" cut only. As you can see from the drawing, the ribs are cut off at two-thirds their length from the backbone (or chine, pronounced "shine").

The primal cut looks like this (opposite, left) when it comes from the wholesaler to your butcher. Nothing has been removed but the hide.

On the fat, notice the purple U.S. Department of Agriculture grade stamp. This particular cut is stamped Prime, or top quality, which means that the beef has firm, pale fat and that the lean is bright red and well marbled. Marbling refers to the white web of fat diffused in three dimensions throughout the lean. The meat has a tender, close-grained, glossy texture. Not all butchers carry top-quality, Prime beef since it is in great demand by hotels and restaurants. (Incidentally, the term "prime rib roast of beef" refers to the beef quality, not to the ribs themselves.) The next grade of beef is labeled Choice and is very good, too, although not as heavy and not as marbled. Frankly, I would not buy a beef roast at all if it were not at least Choice in grade; I would pick another cut or kind of meat.

Under the thick outer layer of fat lie two thinnish pieces, called "cap meat," which though sometimes left on should really be removed since they are for pot-roasting.

The short rib ends should be sawed off close to the end of the rib-eye meat. The ends nearest the shoulder are trimmed of excess fat and may be braised; the others, with less meat, are scraped clean and the meat is used for hamburger. The backbone or chine should be sawed off and all vestiges of it removed for ease in carving. There is also a tough nerve running along the top outside edge, which should be cut out.

Here is a cross section of a rib roast showing the differences between the small or loin end, with its solid eye of meat, and the large or shoulder end. Note that the meat from the shoulder end shows separations and that the eye of the roast is smaller. Note also the cap of meat under the top layer of fat; you are paying roast beef prices for stew meat here.

In other words, the choice end of the roast is the small end; you should know what you are asking for and call it by the right name. If you say you want "the first four ribs," you have made a meaningless and confusing request since ribs are officially numbered from the neck or shoulder end. Ribs numbers 1 through 5 are part of the shoulder. Ribs numbers 6 through 12 are part of the rib roast, and the ribs nearest the loin are the ones you want: numbers 12, 11, 10, 9, and 8—if you want a 5-rib roast. You can also request "a roast from the small end," but you are safer specifying both "small end" and rib numbers.

This is a 5-rib roast from the small end, ribs 8 through 12, trimmed and ready for the

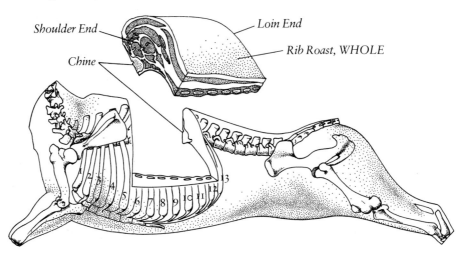

Shoulder End

Chine

Loin End

Rib Roast, WHOLE

oven. It is a Prime roast, weighs 11½ pounds (5¼ kg), and takes 2½ hours in a 325°F/170°C oven—or some 13 minutes per pound—for the internal temperature at the small (loin) end to reach 120°F/49°C, meaning that the loin half will be pinky-red rare, and the large end red rare. It will serve 14 to 16 people. So why buy such a large roast for 6 people when a 3-rib roast would do? Well, if I am going to have a roast of beef at all, I like a big one, since I can use it twice for guests, once hot and once cold. And any leftovers will provide a plush family meal, sliced and carefully reheated in foil.

Meat Temperatures:

We like rare beef in our family, and I find that 120°F/49°C at the small end is just right for us. That means the temperature before the beef is removed from the oven, since it gradually goes up when you take the roast out and soon reaches 130°F/54°C because the hot juices at the outside layer of meat recirculate into the interior, raising the temperature accordingly. Please note, however, that a temperature of 140°F/60°C before the roast is taken out of the oven—meaning 5 minutes or so longer per pound or half kilo, and a pinky-gray color—is the official safe temperature for cooked meats, where salmonella and other sick-making bacteria are surely killed off. Thus we rare-meat lovers eat red beef at our own peril and should be sure of our butchers, restaurateurs, and other purveyors of raw and/or rare beef.

Speaking of temperatures, I do think an accurate meat thermometer is essential for the home cook, and the instant or microwave oven thermometer illustrated here is available in most good cookware shops; put it in the meat and leave 30 seconds to give it time to register, then take it out—it does not roast with the meat. The advantage here, besides accuracy, is that you can test several areas of the meat, since all do not register the same; this is particularly true of legs of lamb, where the circumference varies from one part to another.

Roasting Methods and Roasting Times:

There is certainly more than one way to roast beef. Some cooks swear by the slow roasting method, where the meat goes in a preheated 200°F/95°C oven for 1 hour per pound—per-

Short rib ends and backbone, sawed off

Primal cut

Loin end (above) and shoulder end (below)

fect meat, no loss of weight, and so forth, say they. Other cooks are equally enthusiastic about the Anne Seranne/Craig Claiborne system, whereby you have your ready-to-roast ribs of beef at room temperature and place the meat in a preheated 500°F/260°C oven for exactly 15 minutes per rib; you then turn off the oven and never open its door for 2 hours or even 3 or 4 hours—crunchy brown outside and beautifully rare inside.

As for myself, I like to feel in complete control of my roast of beef, and find that an even 325°F/170°C works well for me with large roasts of three ribs or more. For smaller pieces, which might not brown sufficiently in their shorter roasting times, I sear them first at 450°F/230°C for 15 minutes, then reduce the thermostat to 325°F/170°C for the rest of the roasting, periodically checking the internal temperature with a meat thermometer well before the end of the estimated time. As soon as the instrument registers 105°F/41°C, I check every 5 minutes or so since the temperature can go up rapidly from then on. Here is the meat roasting chart that I use:

Chart for Roast Ribs of Beef

Choice graded roasts will usually be a little lighter in weight and take a little less time per pound to roast than Prime ribs. In addition, the particular way your market trims its roast determines its total weight, such as how much or little fat is left on, how close to the eye—the main muscle of meat—the ribs have been sawed off, how much of the backbone has been removed, and how much of the cap meat remains on the roast. I calculate 13 minutes per pound (or 450 grams) for rare-roasted, fully trimmed Prime ribs, and about 12 for Choice. The following chart gives rib counts and the weights and time estimates I have figured out for roasts of beef, but timing—if your roast weighs less than the rib count shown here—should be based on weight. Any chart, however, is only a guide, and you must rely on your accurate meat thermometer, starting to take temperatures half an hour before the end of the estimated roasting time. As for number of servings, it is safe to count on 2 people per rib of roast beef, which gives generous helpings and perhaps some leftovers.

Rib Count	Approximate Weight	Oven Temperature*	Total Estimated Time	Meat Thermometer Reading (Rare)[†]
2 ribs	4–5 lb (1¾–2¼ kg)	450–325°F** (230–170°C)	60–70 minutes	120°F/49°C
3 ribs	7–8½ lb (3–3¼ kg)	325°F/170°C	1½–1¾ hours	120°F/49°C
4 ribs	9–10½ lb (4–5 kg)	325°F/170°C	1¾–2¼ hours	120°F/49°C
5 ribs	11–13½ lb (5–6 kg)	325°F/170°C	2¼–2¾ hours	120°F/49°C
6 ribs[††]	14–16 lb (6¼–7¼ kg)	325°F/170°C	3–3¼ hours	120°F/49°C
7 ribs[††]	16–18½ lb (7¼–8½ kg)	325°F/170°C	3¼–4 hours	120°F/49°C

*   Be sure your oven thermostat is correct, or your timing will be way off.

**   Sear a 2-rib roast for 15 minutes at the higher temperature, then turn to the lower temperature for the rest of the cooking.

††   I do think you are better off with two 3- or 4-rib roasts than a single 6- or 7-rib one simply because those last 2 ribs at the large end are the least desirable; however, there is no denying the grandeur of that one magnificent spread of meat.

†   Add 2 to 3 minutes more per pound for less-rare beef (125°F/52°C), and medium-rare (130°F/54°C), and 5 to 6 minutes per pound more for medium (140°F/60°C).

Consommé Brunoise

Consommé garnished with very finely chopped fresh vegetables

Homemade consommé is a wonderful treat, and I shan't go into the making of it since it is in both *Mastering I* and *J.C.'s Kitchen*. When I haven't had the time to make my own, however, I have used some excellent canned consommés, one of which is a duck bouillon. Browse among the shelves of your fancy food store, try out several brands, then stock up on your favorites for emergencies. (There is no reason to be a food snob about canned consommés, say I, since one can simmer them with a little wine or dry white vermouth, some chopped onions, carrots, celery, and herbs, and come up with a very respectable brew for the following recipe.)

For 6 people

The garnish

1/3 cup (¾ dL) each of the following vegetables, very finely and neatly diced into 1/16-inch (¼-cm) pieces: carrots, onions, celery, white of leek, white turnips, fresh green beans

2 Tb butter

Salt and pepper

About 2 quarts (2 L) excellently flavored consommé

Several Tb dry Port, Madeira, or sherry

Several Tb minced fresh chervil, parsley, and/or chives

Reserve the beans. In a covered saucepan, cook the other vegetables slowly in the butter until nicely tender but not browned, then season to taste and simmer several minutes in a cup or so of the consommé. Blanch the beans in a quart of lightly salted boiling water just until barely tender, drain, and refresh in cold water.

🕐 May be completed well in advance to this point.

Shortly before serving, pour the remaining consommé into the simmered vegetables and bring to the simmer; add the blanched beans and taste very carefully for seasoning. Off heat, stir in driblets of wine to taste. Pour either into a tureen or into individual soup cups and decorate with the chopped herbs.

Remarks:

You can simmer rice, tiny pasta, or tapioca in the soup to give it more body. You can also finish it off with a poaching of finely diced fresh tomato pulp, which adds a pretty blush of color. You are aiming for delicious flavor as well as colorful effect, and should feel free to let your fancy roam—and that can include diced truffles and mushrooms, too.

Melba Toast

Melba toast couldn't be simpler to make if you can just find the right kind of unsliced bread. The best is a nonsweet sandwich loaf, close grained and a day old—a recipe for just such a loaf is in both *Mastering II* and *J.C.'s Kitchen*. Cut the bread into very very thin slices 1/16 inch (¼ cm) thick; either leave slices whole or cut diagonally into triangles. Arrange, in one layer preferably, on one or two pastry sheets and bake slowly in the upper and lower-middle levels of a preheated 275°F/140°C oven for about 20 minutes, or until the bread has dried out and is starting to color lightly. Cool on a rack.

🕐　May be done well in advance, and recrisped in the oven before serving. May be refrigerated or frozen.

Standing Rib Roast of Beef

A 5-rib fully trimmed Prime or Choice roast of beef (or a 3- or 4-rib roast, timed according to roasting chart earlier in this chapter)

2 Tb soft butter

2 medium-size carrots, roughly chopped

2 medium-size onions, roughly chopped

2 cups (½ L) excellent beef broth (see directions at end of recipe)

　Equipment

A reliable meat thermometer; a low-sided roasting pan (2½ inches or 6½ cm deep); a rack to fit the pan

For accurate timing, particularly if you are doing a 3-rib roast, leave the meat out at room temperature an hour before it is to go into the oven. And, since I always like plenty of leeway, I start my roasting half an hour to an hour ahead of schedule; in other words, I estimate that a 5-rib roast will take 2½ hours, so I start it 3 to 3½ hours before I plan to serve. It is easy to keep it warm, as you will see at the end of the recipe, and I want to be sure I get it done on time.

Therefore, 3 to 3½ hours before serving, have oven preheated to 325°F/170°C and rack placed in lower level. Smear cut ends of beef with the butter and place it fat side up (ribs down) on the rack in the roasting pan. Set in oven, and there is nothing more to do than rapidly baste the cut ends with accumulated fat from the roasting pan every half hour and, about an hour before the end of the roasting time, strew the chopped vegetables into the pan. Then, half an hour later (in this case, after 2 hours of roasting), start checking temperature. When the thermometer reaches 105°F/41°C, watch closely and check every 7 minutes or so, until desired temperature is reached—about 2½ hours in all. The small end will register the highest temperature, and if you want some meat pinky-red rare and the rest very rare, roast to 120°F/49°C. On the other hand, if you want the small end medium rare and the large end pinky red, roast a few minutes more, to 125°F/52°C, and so forth for more doneness. As soon as the temperature has been reached remove the roast from the oven.

🕐   Keeping the roast warm until serving time: If you know your oven is absolutely accurate and that you can keep it at around 115°F/46°C, turn it off, remove roast, leave door open to cool oven for 15 minutes, then set thermostat at 115°F/46°C and return roast to oven. You can safely keep it in the oven for an hour or two, even longer; the meat and its juices, communing together, make for even more delicious eating. Otherwise let the roast cool out of the oven for 15 minutes, then set it over a large kettle of hot but not simmering water; place the top of a covered roaster or a large pan over the beef to keep it warm. Leave meat thermometer in place and check every 15 minutes or so to be sure everything is under control. The temperature will rise some 10°F/5°C at first, then gradually subside; 100°F/38°C is plenty warm enough for serving.

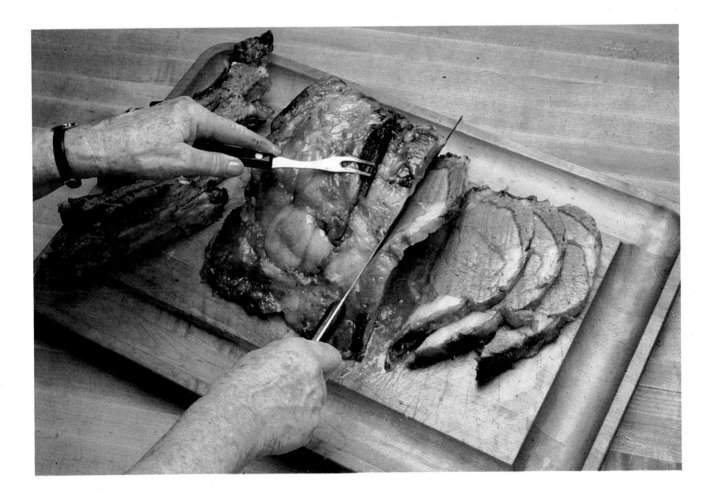

For the sauce or "jus"

Remove beef from roasting pan, pour out accumulated fat, pour in the beef stock, and swish about to dislodge any coagulated roasting juices (there will be little of these if you have roasted to very rare). Pour the liquid and roasting vegetables from the pan into a saucepan and simmer, mashing the vegetables into the liquid. Season carefully to taste, and skim off surface fat. Just before serving, strain into a hot sauce bowl, adding also any juices accumulated from the waiting roast. You should have a tablespoon or so per serving.

To serve

You may wish to bring the roast to the table just as it is, perhaps garnishing the platter with watercress or sprigs of parsley. However, I like to remove the rib bones in the kitchen (another reason for getting the roast done ahead of time); I turn it upside down and cut close against the line of bones, then cut the bones apart. To serve, I set the roast right side up on a big carving board, place the bones at one end, and if there is no enthusiastic carver at the table, I slice a first helping of meat and arrange that at the cut end of the roast. This makes for easy serving, plus the promise of big bones on the plates of those who love them.

Beef Stock:

Brown a pound or more of chopped meaty raw beef bones in a little cooking oil with a chopped onion and carrot, then add a medium-size chopped but unpeeled tomato, 1 cup (¼ L) dry white wine or vermouth, water to cover ingredients by 2 inches (5 cm), and the following, tied in washed cheesecloth: 1 bay leaf, ½ teaspoon thyme, 6 parsley sprigs, and 2 cloves unpeeled garlic. Simmer partially covered for 3 to 4 hours, adding more water if liquid evaporates below level of ingredients. Strain, degrease, and refrigerate or freeze until needed. You will want 1 cup (¼ L) for 6 people; double the amount for 12 to 14.

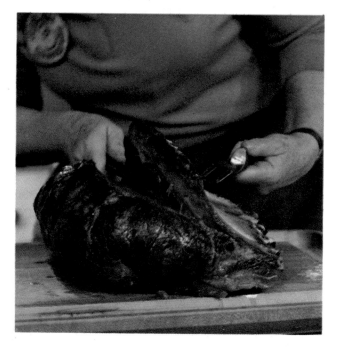

Timbale of Fresh Corn

For an 8-cup baking dish, serving 8 people

12 or more ears fresh corn (to make about 3 cups or ¾ L cream-style grated corn)

6 eggs

2 to 3 Tb grated onion

1 tsp salt

4 to 5 Tb fresh minced parsley

⅔ cup (1½ dL) lightly pressed down crumbs from crustless nonsweet white bread

⅔ cup (1½ dL) lightly pressed down grated cheese (such as a mixture of Swiss and/or Cheddar or mozzarella)

⅔ cup (1½ dL) heavy cream

6 drops hot pepper sauce (or ⅛ tsp Cayenne pepper)

8 to 10 grinds fresh pepper

Equipment

A corn scraper or grater; a straight-sided 8-cup (2-L) baking dish, such as a charlotte mold 5 to 6 inches (13 to 15 cm) deep, and a larger baking dish in which to set it

Scrape or grate the corn and turn into a measure to be sure you have about 3 cups or ¾ liter. Beat the eggs in a mixing bowl to blend; then add all the rest of the ingredients listed, including the corn.

🕐 Recipe may be completed even a day in advance to this point; cover and refrigerate.

Preheat oven to 350°F/180°C. About 2 hours before serving, butter the 8-cup (2-L) baking dish and line bottom with a round of buttered wax paper. Stir up the corn mixture to blend thoroughly and pour into the dish. Set corn dish in larger dish and pour boiling water around to come two-thirds up the sides of the corn-filled dish. Bake in lower-middle level of oven for half an hour, then turn thermostat down to 325°F/170°C. Baking time is around 1¼ to 1½ hours, and water surrounding timbale should almost but never quite bubble; too high heat can make a custard (which this is) grainy. Timbale is done when it has risen almost to fill the mold, the top has cracked open, and a skewer plunged down through the center comes out clean. Let rest 10 minutes or more in turned-off oven, door ajar, before unmolding.

🕐 May be baked an hour or so before serving; the timbale will sink down as it cools, but who would ever know how high it might have been, once it is unmolded?

Brussels Sprouts Tossed in Butter

Here is one method for serving Brussels sprouts that are fresh and bright green. Blanch them until just cooked through, drain and cool them, halve or cut them into thirds, and set aside until just before serving. Then toss them in a big frying pan in hot butter and seasonings, just to heat them through, and serve them forth. A marvelous vegetable when done this way.

For 6 people

Two to three 10-ounce (285-g) packages fine fresh green hard-headed Brussels sprouts

Salt

4 or more Tb butter

Pepper

Equipment

A kettle large enough to hold at least 6 quarts or liters water

Preparing sprouts for cooking

One by one, pull any small or withered leaves off root end of sprouts, shave root close to base of remaining leaves (but not so close that leaves will come loose); with a small knife,

pierce a cross ⅜ inch (1 cm) deep in root ends —to make for fast and even cooking. Throw out any wilted or soft-headed sprouts.

🕐 May be prepared in advance even a day before cooking; cover and refrigerate.

Preliminary cooking—blanching

Fill a large kettle with at least 6 quarts or liters of water, adding 1½ teaspoons salt per quart or liter. Cover and bring to the rapid boil. Meanwhile wash the sprouts under cold running water. (Old recipes call for soaking sprouts in salted water, presumably to make them disgorge bugs, weevils, ants, and whatnot. I have never found any such fauna in any of my Brussels sprouts, and have therefore never done more than simply wash them rapidly.) When water is boiling, plunge in the sprouts, cover kettle, and as soon as water boils again uncover and boil slowly for 4 or 5 minutes. Sprouts are done when just cooked through but still slightly crunchy and bright green—taste one or two, to verify the cooking. Drain them at once, by holding a colander in the kettle and pouring off the water. Then, with colander still in place, run cold water into the kettle to refresh the sprouts, to set the green color, and to preserve the fresh texture. Drain in a moment or two, then halve the sprouts lengthwise, or cut into thirds, to make them all the same size.

🕐 May be prepared several hours in advance to this point; arrange in a bowl, cover, and refrigerate.

Final cooking

Between courses, and just before serving, melt as much butter as you think sensible and/or decent in a large frying pan, add the sprouts, and toss and turn (shaking and twirling pan by its handle rather than stirring with a spoon). Season to taste with salt and pepper, and sample a sprout or two to be sure they are thoroughly heated through.

Serving

Either turn the sprouts into a hot vegetable dish or surround the preceding unmolded timbale of fresh corn.

Macédoine of Fruits in Champagne

Plan as attractive a mixture of cut-up fruits as you can muster, considering the season of the year. Summer is ideal, of course, with fresh apricots, peaches, cherries, berries, and all the bounties the warm months can offer. December is more of a problem. However, one can still have fresh oranges and grapefruit cut into skinless segments, an occasional strawberry or melon, pineapple, bananas, and grapes to peel and seed. And there are nuts to sliver or chop, and shavings of ginger (either candied or fresh). And, of course, the canned and frozen fruits that can marry with the fresh. Among canned fruits I do like figs in syrup, dark purple plums, and sometimes mandarin or tangerine segments, as well as the exotic fragrance of a few kumquats, sliced thin and seeded. Frozen blueberries have the charm of deep purple for color, and sometimes whole strawberries are successful. I shall not offer a combination since it is too personal and seasonal a dish, but I do suggest a careful design plan for the arrangement, squeezings of lemon, and sprinklings of kirsch, white rum, or Cognac, if you like such additions. Let the fruits macerate together in their covered serving bowl in the refrigerator for several hours, and taste frequently in case more lemon, or even orange juice, or liqueurs are needed—and you may want to drain off some of the juices before serving. Then, at the table, and just before ladling out, pour some Champagne from the bottle either into the serving bowl or into each dish—that fizzling sudden sparkle of foam transforms a simple collection of cut-up fruits into a dressy *macédoine au Champagne.* Then pour out a glass of the same Champagne for each guest, to accompany the fruit.

Bourbon-soaked Chocolate Truffles

For 12 to 18 pieces

7 ounces (200 g) semisweet baking chocolate
1 ounce (30 g) unsweetened baking chocolate
4 Tb bourbon whiskey or dark Jamaica rum
2 Tb strong coffee
1 stick (4 ounces or 115 g) unsalted butter, cut into 1-inch (2-cm) pieces
6 ounces (180 g) best-quality gingersnaps (to make ¾ cup or 1¾ dL pulverized)
½ cup (1 dL) unsweetened cocoa powder
¼ cup (½ dL) powdered instant coffee
Equipment
Paper or foil candy cups

The mixture

Break up the two chocolates and place in a small saucepan with the bourbon or rum and the liquid coffee. Cover, set chocolate pan in a larger pan of boiling water, and turn off the heat under it. When chocolate is melted and smooth, in 5 minutes or so, beat in the butter piece by piece (a portable electric mixer is useful here), then the pulverized gingersnaps. Chill for several hours.

Forming the truffles

Mix the cocoa powder with the powdered coffee and spread on a plate. With a soup spoon or teaspoon, depending on the size you wish, dig out gobs of the chocolate mixture and form into rough, roundish, rocklike, trufflelike shapes. Roll in the cocoa and coffee powder, and place in candy or cookie cups. Refrigerate in a covered container until serving time.

🕐   Truffles may be kept under refrigeration for several weeks or frozen.

🕐 *Timing*

Since this menu calls for two dishes that need oven cooking, the beef and the corn timbale, can you manage with only one oven? If it's big enough you can put the corn in with the beef. Since you can roast the beef and keep it warm over hot water, as described in the recipe, you can bake the corn after you remove the beef. But with only one oven, you may wish to substitute another vegetable for the corn timbale, attractive as it is; suggestions for other vegetables are in the following section.

In any case, you have few last-minute jobs. The Brussels sprouts, which have been lightly precooked, are tossed in hot butter between courses while you arrange the beef for serving. The timbale stays warm in its baking dish and is unmolded just before serving, and then you can surround it with the hot sprouts. All you do before dinner is check on your beef, remove its ribs if you wish to do so, and reheat the consommé.

An hour before your guests arrive, the timbale goes into the oven and, if you can control oven temperatures, your roast is done and cooling, to be kept safely at 115° to 120°F (45° to 50°C) until you are ready to serve it.

Two hours before dinner, chill the Champagne, stir the final flavorings into your macédoine of fruits, and let it continue macerating in the refrigerator.

Three to three and a half hours before serving, put the roast in the oven. You have set it out at room temperature an hour beforehand, and the oven has been preheated.

In the morning, prepare the vegetables for the soup, blanch the beans (also for the soup), trim and blanch the sprouts, prepare the timbale, and compose the fruits for the dessert.

If you are making your own consommé, you can do so days in advance—it freezes nicely, as do the chocolate truffles and the simple beef stock for the roasting sauce.

Menu Variations, of a Conservative Sort

The soup: Consommé variations are infinite, as a quick trot through Escoffier or even *J.C.'s Kitchen* will show you. You could change from consommé to clams or oysters, or cold lobster or crab as an appetizer. I'm always partial to fish soup, but that might offend a conservative meat-and-potato palate. Better stick to consommé or shellfish.

The roast: Substitute a rib eye of beef (meaning the roast is boned); a sirloin strip—a fine boneless roast this is, less dramatic than the rib but easy to carve; a well-aged Prime rump roast; or a tenderloin. Try a roast leg of veal, if you can get a large, Prime, pale, and perfect piece—not easy. Or roast leg of lamb, if you have an expert carver to handle it. Saddle of lamb is elegant but needs carving expertise, too. Though a roast loin of pork and fresh ham are delicious, they are never considered as dressy for this kind of occasion, unless you know the tastes of your principal guests.

The vegetables: Instead of fresh corn for the timbale, you could use spinach, broccoli, or cauliflower—but these alternative vegetables should be blanched, chopped, and turned in butter first; grated zucchini should be squeezed dry and sautéed in butter. Cauliflower or zucchini timbale surrounded by fresh peas would be lovely. Sautéed mushrooms could surround a timbale of spinach or broccoli. Rather than using a high molded structure for the timbale, you could bake it in a ring mold and pile the other vegetables in the middle for serving. You could get away from the timbale idea entirely and serve braised lettuce or endive and cleverly cut sautéed potatoes or scalloped potatoes, with something colorful and red, like tomatoes Provençal or baked cherry tomatoes.

The dessert: Serve a homemade sherbet of strawberries or grapefruit, or the delectable Fresh Pear Sherbet on page 89. Or fresh fruits, like a fine ripe pineapple, or melon with grapes, or freshly poached fresh peaches sauced with raspberry purée. With fresh fruit, homemade cookies, like almond tuiles, walnut wafers, or madeleines, would be attractive, and you could omit the bourbon and chocolate truffles.

Leftovers

The consommé: Eat it cold or reheated; use for stock; or freeze. The *brunoise garnish,* if not overcooked, makes a nice hot or cold *macédoine* to garnish a platter.

Roast beef: One advantage of a conservative menu with simple (as opposed to composite) dishes is the fine array of possibilities for leftovers. Perhaps you planned in any case to arrange a beautiful cold beef platter for another party; it could be accompanied by a salad or made into one with potatoes, cherry tomatoes, and hard-boiled eggs on lettuce—a Salade de Boeuf à la Parisienne.

I'd save any well-done roast beef, or the coarser parts surrounding the eye, to dice for a hearty roast beef hash, to grind for shepherd's pie, or to grind and combine with sausage meat in patties.

To reheat slices as is, layer them on a platter, cover with foil, and set in the oven at

375°F/190°C; watch carefully and remove when just warmed through. To reheat in a sauce, try adding mustard and cream to your gravy or to some beef broth, or fresh tomato pulp with garlic and fresh basil or dried thyme; if you add red wine, then season it with tomato paste, bay leaf, and thyme, and reduce it by half, you have a great sauce which, if you add poached beef marrow, becomes à la Bordelaise. Or finish your gravy with savory *pistou* or *pipérade*. (For these two preparations, see *Mastering II*. Detailed descriptions of the previous dishes are in *J.C.'s Kitchen*.)

If you have enough of the fine lean eye section, still very rare, you could slice and combine it with mushrooms, onions, and sour cream for beef Stroganoff, or spread it with mushroom *duxelles* and bake in a pastry case for beef Wellington. Or, to serve cold, try it with drinks, in spiffy canapés (on buttered toast, for instance, with a corner spread with caviar); cut in chunks, with a spicy hot or cold dip; or sliced thin and spread with a horse-radish and cream cheese mixture, rolled, and sliced across. Or line cornet molds with small perfect slices, stuff with a piquant mousse or *macédoine*, coat with aspic, and chill till firm —to decorate a cold main dish.

Brussels sprouts: Even if they have been buttered and heated, they should still be green and crisp. You can simply reheat them, or add them to soup, or, if you have lots, make a timbale by the method in this chapter (allowing more milk) or as suggested in *Mastering I*.

If the sprouts have been blanched but not buttered, you have accomplished the first step in a choice of classic dishes. One group, described in *Mastering I*, includes sprouts braised in butter, with cream, or with chestnuts, or gratinéed à la Mornay, or coated with cheese and browned.

Or have the blanched sprouts cold in salad or with drinks. To be posh, you could hollow them out and pipe in a squirt of ham mousse or some savory mixture.

Corn: Any timbale leftovers can be sliced and eaten cold, or easily turned into a hot soup.

As the ears vary so in yield, you may have extra pulp and milk on hand. If so, try corn chowder (see "New England Potluck Supper"), or make skillet corn dowdy, corn flan, or corn crêpes (for directions, see "From Julia Child's Kitchen" in the September 1977 *McCall's*). Or have corn fritters for breakfast; or combine the pulp with other crunchy bits of vegetables, in puffy eggs fu yung.

The dessert: Any fruit which has been champagne'd should be eaten right up. But if you kept some fruit in reserve, the possibilities (according to the combination you chose) are endless. To keep cut fruit, pack it close in careful layers in a glass bowl, pour over orange juice to cover, shake to make sure there are no unfilled crannies or airholes, cover well, and refrigerate; it keeps 2 or 3 days. Serve as is or drained, in a melon case or ripe papaya cases. Or make a fruit salad, or mold the fruit in aspic (but omit fresh pineapple as it's anti-jelling). Or try a hot fruit curry on steamed rice.

There are lovely compotes, hot or cold, with the fruit juices reduced with wine and cinnamon or flavored ad lib with liqueurs or pure vanilla or almond extract; you can present them baked deep-dish fashion under a meringue or pastry lid. Or make a fruit tart in a rich pastry case. A mixed-fruit sherbet is easy (see "VIP Lunch" for a basic method); or fruit can be liquefied for a refreshing punch. And if a few fine sections or specimens remain, glaze them in their own well-reduced syrup to garnish an elegant platter.

Postscript

About beef there is always so much more to learn. Since meat is such a big budget item, the whole subject is well worth study, and here are some books you may find useful. All of them were written not as texts but for the consumer.

Barbara Bloch, with the National Live Stock and Meat Board, *The Meat Board Meat Book.* New York: McGraw-Hill Book Company, 1977.

Merle Ellis, *Cutting-Up in the Kitchen: The Butcher's Guide to Saving Money on Meat and Poultry.* San Francisco: Chronicle Books, 1975.

Travis Moncure Evans and David Greene, *The Meat Book: A Consumer's Guide to Selecting, Buying, Cutting, Storing, Freezing and Carving the Various Cuts.* New York: Charles Scribner's Sons, 1973.

Leon and Stanley Lobel, *All About Meat,* edited by Inez M. Krech. New York: Harcourt Brace Jovanovich, 1975.

Phyllis C. Reynolds, *The Complete Book of Meat.* New York: M. Barrows & Company, 1963.

For families who like to cook and eat together, this homey, savory menu starts from the ground up with jobs for all ages.

Sunday Night Supper

Take 1 cup (140 g) flour, add enough salt to render it unappetizing, and blend in vegetable dye by droplets, kneading with enough water to form a stiff, elastic dough. Yield: 2 good fistfuls, depending on age. Keeps well in a wide-mouthed screw-top jar. Some cookbook this is; but I mention play dough, the toddler's joy, to remind you of the deep satisfaction we all, even babies, derive from kneading and manipulating dough. In the Child clan, we like to save Sunday night for a do-it-yourself family cooking bee; and anyone old enough to stay up is welcome. The most popular project with all ages is noodle-making-and-eating; all the more so since Paul and I acquired a thrifty, efficient little hand-cranked machine which makes lumps into sheets and then into ribbons— wavy, pale gold strips a yard long which are briefly dried over a broomstick suspended between two chairs. At table the younger members learn, by practicing it, the small, gratifying art of eating noodles deftly: the fork, held vertically to the plate, engages a few strands with the tines and rotates against the inside of a spoon, making a neat parcel. Decorum reigns, unless Paul elects to demon-strate noodle eating as we learned it in China during World War II. I am sorry to say that his deafening inhalations are widely copied.

However you eat them, noodles are not only amusing but delicious—and almost uni-versal, as you discover in any wheat-growing corner of the world. Just how delicious, you won't discover until you make your own. The machine does practically all the kneading and all the rolling and cutting. It's a pleasure to use, and we all take turns cranking it and catching the ribbons as they fall from the cutters. Homemade noodles have a lovely nutty flavor and a tender texture. They cook in half the time of store-bought noodles and cost precisely half as much. We reckoned it out that the compact, well-built machine had paid for itself after 76 two-egg batches … rather soon, in other words, since people borrow it constantly.

Noodles are good with almost anything, but once or twice a year Paul and I start well in advance and corn our own meat for a Sunday party. I suppose this sounds like reinventing the wheel! Meat used to be corned (salted and spiced) in order to preserve it, which in these days of refrigeration is unnecessary; and, if you do like corned beef, you can buy it anywhere. But we like corned pork sometimes (which you can't often buy); we prefer short-fibered cuts to the usual brisket; and, finally, we fancy our own combinations of spices and

the appetizing light brown color of meat corned without nitrates (potassium salts) to turn it commercial red. Before refrigerators, the process was cumbersome: you needed a big stone crock with a lid fitting inside it like a piston in a cylinder; weights for the lid; and, most important, a cold room or outbuilding where the temperature stayed at 37°F/3°C. But this is usual refrigerator temperature, and a plastic bag works just as well as a crock—provided you remember to massage the package daily for a minute or two. (Using a crock, you didn't have to do that, since the meat was surrounded with brine; in a bag, the salt and meat juices create a brine, but you have to be sure it cures the meat on all sides.)

While the meat is cooking and the noodles are being kneaded, extruded, draped, and dried, other pairs of hands are preparing a bouquet of beautifully trimmed vegetables for the steamer. And the smallest hands are at work on a decoration for our dessert of store-bought strawberry sherbet or ice cream, a soft fresh flavor to round off a savory dinner. The makings are a tray of plump strawberries with a bowl of quickly prepared royal icing to dip them in; it clothes each berry in a little white velvet shirt—hence the name *en chemise*. A few strawberries always seem to disappear at this stage—which is only fair, since we elders are sipping away as we putter. There are fresh tomatoes to be peeled, seeded, juiced, and chopped, and a pot to be watched as the pale, subtle cream of garlic sauce is reduced and a touch of horseradish added.

Since we are, after all, busy accomplishing something, our drink is a mild one, something I first tasted in California. With its mixed vermouths and the light filming of gin (not for kick, but for flavor and satiny flow), it's finely, richly aromatic. And lovely to behold. Properly served in a big goblet of ice, with a goldfish-sized curve of orange zest, it looks so full and glowing that I wonder if my brother-in-law, who invented it, was inspired by the California sunset. Anyway, the family has named it Ivan's Apéritif for him, and we always like to have it together on the night that rounds off the week.

Preparations

Recommended Equipment:

For corning the meats, you'll need sturdy plastic bags with fasteners, a large bowl with a plate or pan that fits inside it, and a 10-pound (5-kg) weight to set on it.

For making noodles, a hand-cranked pasta machine (which also makes lasagne and thin noodles) is desirable. The electric models are at least five times the price and are supposed to be good, but I've never tried one.

To cook dinner, you'll need three big pots, at least two of them with well-fitting lids, and a metal colander which fits one of the pots (or else—and preferably—use the steaming rack illustrated in "Lo-Cal Banquet," page 44).

Marketing and Storage:

If you are going to do the corned meats for this menu, you'll need to start two weeks in advance, so I have marked the items for corned meat making with an asterisk on the list.

Staples to have on hand

Table salt
*Coarse or kosher salt
*Black and white peppercorns
*Powdered spices and herbs: allspice, thyme, sage, paprika, bay leaf
*Optional: juniper berries
Whole cloves
Whole imported bay leaves
Prepared horseradish
Olive oil
*Granulated sugar
Confectioners sugar
Cornstarch
Flour
Eggs (about 6 "large")
Butter
Heavy cream (1 cup or ¼ L)
*Garlic (2 heads)
Parsley
Optional: chives
Shallots and/or scallions
Lemons (2)
Oranges (2)
Cognac

Specific ingredients for this menu

*Beef and/or pork, braising cut (see recipe)
*Carrots
White turnips (at least 3 or 4)
*Rutabaga (1 large)
*Onions and/or leeks
Celery
Optional: green beans (1 pound or 450 g)
Tomatoes (8 to 10; see "Tomato Talk," page 159)
Strawberries (24 large)
Strawberry sherbet or ice cream (2 quarts or liters)
Sweet white French or Italian vermouth
Dry white French vermouth
Optional: milk, cider, apple juice

Ivan's Apéritif

Mixed vermouth with orange

Ingredients per drink

1 jigger dry white French vermouth (Noilly Prat, Martini & Rossi, or Boissière)

1 jigger sweet white vermouth (Cinzano, Gancia, Lillet, or white Dubonnet)

1 Tb gin

1 fresh zest of orange (a 2½-inch or 6-cm strip of the orange part of the peel)

Equipment

A large, clear, stemmed wineglass; ice cubes

Fill the wineglass with ice cubes, stir in the vermouths, float the gin on top but do not stir in, squeeze the zest over the glass, then rub the rim of the glass with it and drop the zest into the glass.

A Junior Version:

For the vermouths and the gin, substitute apple juice or cider. The orange zest, the big glass, and the ice are the important parts.

Corned Beef and Pork

Potted, salted, and/or spiced meat— home cured in plastic bags rather than in a crock or pot

Salt and Spice Mixture:

For 10 to 12 pounds or 4½ to 5½ kg meat

1⅓ cups (3¼ dL) coarse or kosher salt

3 Tb granulated sugar

1 Tb cracked peppercorns

2 tsp each powdered allspice and thyme

1 tsp each powdered sage, paprika, and bay leaf

Special Optional Aromatic Vegetable Mixture for Beef:

For 4 to 5 pounds or 2 to 2½ kg meat

½ cup (1 dL) each: minced rutabaga, onion, and carrot

2 large cloves garlic, minced

Special Optional Addition for Pork:

For 4 to 5 pounds or 2 to 2½ kg meat

2 Tb crushed juniper berries

The Meat—One Kind or Cut, or a Mixture:

Beef: brisket, chuck, eye round roast, bottom round

Brisket.

Pork: shoulder arm picnic or blade (butt); loin, blade end (bone-in or boneless for either shoulder or loin)

Equipment

Sturdy plastic bags, one for each piece of meat; secure fastenings for bags; a large bowl or other receptacle to hold meat; a plate or pan to cover meat; a 10-pound (5-kg) weight to set in plate or pan; washed cheesecloth

Curing the meat

Trim meat of excess fat (and bone it, if you wish, but do not tie it until the curing is finished). Blend the salt and spice mixture in a bowl, set the meat on a tray, and rub mixture into all sides of meat and down into crevices. Set each piece into a bag, divide remaining salt and spice mixture among the bags (including all that has dropped onto the tray). Add optional ingredients. Close bags, squeezing out as much air as possible, and pack into bowl, cover with plate or pan, and weight. Set in the bottom of the refrigerator, where temperature should remain between 37° and 38°F/3° and 4°C. Within a few hours juices will begin to seep into bag, showing that the curing process is taking place. Turn bags and massage meat daily to be sure salt is penetrating all sides. Curing takes a minimum of 2 weeks, but you may let meat cure for a month. (If you leave it longer or if bags leak or break, repackage the meat, returning all juices and half again as much new salt to the new bags.)

Preliminary soaking before cooking

Wash off meat in cold water, and soak in a large bowl of cold water, changing it several times—I soak mine for 24 hours to be sure excess salt is out. As the salt leaves the meat, the meat softens and will feel almost like its original self. (Tie with white butcher's twine if you think meat might fall apart during cooking.)

Remarks:

You will note that there is no saltpeter, nitrite, or nitrate in the curing pickle here; thus the cooked meat will be turning a brownish, rather than the store-bought reddish, color.

Clockwise: boneless chuck, top round, and fresh pork shoulder

Corned Beef or Pork Boiled Dinner

For 4 to 5 pounds or 2 to 2½ kg meat

1 onion stuck with 4 cloves

1 large carrot

2 celery stalks

A large herb bouquet (8 parsley sprigs, 3 bay leaves, 1 tsp thyme, 3 cloves unpeeled garlic, tied in washed cheesecloth)

Set the meat in a kettle with cold water to cover by 2 inches (5 cm); add the onion, carrot, celery and herb bouquet. Bring to the simmer, skim off any scum for several minutes, set over it a cover slightly askew for air circulation, and simmer slowly—usually for 3 to 3½ hours, or until meat is tender when pierced with a fork. (Add boiling water if liquid evaporates below level of ingredients; after 2 hours taste meat and add salt to water if needed.)

🕐 May be cooked an hour or more in advance and left, partially covered, in its cooking bouillon; reheat slowly before serving.

Serving suggestions

Carve the meat into serving pieces and arrange on a hot platter with, if there is room, the steamed vegetables in the following recipe. Garnish with sprigs of parsley. Moisten with a ladleful of degreased cooking bouillon and pass a pitcher of bouillon, along with the garlic and tomato sauces, for the meat and noodles.

Remarks:

Solid pieces of meat can be carved more attractively than pieces with muscle separations—like those in the beef chuck and in the pork shoulder and the blade end of the pork loin. This is probably why the beef brisket, even though rather stringy in texture, is always popular—it slices evenly; but do note that if you get an edge cut (or double) brisket, you should separate it before carving since you have two muscle layers, each going in a different direction.

A Mixture of Steamed Vegetables

To accompany a boiled dinner and noodles

For 8 people

6 carrots

1 large rutabaga

3 or 4 (or more) white turnips

8 leeks and/or white onions

Enough boiled-dinner bouillon to fill steaming-kettle by an inch or so

Fresh parsley

Equipment

A steamer rack (see illustration, page 44) or metal colander; a kettle to hold whichever you use; a close-fitting cover

Preliminaries

Since these vegetables all take about the same time to cook, you can arrange them together on the steamer or in the colander; or cook them separately. The number and variety is up to you and the appetites of your guests. To prepare the vegetables, peel the carrots, cut into quarters, and cut the quarters in half. Peel the rutabaga and cut into pieces about the size of the carrots, and do the same with the turnips. Cut the roots off the leeks and cut leeks into 3-inch (8-cm) lengths (saving tender green part of tops for soup); if the leeks show any sign of sand or dirt, split into quarters lengthwise down to within 1 inch (2½ cm) of the root end and wash thoroughly under running water. Drop onions into boiling water, boil 1 minute, then shave off the two ends and slip off the peel; for even, nonburst cooking, pierce a cross ¼ inch (¾ cm) deep in root ends.

🕐 Vegetables may be prepared several hours in advance; cover with dampened paper towels and refrigerate in a plastic bag.

Steaming

About half an hour before serving, arrange the vegetables in separate piles on the steamer or in the colander, pour the bouillon into the kettle, and cover closely—if need be, arrange foil over the steamer or colander to make a close seal. Bring to the boil on top of the stove and steam slowly until vegetables are tender; do not overcook—vegetables should just be done.

🕐 If done somewhat ahead, it is best to undercook; set aside partially covered and reheat just before serving.

Serving

Arrange the vegetables either on the platter with the meat or on a separate hot platter; ladle a little of the steaming-liquid over them and decorate with parsley sprigs. Add the rest of the savory vegetable steaming liquid to the bouillon you pass with the meat.

Fresh Green Beans Simply Boiled

The fresh green beans here are mostly for color and need no formal recipe since they are so easy to do the French way. Choose crisp snappy ones, rapidly pull off one end, drawing it down the bean to remove any lurking string, and do the same with the other end. Wash in cold water, drain, and, if you are not cooking them soon, wrap in paper towels and refrigerate in a plastic bag. When ready to cook them—which you can do several hours in advance—have a large kettle with 6 quarts or liters rapidly boiling salted water at the ready (for 1 to 2 pounds or ½ to 1 kg beans; you will need the smaller amount for this dinner), drop in the beans, cover the kettle until the beans come back to the boil, then uncover and let beans boil rapidly for 5 minutes or so. Test by eating one or two, and as soon as just cooked through, set a metal colander curved side down in the kettle and tip to drain the beans. Then, with colander still in, refresh the beans for several minutes in cold water—you can even add ice cubes to the water to speed the cooling. This sets the fresh green color and the texture.

🕐 If boiled in advance, drain thoroughly and refrigerate in a clean towel.

Shortly before serving, toss in a large frying pan for a moment to evaporate excess moisture, then toss with butter, drops of lemon juice, and salt and pepper to taste. Or, drop for a minute or so in a kettle of boiling salted water, drain, and serve at once. (Or serve cold, with oil and lemon dressing, a sprinkling of minced shallots or scallions, and parsley.)

Cream of Garlic Sauce with Horseradish

To serve with boiled dinners, boiled fish or chicken, boiled potatoes

For about 2 cups or ½ liter

1 large head garlic

2 Tb butter

½ cup (1 dL) dry white French vermouth

1 Tb cornstarch

2 cups (½ L) bouillon from the boiled dinner, or from another source

1 or more Tb white prepared horseradish

1 egg yolk

4 Tb heavy cream (a little more if you wish)

Salt and white pepper

2 Tb fresh minced herbs, such as parsley and chives

To peel the garlic cloves, separate them from the head and drop into boiling water for 1 minute; the skins will slip off easily. Then simmer with the butter in a small saucepan for 5 minutes without browning; add the vermouth, cover, and simmer 10 to 15 minutes more or until very tender and liquid has evaporated completely. Purée by rubbing through a sieve with a wooden spoon, then scrape garlic off sieve back into saucepan. Blend in the cornstarch, gradually beat in the bouillon, and bring to the simmer, stirring. Simmer 2 minutes and remove from heat. In a small bowl, blend 1 tablespoon horseradish, the egg yolk, and 4 tablespoons cream; by dribbles beat in half of the hot sauce, then by dribbles beat this mixture back into the pan with the rest of the sauce. Bring again to the simmer, stirring, and taste carefully for seasoning, adding salt and pepper and more horseradish and cream if you wish.

🕐 May be prepared in advance. Set aside off heat, and float a spoonful of cream over surface of sauce to prevent a skin from forming.

Reheat just before serving, stir in the herbs, and pour into a warm sauce bowl.

Fresh Tomato Fondue

A sauce to serve with boiled meats—or with fish, eggs, soufflés, and so forth

For about 2 cups or ½ liter

8 to 10 firm ripe red tomatoes—plus some drained and strained Italian plum tomatoes for added taste and color if you feel them needed

2 Tb olive oil

2 Tb minced shallots or scallions

1 clove minced garlic (optional)

¼ tsp thyme

1 bay leaf

Salt and pepper

Peel, seed, and juice the tomatoes (see "Tomato Talk," page 159), and dice them into pieces of about ⅜ inch (1 cm). Heat the oil in a medium-size saucepan, stir in the shallots or scallions and optional garlic, simmer a moment, then add the tomato (and strained canned tomato if you are using it). Add the thyme and bay and simmer several minutes, tossing and folding, until tomatoes have rendered their excess juice and have formed a fairly thick sauce. Season carefully with salt and pepper. Serve hot, warm, or cold—without the bay leaf.

🕐   May be cooked in advance.

Homemade Noodles

Kneaded and cut in a noodle machine

For about 24 ounces (675 g) noodles, or the equivalent of 2 standard boxes of commercial egg noodles, serving 8 people generously

The Noodle Dough:

1 ¾ cups (4 dL) all-purpose flour

2 "large" eggs

2 to 4 Tb cold water

Equipment

A mixing bowl, wooden spoon, and rubber spatula, or a food processor; a noodle machine (either hand-crank or electric); 1 or 2 clean broom handles to be suspended (for instance, between 2 chairs)

Forming the noodle dough by hand
Place the flour in a mixing bowl, make a well in the center, and break in the 2 eggs; blend them with 2 tablespoons of the water, and gradually mix in the surrounding flour with a wooden spoon or a spatula. Blend vigorously to make a stiff dough; turn out onto a work surface and knead vigorously with the heel of your hand, adding droplets more water to unblended bits. Dough should just form into a mass—the machine will do the rest.

For the food processor

Add all ingredients to the machine, using 2 tablespoons water, and process (using metal cutting blade); in about a minute, if you have enough water for the temper of the day, the dough will usually form itself into a ball on top of the blade. Sometimes the dough will not form a mass but seem to be made up of granular particles; however, as long as you can squeeze it into a coherent mass when removed from the food processor, all is well. In any case, experience will be your judge as to whether or not to add droplets more water. Turn dough out onto work surface and knead together to blend. Dough should be firm; if soft and/or sticky, knead in a sprinkling of flour.

Remarks:

A little too much water, in my book, is no disaster, since you can always knead in more flour to make the requisitely stiff dough. Again, your own experience will guide you, eventually, but don't be afraid of the dough. Not much can go wrong as long as it is stiff enough and dry enough to pass through the kneading and cutting rollers of your machine. Tenderness and exquisiteness of texture can come later, and will be part of your own particular secret genius with the noodle.

❶ Dough may be formed half an hour or so in advance, and some practitioners prefer to let the dough rest before forming it; in this case, wrap it airtight in plastic to keep it from crusting over. (I have found, by the way, that dough made with unbleached flour turns a grayish yellow when refrigerated overnight; however,

it kneads and cooks up satisfactorily when cooked the next day.) Freshly made dough may be frozen.

Finishing the dough and forming noodles

Cut the dough in half and cover one piece with plastic while forming the other. Flatten this piece of dough into a cake the size of your palm, and pinch one edge so it will fit into the machine. Set smooth rollers to their widest opening—number 8 on most machines. Crank the dough through. Fold dough in half, end to end, and crank through several times until dough is smooth and fairly evenly rectangular; as necessary, brush dough with flour before passing through rollers, since it will stick to the machine if it is too damp.

When dough is smooth, reset rollers to the next lower setting and crank it through, then to the next lower, and the next—which is usually number 5. By this time your strip of dough will be so long you will probably want to cut it in two; now pass the first and then the second half through number 4, the setting that gives, I think, the right thinness for noodles and lasagne. Hang each strip as it is finished on a broom handle to dry out briefly (but not to stiffen—4 to 5 minutes are usually enough). Repeat the process with the reserved piece of dough, then crank the dried strips through the noodle roller, set at number 4, and hang noodles on broom handles as you cut them.

❶ Noodles may be formed and cooked at once, or formed in advance and cooked later. For instance, you may let them hang on the broom handles until they have dried thoroughly, and then package them. Or you

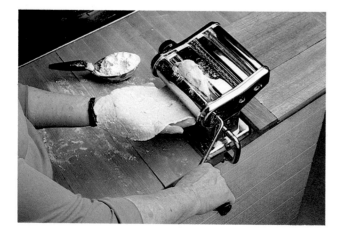

may like to preserve them in a semifresh state. In this case, arrange a layer of noodles on a tray, sprinkle corn flour over lightly (if you can't find corn flour, pulverize cornmeal in your blender), cover with wax paper, and continue with successive layers of noodles, ending with wax paper; set in the refrigerator overnight, or until dry, then package in their laid-out state, and freeze. (If you freeze noodles when they are damp they will stick together, and it is almost impossible to separate the strands while they cook.)

Cooking Noodles:

A large kettle filled with at least 8 quarts or liters rapidly boiling water

2 tsp salt per quart of water

A large colander (for draining)

Butter and olive oil (or your choice of dressing)

A hot platter and 2 large forks for tossing and serving

Salt and pepper

About 5 minutes before serving, plunge the noodles into the rapidly boiling water and cover until boil is reached. Then boil uncovered, frequently testing the noodle cooking by eating a strand or two—fresh soft noodles take but a minute of cooking, while semifresh and dry noodles take a minute or two longer. Do not overcook or the noodles will be mushy—better slightly under- than slightly overcooked.

Once they are done, drain in a colander, shaking vigorously to remove excess water. Spread a little butter and oil (or dressing) in the platter, turn into it the steaming noodles, and toss with the forks, adding salt and pepper, more butter and oil (or dressing), and tasting to be sure all is perfectly seasoned. Work rapidly and rush them to the table, still steaming.

Strawberries en Chemise

Icing-coated strawberries, to decorate desserts and ice cream

For 24 large strawberries

1 cup sifted confectioners sugar (a little more if needed)

1 tsp raw egg white (a little more if needed)

¼ tsp fresh lemon juice

Drops of Cognac or more lemon juice (as needed)

Fresh strawberries, washed rapidly and laid on a rack

Equipment

A portable electric mixer or a wire whip

Place the sugar, egg white, and lemon juice in a smallish high-sided mixing bowl and beat a minute or more with electric mixer or wire whip until sugar forms a quite stiff mass that "forms the beak"—makes stiff points when a bit is lifted in the blades of the beater. Thin out with a droplet or two of Cognac or more lemon juice—icing should be thick enough to enrobe strawberries. Holding a berry by its topknot, swirl it in the frosting to cover two-thirds the way up its sides, and replace on rack.

🕐 May be done an hour in advance.

Arrange over strawberry sherbet or ice cream just before bringing to the table.

🕐 *Timing*

Boiling and draining the noodles is *the* last-minute job for this dinner. They must be eaten the moment they're done, and homemade ones take only minutes to cook. About 20 minutes before putting on the water for the noodles, start the vegetables steaming. *N.B.:* If you plan to add the optional green beans to the vegetable bouquet, blanch them and refrigerate that afternoon, and toss in butter right after you've put the noodles into the pot.

The two sauces are quick to make, and the strawberries, to dip. But remember to put the sherbet or ice cream in the refrigerator to soften at about the time you sit down to dinner.

You should start cooking the corned meat about 3½ hours before you eat it, and it must be soaked for 24 hours before that. Salt and spice it at least 2 weeks in advance, though it can stay in its brine for 2 months. And don't forget to massage and turn it every day during that 2-week period.

One nice thing about shopping for this dinner is that every ingredient except the strawberries (and, if you're having them, the green beans) can be bought days in advance.

Pasta primavera—cooked noodles have been tossed in slivered garlic and oil, then simmered in heavy cream (or béchamel); now blanched, diced, buttered fresh vegetables are added; and finally cheese is sprinkled over all.

Menu Variations

The main course: Rather than cured meat, you may like fresh meat with noodles, or a boiled fowl; if you do either, I'd suggest adding a cooking sausage, such as chorizo or Polish kielbasy. Salted goose or duck would be elegant and is made in exactly the same way as corned meat. Both are simple cousins of the French preserve, or *confit*.

Noodles are delicious tossed in olive oil in which you have sautéed a clove of garlic; they are then simmered in cream and tossed with cheese. You could elaborate on this, especially in summer, by adding a bouquet of bright diced and cooked vegetables and tossing again for a Pasta alla Primavera. Going further, you could add diced ham.

The pasta machine Paul and I have makes either thin or medium-width noodles; and, as you know, noodle dough tastes quite different in its many forms. A lasagna made with uncut homemade noodle dough is an experience (for a nice recipe, see the French-Italian one in *J.C.'s Kitchen*). Most general cookbooks—and most ethnic ones, for that matter—have useful suggestions for other, myriad uses of this dough.

The dessert: I do think something light and fruit flavored will taste best to you after noodles and cured meat: a homemade sherbet, perhaps (see "VIP Lunch," page 89), or a fruit compote (see "Dinner for the Boss," page 129). Or you could offer a basket of fresh fruit. The children will enjoy arranging a lovely still life and maybe learn to eat even such difficult delights as ripe figs in the French manner, with knife and fork.

Leftovers

You can rinse leftover cooked *pasta* by a quick plunge in boiling water; then drain well and serve hot with any of an enormous variety of accompaniments. Or use it, rinsed in cold water after draining and drained again, in a composed salad. Leftover raw pasta can be frozen.

Cured meat can be reheated, even several times. Sliced, it makes splendid sandwiches, or can be served as a salad platter, close cousin to Salade de Boeuf à la Parisienne (see "Dinner for the Boss," page 131). Ground and mixed with chard, cheese, and egg (see *Mastering II*), it makes a fine hamburger. I'd add sausage meat if I planned a meat loaf or patties. You can make a vegetable-and-meat loaf, to serve with tomato sauce, as follows: run leftover vegetables, along with noodles, through the food processor; then process twice as much meat. Combine these ingredients, then add 1 egg for each 2 cups (½ L) of the mixture, add a bit of sausage meat for richness, mix, and bake. To make that delicious classic, corned beef hash—or for that matter, corned pork hash—see page 172. Also, if you have boned your own pork loin for corning, you'll find you have enough pork meat clinging to the bone to make scrapple, page 174.

The bouillon is delicious; why not add to it some of the leftover noodles, some of the meat, and some of the vegetables for a splendid soup? A bit of the *garlic sauce* would be excellent with either this soup or the meat loaf.

Postscript: On cooking with children

Influenced, perhaps, by my early experience at a Montessori school, and surely by living in a clan full of carvers, painters, carpenters, and cooks of all ages, I am all for encouraging children to work productively with their hands. They learn to handle and care for equipment with respect. It is good to give them knives, for instance, as early as you dare. A knife is a tool, not a toy. A sharp, clean knife is safer to use than a dull, rusty one—easier too: a four-year-old will discover that for himself as you teach him to slice a hard-boiled egg neatly and then to fillet a fish. Talk to children as you plan menus. Let their small, sensitive noses sniff the fish as you shop. Work together at the counter and let your children arrange platters. Nothing gives them more pleasure than setting things in rows and rosettes.

The small rituals, like the clean hands and clean apron before setting to work; the precision of gesture, like leveling off a cupful of flour; the charm of improvisation and making something new; the pride of mastery; and the gratification of offering something one has made—these have such value to a child. And where are they so easily to be obtained as in cooking? The patience and good humor demanded of you by cooking with a child are a good investment.

Do taste everything together, at every stage, and serve to children what you eat yourself. Once they have enough teeth to cope with any food, children, with their unjaded palates, are a keen, responsive audience for an enthusiastic cook. And I suspect that those who learn the use of wine early and sensibly will be less tempted to its abuse later on.

Advance preparation, easy service, and a charming main dish adapted from a classic of the haute cuisine; *special treats for a big crowd.*

Buffet for 19

Menu

Oysters on the Half Shell

❧

Turkey Orloff—turkey breast scallopini gratinéed with mushrooms, onions, rice, and cheese
Fresh Green Beans with Watercress and Tomatoes, Oil and Lemon Dressing
French Bread

❧

Jamaican Ice Cream Goblet

❧

Suggested wines:
Chablis, Muscadet, or Riesling with the oysters; red Bordeaux or Cabernet Sauvignon with the turkey

Supper for a crowd nowadays means buffet service. I ask of a good buffet main dish that it be easy to serve, hold heat well, be reasonably compact to save oven and table space, that-it be neither expensive nor pretentious, and that it may be prepared largely in advance. At once I add: the dish must be delicious, handsome, and a little unusual. Just because the guests have been invited en masse, they mustn't be let think that their dinner has been indifferently chosen or perfunctorily prepared.

Except for our kitchen Cocktail Party, none of the menus in this book requires a special setting or unusual kitchen facilities. But a meal for a big crowd puts special demands on almost any house, host, and hostess. I am not mad about buffet dining, but when it is unavoidable I like guests to help themselves to the main course, then be served more wine and second helpings. I like their plates to be cleared and the dessert to be passed to them.

In this menu, the oyster bar makes for fun and informality, but it does need a special place of its own. After serving them, arrange with a good friend, or your helper if you have one, to dismantle the remains of the once splendid set-up while the guests are moving on to the main course. At home, Paul and I have enough room so we can enjoy our oysters in one place and then grandly waft everyone off to another for the sit-down part of dinner. We generally arrange platters at either end of our long table, so that people can help themselves quickly and find a place to sit down.

In any crowd, there are invariably a few people who simply cannot face oysters, so we offer them a simple alternative like cheese or thinly sliced salami. We allow three oysters per person, which seems to average out for those who can leave them and those who so love them that they will eat four or five or even more. Now that we have learned to open them easily, we do so as we serve them, which is always advisable anyway. Once our guests get the knack of prying up the shells with a beer can opener, or, as college wags used to put it, a church key, we find that most of them find it great fun doing their own. We set out plates and napkins, oyster forks for the conventionally minded, and spoons for those who eat oysters, as we do, in one voluptuous slurp. We add lemons and a pepper grinder—but no cocktail sauce!—and buttered dark bread.

The Turkey Orloff is a modern, streamlined cousin of an elaborate dish, Veal Prince Orloff, named for a notable Russian gourmet of the nineteenth century by some forgotten Paris chef. It is a saddle of veal that is roasted, sliced, then re-formed with a stuffing of mushrooms and *soubise* (rice braised with onions) and gratinéed with a rich creamy sauce. It is a noble dish; but its price is almost prohibitive since you must use a very choice cut of veal, and it is almost fiendishly fattening. The turkey variant is much less expensive, less rich—and less work. But it is a recipe designed for the food processor, where you can make light of slicing 15 cups of onions and mincing quarts of mushrooms. If fresh sliced turkey

breast is not available at the supermarket, frozen breasts always are. The finished dish, whose layers of white turkey meat are interleaved with a rice, onion, and mushroom stuffing and finished off with a golden gratin, has a deep, subtle flavor and an agreeable, fork-tender texture.

When you're planning a vegetable here, you have to think about the number of people you're serving, and about your kitchen facilities. A great platter of hot broccoli, fresh peas, or beans would be lovely. But for 19 people? That's much too difficult, I think. I'd rather have something cold, but not the usual green salad. Instead, I have chosen a beautiful platter of fresh green beans, cooked, chilled, and lightly dressed with oil, lemon and mustard, and brightened up with red onion rings and tomatoes.

Dessert for a crowd. You want it dressy, delectable, original, but easy to handle. The idea here is simple indeed: store-bought vanilla ice cream, each serving topped with a spoonful or two of dark rum, then dusted with powdered coffee. It's a surprise dessert with a sophisticated air—and there's something wonderfully sensuous about spooning up this ambrosial combination from a big opulent goblet that a pedestrian old bowl simply doesn't supply.

Preparations

Recommended Equipment:

For your oyster bar, you will need a space about the size of two card tables, a big tub and plenty of chopped ice for the oysters, some kind of receptacle for their shells, a pepper mill or two, and several beer can openers. (Or see the set-up described in "Cocktail Party," pages 93-4). Have paring knives for separating the muscles from the shells and a conventional oyster knife or two for recalcitrant cases.

For every multiple of the turkey recipe (which is given for 8 persons), you'll want a baking-and-serving dish 2 inches (5 cm) deep. As I've said, the turkey recipe is designed for the food processor; if you don't have one, see suggestions for other main courses in Menu Variations.

Marketing and Storage:

A note on quantities: the recipes, and therefore the lists below, are for 8 "average" appetites. Multiply by 2½ if the dinner is for 19—or even 20—people.

Staples to have on hand

Salt
Peppercorns
Mustard (the strong Dijon type; see Remarks, page 6)
Herbs: dried tarragon, thyme or sage, imported bay leaves
Flour
Celery, onions, and carrots (small quantities for making stock)

Garlic
Powdered instant coffee (for the dessert topping)

Specific ingredients for this menu

Turkey breast (either 2½ pounds or 1¼ kg fresh slices or half a frozen 9-pound or 4-kg bone-in breast) ▼
Fresh oysters in the shell (24 to 30)
Salami (16 thin slices)
Cheese (if you wish it, as an alternative to oysters)
Cocktail sausages (16)
Olive oil or salad oil (4 ounces or 1 dL)
Plain raw white rice (2 ounces or 60 g or ¼ cup)
Thin-sliced dark bread (20 slices), pumpernickel or rye
French bread, 2 loaves
Butter (½ pound or 225 g or 2 sticks)
Eggs (3)
Low-fat cottage cheese (4 ounces or 115 g)
Mozzarella cheese (4 ounces or 115 g), coarsely grated
Fresh mushrooms (½ pound or 225 g)
Yellow onions (1 pound or 450 g, or 5 or 6 medium-size)
Red onions (2 medium-size) or scallions (1 bunch)
Cherry tomatoes (1 quart or 1 L) or ripe red regular tomatoes (3 or 4)
Watercress (2 or 3 bunches) or romaine (1 head)
Fresh green beans (2½ pounds or 1¼ kg)
Fresh parsley
Lemons (5)
Vanilla ice cream (1½ quarts or 1½ L), best quality
Dark Jamaica rum (8 ounces or ½ L)
Crushed ice for the oysters and ice cubes for drinks

▶ *Remarks:*

In providing for non-oyster-eaters with cheese, salami slices, and hot cocktail sausages, I allow about 2 ounces of each per person, since some oyster eaters will consume both. I also count on 2 or 3 slices of dark bread per person, and 2 tablespoons softened butter to spread on each 10 to 12 pieces. *Turkey breast:* Fresh ready-sliced turkey breast meat is available in many markets: look in the poultry section, where it is usually attractively packaged in flat see-through trays. If you are buying frozen breasts, the best size, I think, is around 9 pounds (4 kg); have the breast sawed in half lengthwise if you are doing the turkey recipe for only 8 people, and you can store the other half in your freezer. It is always best to defrost frozen turkey slowly in the refrigerator, since you will then have juicier and firmer meat.

Turkey Talk:

You can begin with sliced raw fresh turkey breast meat, or with half a 9-pound (4-kg) frozen turkey breast. Once a turkey breast has thawed, peel off and discard the skin, remove the breast meat in one piece from the bone, and cut it into 12 or more serving slices about ⅜ inch (1 cm) thick with a very sharp knife.

The Stock:

Chop up the carcass and simmer it and any turkey meat scraps for 2 hours in lightly salted water to cover, with a chopped carrot and onion, 2 celery ribs, and an herb bouquet (8 parsley sprigs, 1 large imported bay leaf, and ½ teaspoon thyme or sage tied in washed cheesecloth); strain, degrease, and refrigerate until needed.

If you've no homemade stock, use canned chicken broth but flavor it as follows: for each 2 cups (½ L), simmer for 30 minutes with 3 tablespoons each sliced onions, carrots, and celery, ½ cup (1 dL) dry white wine *or* ⅓ cup (¾ dL) dry white French vermouth; then strain.

Turkey Orloff

Turkey breast scallopini gratinéed with mushrooms, onions, rice, and cheese

For 8 people

¼ cup (½ dL) plain raw white rice
Salt
1 pound (450 g or 5 to 6 medium-size onions
1½ sticks (6 ounces or 180 g) butter
1 egg plus 2 egg yolks
½ pound (225 g or 3 to 3½ cups) fresh mushrooms
A handful fresh parsley sprigs (to make 3 Tb minced)
½ tsp fragrant dried tarragon
Pepper
12 or more turkey breast slices (see notes preceding recipe)
5 Tb flour for sauce, plus extra for turkey sauté
1 Tb vegetable oil
3 cups (¾ L) hot turkey stock (or chicken stock—see notes preceding recipe)
½ cup (1 dL) low-fat cottage cheese
1 cup (¼ L or 4 ounces) lightly pressed down coarsely grated mozzarella cheese

Rice and onion soubise

Preheat oven to 325°F/170°C. Drop the rice into a saucepan with 2 quarts (2 L) rapidly boiling salted water and boil uncovered for exactly 5 minutes; drain immediately and

reserve. Meanwhile peel and then chop the onions in a food processor; (it needs no washing until after its last operation). To do onions, prechop roughly by hand into 1-inch (2½-cm) chunks and process them 1½ cups (3½ dL) at a time, using metal blade and switching machine on and off 3 or 4 times at 1-second intervals to chop onions into ⅜-inch (1-cm) morsels. Melt 4 tablespoons of the butter in a flameproof 6- to 8-cup (1½- to 2-L) baking dish, stir in the chopped onions, the drained rice, and ¼ teaspoon salt, mixing well to coat with the butter; cover the dish and bake in middle level of oven for about 1 hour, stirring up once or twice, until rice is completely tender and beginning to turn a golden yellow. When the rice is done and still warm, beat in the egg; taste carefully and correct seasoning.

🕐 May be done a day or two in advance.

Mushroom duxelles

While rice and onion *soubise* is cooking, trim and wash the mushrooms. For the food processor, first chop roughly by hand into 1-inch (2½-cm) chunks, then process into ⅛-inch (½-cm) pieces, using the 1-second on-off technique. Mince the parsley in the machine afterward. By handfuls, either twist mushrooms hard in the corner of a towel or squeeze through a potato ricer to extract as much of their juices as possible. Sauté the mushrooms in 2 tablespoons of the butter in a medium-size frying pan over moderately high heat, stirring and tossing until mushroom pieces begin to separate from each other—5 to 6 minutes. Stir in the tarragon and parsley; season to taste with salt and pepper. Stir half of the mixture into the cooked rice and onion *soubise;* reserve the rest.

🕐 Mushroom *duxelles* may be cooked in advance and may be frozen.

Preparing the turkey scallopini

Pound the slices between 2 sheets of wax paper, with a rubber hammer, a rolling pin, or the side of a bottle, to expand them about double and to thin them down by half. These are your turkey scallopini; cover and refrigerate them until you are ready to sauté them.

Sautéing the turkey scallopini

Salt and pepper the turkey slices lightly, dredge in flour and shake off excess, sauté for about a minute on each side in 1 tablespoon of the oil and 2 tablespoons of the butter (more if needed)—just to stiffen them and barely cook through. Set slices aside on a plate as you finish them.

The gratinéing sauce

Make a turkey *velouté* sauce as follows. Melt 4 tablespoons of the butter over moderate heat in a heavy-bottomed 2-quart (2-L) saucepan, blend in the flour, and cook, stirring with a wooden spoon until flour and butter foam and froth together for 2 minutes without turning more than a golden yellow. Remove from heat and, when this *roux* has stopped bubbling, pour in 2 cups (½ L) of the hot turkey or chicken stock and blend vigorously with a wire whip. Return to heat, stirring slowly with wire whip to reach all over bottom, corner, and side of pan, and boil slowly for 2 minutes. Taste and correct seasoning. Sauce should be thick enough to coat a wooden spoon nicely, mean-

ing it will coat the turkey. Beat in more stock by droplets if sauce is too thick. In the food proccssor or an electric blender, purée the egg yolks with the cottage cheese (or push through a fine sieve and beat in a bowl with a wire whip); by dribbles, beat the hot sauce into the egg yolk and cheese mixture.

Assembling the dish

Choose a baking-and-serving dish about 10 by 14 by 2 inches (25 x 35 x 5 cm); butter the inside, and spread a thin layer of sauce in bottom of dish. Make a neat, slightly overlapping pattern of the turkey slices down the center of the dish, spreading each, as you go, with the *soubise*. Spoon remaining mushroom *duxelles* down the sides. Spoon remaining sauce over the turkey and spread the mozzarella cheese on top.

🕐 Recipe may be prepared a day in advance to this point; when cool, cover and refrigerate. If, before proceeding, you note that the sauce does not cover some parts of the meat, spread more mozzarella on these areas.

Final baking and serving

Turkey will take about 25 minutes to heat and for the top to brown; it should be served fairly promptly since the meat will be juicier if it does not have to wait around. Set uncovered in upper third of a preheated 400°F/200°C oven until contents are bubbling hot and sauce has browned nicely.

Fresh Green Beans with Watercress and Tomatoes, Oil and Lemon Dressing

For 8 people
2½ pounds (1¼ kg) fresh green beans, trimmed and blanched (see page 40)
Salt and pepper
2 or 3 bunches watercress, or 1 head romaine
For the dressing
1 lemon
1 small clove garlic (optional)
1 tsp prepared mustard, Dijon type
6 or more Tb olive oil or salad oil
2 medium-size mild red onions, or 1 bunch scallions
1 quart (1 L) cherry tomatoes, or 3 or 4 ripe red regular tomatoes

Prepare the beans in the morning, wrap in a clean towel and then in a plastic bag, and refrigerate. Also remove tough stems from watercress, wash the cress, and fold in a clean towel and plastic; refrigerate (or if using romaine, wash, separating leaves, wrap like the cress, and refrigerate).

An hour or so before serving, prepare the dressing as follows. Cut the zest (yellow part of

peel) off half the lemon and mince very fine. Place in a small mortar or heavy bowl with the salt; purée in the optional garlic. Pound into a fine paste with a pestle or the end of a wooden spoon, then beat in the mustard, a tablespoon of juice from the lemon, and the oil. Carefully correct seasoning—dressing should not be too acid, only mildly so because of the wine you will be serving with the dinner.

Peel the red onions and slice into thin rings; toss in a bowl with the dressing (or mix chopped scallions with the dressing); cover and refrigerate. Halve the cherry tomatoes, place cut side up in a dish, and salt lightly (or peel, slice, and lightly salt regular tomatoes); cover and refrigerate. If you are using romaine rather than cress, gather leaves by handfuls and slice crosswise into ⅜-inch (1-cm) julienne strips; refrigerate in a plastic bag.

Shortly before guests are to arrive, arrange the watercress or romaine in the bottom of a wide salad bowl or platter and toss with a sprinkling of salt. Toss the blanched beans in a bowl with the onions or scallions and dressing, taste carefully for seasoning, and arrange attractively over the cress or romaine, with the tomatoes around the edges. Baste tomatoes and beans with dressing left in bean bowl. Cover and keep cool until serving time.

Jamaican Ice Cream Goblet

This dessert needs no actual recipe since it consists only of a healthy helping of the best vanilla ice cream in a big goblet (if possible! or a pretty bowl or a dessert plate), a spoonful or two of dark Jamaica rum, and a sprinkling of powdered instant coffee (if you have only the freeze-dried granular type, pulverize it in a blender). It couldn't be simpler, but the rum and coffee blending into that vanilla cream combine into a marvelous medley of tastes. I usually assemble this in the kitchen, with a friend or two to help pass it around. But with not too big a crowd, it's rather fun to pass the goblets of ice cream and let guests help themselves to the rum, in a pitcher with ladle, and to the coffee, in a bowl with teaspoon.

P.S. Bourbon whiskey can substitute for rum—but in that case it must be called a Bourbon rather than a Jamaican goblet.

⏱ *Timing*

Midway through your menu, perhaps when you move on from the oysters to the turkey, remember to take your ice cream out of the freezer and put it into the refrigerator to soften.

Just before the guests arrive, assemble the salad platters while you heat the cocktail sausages or crisp the French bread.

Since Turkey Orloff shouldn't sit around too much after its 25- to 30-minute baking, when you put it in depends on your party-giving style.

An hour or so before the guests are to arrive, slice the onions, tomatoes, and other green bean fixings. Set up the oyster bar.

In the morning, blanch and chill the beans, wash and pick over the cress or wash the romaine. Butter the brown bread for the oysters, etc.; stack the slices on a tray between sheets of wax paper and chill, ready to be arranged on a board or platter when you set up the oyster bar. Buy the ice.

You can assemble the Turkey Orloff in the morning or the day before, and as you'll see from the recipe, parts of it may be made days in advance.

A day or even two or three before the party, buy the oysters, clean them, and stack them.

Buy the wines and other drinkables well ahead, so that those needing remedial rest will have their due.

Menu Variations

Oysters: You could also include clams and cooked shrimp. For a quite different dish—but similar in also being something raw, not too highly flavored, and obviously very special— serve Steak Tartare. Grind it yourself from beef tenderloin butts or tails, season lightly with salt and pepper, beat in raw egg yolks (one per half pound), and serve the trimmings separately: more salt, a pepper grinder or two, capers, anchovy fillets, finely minced onion, and chopped fresh herbs like parsley and chives. Guests pile their own on buttered dark bread and mix in the trimmings of their choice.

Turkey Orloff: For other dishes comprising poultry with an elegant stuffing, you might consider a boned stuffed turkey *ballottine* (as described in *The French Chef Cookbook*), or the Chicken Melon (see page 20) served hot, or boned ducks or chickens in pastry crusts. You could make your Orloff dish with chicken, veal, or thinly sliced loin of pork.

Vegetable or salad: Delicious, in season, would be fresh asparagus vinaigrette, or artichoke hearts with a few halved cherry tomatoes for decorations. A platter of sliced cucumbers with a light dressing and a wreath of watercress is another green idea, or that always amenable standby, fresh broccoli vinaigrette. Finally, just have fine big bowls of fresh mixed salad greens.

Dessert: You could make peach Melba, or serve your ice cream with poached pears and chocolate sauce (*poires belle Hélène*), or garnish the ice cream with canned peaches simmered in their own syrup that has been boiled down with wine and cinnamon. And there are a thousand ways of using liqueurs, of freezing store ice cream into a bombe, and of serving it with meringues. Or change from ice cream to fruit and have the macédoine suggested on page 129, or one of its variations; and with it you could serve cake or cookies.

Leftovers

Oysters: See the Leftovers section in "Cocktail Party," page 109.

Turkey Orloff: You can reassemble, sprinkle on more cheese, and regratiné the dish; it will not have quite its original glory, but it will still make very good eating. You can chop the turkey bits, mix everything together, and use for stuffing crêpes; or make an elegant turkey hash. Or grind everything up in a food processor, add a little fresh sausage meat, and 1 egg per cup of mixture, and turn it into a meatloaf. Or chop or grind up everything and simmer with a chicken stock to make a rich and hearty soup.

Green beans: I would prefer not to have leftovers in this category since the beauty of the fresh bean is fleeting. Serve them again the very next day as a salad would be my suggestion. However, you could try dropping the whole mixture briefly in boiling water to wash off the dressing, draining, and boiling up in a soup.

Postscript

Luxury and quantity, like the lion and the lamb, don't often consort; and it is not easy to serve a really fine meal to great numbers, especially without expert household help. I won't bore you with admonitions about counting silver, shifting furniture, and all those preparatory chores; but it is very certain that planning is the essence of a successful party, and I do think too many hosts skimp on menu planning, though this is the most important thing of all. My own practice is to choose a simple workable menu and to do as much as possible in advance, such as freezing what can be frozen of the menu's elements, like the *duxelles,* precooking the stock and *soubise* for the turkey, and saving a bit of that valuable last-minute time for some truly special touch. Nothing gives a party so much personal warmth as the guests' sense that you wanted to give them a particular treat. One remarkable dish has twice the effect of several run-of-the-mill ones.

Steak Tartare with trimmings.

Essay

A basketful of common varieties of tomatoes, green and ripe, with Italian plum cooking tomatoes and small cherry tomatoes beside them.

Tomato Talk

Tomatoes come in all sizes; cherry tomatoes are the smallest sold, but "currant" types exist. Except for the rare yellow varieties, the skin and flesh of fine tomatoes are intensely, evenly red. The perfect tomato is plump, heavy, smooth, and unblemished, though "cat faces," or scars around the blossom end, are harmless; and the locules, the interior chambers containing jelly and seeds, should be few. Our gardening friends tell us that the plants are thrifty, bounteous, and easy to cultivate. For home consumption, they grow the thin-skinned, deep-flavored varieties, and pick them at their peak of ripeness—at which point a day's chilling in the fridge will do no harm, if you can wait that long to bite into these summer miracles of sun and light sweet soil, and gentle handling.

How to choose them

Varieties like these are too fragile for commercial cultivation and shipping; nor, except in rare instances, can you expect to buy market tomatoes which were picked at full ripeness. At their best, typical market tomatoes will have been picked fairly near ripeness and are then termed "greenhouse" or "hothouse." The calyx, the little star of leaves at the stem end, will be fresh and bright green; and, if a bit of stem is left on, the tomato will keep better—but stems are a packer's bane, for they puncture the tomato's neighbors in the crate. Next best is the "vine-ripe" tomato, which was harvested when merely pink. Third best is "mature-green," which you won't see often, since the wholesaler usually holds it until it has reddened in his ripening room.

Perfect or not, the market tomato is an indispensable item. It has lots of Vitamin C and some A, its appearance is pretty, its texture and flavor are unique, it is a basic and versatile element in most Occidental cuisines, and it is available all year round. When you consider what treatment it undergoes before you ever see it, you may think its reliable presence a commercial miracle. Typically the poor thing is picked, packed in field crates, shipped to the packing house, unloaded, weighed, checked, washed, dried, waxed, sorted, graded, sized, packed for transport, loaded and shipped, unpacked for federal and/or state inspection, repacked, shipped again, unloaded, sorted (several operations here), repacked, trucked to the ripening room, unpacked, shelved till it's pink or red, repacked, trucked to the market, trucked to the retailer, probably unpacked and repacked again in trays, marked with an appalling price, and set out at last to wait for you. Not only can it be bruised or punctured at any of these stages, it is extremely vulnerable to chill from cold weather or imperfect storage. The effect of cold below 55°F/13°C on a tomato is to inhibit, even prevent, its ripening; and the effect is cumulative. A cold snap in the field, plus a day in a gelid refrigerator car, plus a few more on a sidetrack in winter can cause imperceptible damage which dooms the fruit (that's what it is, botanically: a berry, in fact—so's a banana) to die unripened.

The tomato hides its griefs. Internal damage is hard to spot, but beware of flattened or indented sides, skin discolorations, and skin cracks which invite bacteria. A few yellowish spots near the stem end are common, though not desirable. If when you cut it a tomato turns out to be puffy—watery flesh plus empty pockets in the locules—it's a total dud. Complain to your market.

Well. Suppose you have bought a presentable tomato, *do not chill it*. Don't leave it in sunlight, either, or at a temperature above 80°F/27°C. Unless you got it from the garden or a local stand, it needs to ripen for a few days, at room temperature and preferably in a container which will trap the ethylene gas all fruit exudes as it ripens. When the tomato's color has deepened and its scent intensified, it's ready.

How to use them

I like to eat a fine summer tomato just as it comes, or sliced and sprinkled with minced herbs and a *vinaigrette* dressing; and I love the thin tomato sandwiches which are so popular at English summer tea parties: the trick is to spread the butter thinly but carefully, to seal the bread against sogginess. If you slice tomatoes vertically, the jelly won't ooze out.

In cooking it's best to use the pulp only, since the jelly juice has little flavor, and the seeds harden as they heat. To skin a tomato, drop it in boiling water to cover, count off ten seconds exactly (slowly intoning, "one thousand, two thousand" up to ten), then cut out the stem and pull off the skin. To empty the locules of seeds and jelly, cut the tomato in half crosswise, and squeeze each half gently; or cut off the top and ream out each pocket with your fingertip. To extract more juice, you may salt the cavities lightly and set the tomato upside down. Juice will gradually exude.

The chopped, sliced, or diced pulp is a basic kitchen ingredient. If you judge it weak in flavor, add canned pear-shaped tomatoes, drained and sieved; for even more intense savor and color, blend in canned tomato paste.

Start cautiously, since the sugary, herbal flavor of tomato paste can overpower a dish: try one tablespoon per cupful of fresh tomato pulp, and taste before adding more.

On cooking tomatoes whole or halved: leave the skins on, so they'll keep their shape, but seed and squeeze them; and cook them at the last minute. Since they blacken so quickly, instead of broiling them, I bake them for about ten minutes at 400°F/200°C. For a fine full Provençal flavor, try a classic French stuffing: mix fresh (not dry) white bread crumbs with a good sprinkling of fresh minced herbs and garlic; flavor to taste with dried herbs, salt, and pepper; fill the tomatoes and drizzle on a little olive oil. About a cupful of stuffing should suffice for 6 good-size tomatoes. Or give them an American accent by tossing the bread crumbs in melted butter with a little brown sugar, salt, and several generous grindings of fresh black pepper.

As a garnish, cherry tomatoes, raw or quickly baked, are a familiar pleasure. Less well known but delicious is tomato fondue, tomato pulp cut in neat strips or diced and cooked briefly in oil with minced shallots or scallions, to lend piquant flavor and pretty color to a soup or a dish of vegetables—cauliflower, for example, or puréed spinach.

However you use them—and there are hundreds of ways—do have the patience and take the pains to buy tomatoes beforehand, store them right, and wait, to taste them at their best.

Your own sausage and scrapple, and a home-made muffin worthy of eggs Benedict, a noble dish whose true tale now stands revealed. And other contributions to Joy in the Morning!

Breakfast Party

There are reasons, and then there are excuses. The excuses for being festive at breakfast time (whatever that is at your house) can be anything—a football game to follow, perhaps. For me the best of all reasons is that it's an occasion to serve that beloved combination, eggs Benedict: an easy dish to mass-produce, yet one that everyone considers a special treat. It's an American dish, quite different from the French *oeufs à la Bénédictine* (a tartlet lined with *brandade de morue*—a garlicky purée of salt cod—which is surmounted by a poached egg and napped with a creamy sauce). I had understood that it was originated at the New York Yacht Club by Commodore E. C. Benedict. However, a recent check with the club's librarian, Sohei Hohri, and with Mrs. Allan Butler of Vineyard Haven, Massachusetts, has set the record straight. It seems it wasn't Mr. Benedict (who wasn't commodore at the N.Y.Y.C., but somewhere else), but his cousin Mrs. LeGrand Benedict, Mrs. Butler's great-aunt, who invented the dish; and the place wasn't the N.Y.Y.C. but Delmonico's, an elegant place to lunch at the turn of the century. Mrs. Benedict, bored with the luncheon menu, asked the maître d'hôtel to suggest something new; he asked her if she had any ideas... and, just like that, she said, "What if you put a slice of ham on half an English muffin, and a poached egg on the ham, and hollandaise sauce on the egg, and truffles on top?" And lo, a star was born.

Honor, then, to our benefactress Mrs. Benedict; and honor, too, to the butter-loving British. The object of the English muffin is to be a butter mop, and that's why it is so honeycombed with little holes, or butter wells. The recipe I use is for something between a muffin and a crumpet—cruffin? mumpet?; it is baked in rings on a griddle and made of a very spongy yeast batter, not a dough. Since I am not about to get up at 3 a.m. to cook breakfast, I make my muffins days or weeks in advance. And, when I do make them, I mix the batter the night before and let it rise once, then stir it down and often give it a second rising in the refrigerator, where it can await my pleasure. Coming down next morning, I find a swollen, adhesive, bubbly mass that looks uncannily alive. And the little yeast plants are alive, of course, and lively, because they have been gorging on starch all night. As soon as one scoops up this mass and drops it into the baking rings, set on their hot griddle, the batter becomes excited by the heat. Bubbles form at the bottom, rise upward, and seem to wink as they burst on the surface, leaving behind them little vertical wells. So graphic is this illustration of the vigor of yeast that it might give pause to believers in the transmigration of souls, the "Don't swat that fly, it might be Grandma" people.

It's nice to have the poached eggs already cooked, ready to be reheated in warm water, so famished guests can fall to at once; but what if they want seconds? Let those who want to poach them make their own. Why not? And if you have a flameproof glass saucepan, let them try the old-fashioned whirlpool method, so that they can crouch down to observe the process: the yolk twirling in its veil of white, trapped in the cone-shaped vortex. Some might want their second eggs with different underpinnings, so have some scrapple or fresh pork sausage waiting, and/or some crusty corned beef hash or sausage cakes, and a bowl of fresh tomato sauce or warm chili sauce or ketchup to splosh on top. Or perhaps they'd enjoy eggs Henriette, so have some sautéed chicken livers ready too. And stacks of pancakes, with hot butter and maybe syrup or honey to slather on.

If you have room in your kitchen, it's a great place to give this kind of party. We like to eat right there, at the big table where the morning sun falls brightest, so we set out our cold offerings on the counter tops: pitchers of milk and of orange and tomato juice—with the Bloody Mary pitcher clearly distinguished so that guests who feel fragile in the morning won't get any untoward surprise—and a great bowl of the loveliest fresh fruit we can find. From the warming drawer we bring forth platters of homemade doughnuts and coffee cake or Danish pastry. And the stove, or part of it, becomes our hot table. The bowls of chicken livers and of warm sauce are set in water-filled shallow roasting pans over low heat; platters sit on cake tins, also full of water to keep them warm; and that still leaves us a burner or two for poached egg experiments.

Right on the table we set two cozy little warming lamps, over which go two fat pots, one of strong fresh coffee and one of our favorite China tea. Made our way—we carefully measure out both boiling water and tea, and brew it in a stainless-steel pan, then strain it through a very clean stainless-steel sieve into our teapot—it keeps perfectly for hours. And it will have to. Guests at this comfortable meal will eat to bursting and then stay around to chat drowsily cuddling their warm mugs, until it's practically sunset. Don't say I didn't warn you!

Preparations

Recommended Equipment:
For homemade English muffins, you will need muffin rings, crumpet rings, or shallow tin cans with the tops and bottoms removed, and a griddle or heavy frying pan. See recipe for details.

For the other dishes, all kinds of makeshifts will work. Be sure to check out the recipe for poached eggs in advance, as various methods depend on various gadgets.

Marketing and Storage:
Staples to have on hand

Salt
Peppercorns
Herbs and spices: dried sage, oregano, thyme, tarragon; paprika, mace, and allspice
Double-acting baking powder
White vinegar or cider vinegar
Olive oil or cooking oil
Chicken bouillon and/or meat bouillon (see recipes for Corned Beef Hash, Sautéed Chicken Livers, and Scrapple for kinds and quantities)
Flour, butter, and eggs (see recipes for quantities needed)
Milk
Parsley
Fruit juices to your taste
Coffee and/or tea to your taste

Specific ingredients for this menu
All ingredients calculated for 6 people unless otherwise indicated in recipes

For Homemade English Muffins:
Dry active yeast (1 Tb)
Instant mashed potatoes (2 Tb) or raw potatoes (1)

For Eggs Benedict:
  Sliced boiled ham (about
  ½ pound or 225 g)
  English muffins (6) ▼
  Lemons (1)
For Corned Beef Hash:
  Cooked corned beef (4 cups or 2 pounds
  or 1 kg), preferably homemade
  (see page 138)
  "Boiling" or all-purpose potatoes (6 to 8)
  Onions (3 or 4)
  (Optional: heavy cream (½ cup or 1 dL)
  Fresh tomato sauce (see page 143) or chili
  sauce or ketchup
For Sautéed Chicken Livers:
  Chicken livers (1 pound or 450 g)
  Optional: fresh mushrooms (½ pound
  or 225 g)
  Port, Madeira, or dry white French ver-
  mouth
For Sour Cream and Bread Crumb Flapjacks:
  Nonsweet white bread (to make 1 cup or
  ¼ L crumbs)
  Wondra or instant-blending flour (½ cup
  or 70 g)
  Sour cream (½ cup or 1 dL)
  Syrup, honey, or whatever you fancy
For Scrapple:
  Sausage meat (4 cups or 1 L),
  preferably homemade (see page 175)
  Yellow cornmeal (1 cup or ¼ L),
  preferably stone ground
  Fragrant leaf sage
For Fresh Sausage Meat:
  Fresh ground pork (8 cups or 2 L)
  Dry white wine or vermouth
Fresh fruits in season
Optional: Assorted coffee cakes, doughnuts,
  and/or Danish pastry

▶ *Remarks:*

English muffins: Let's not be muffin snobs;
store-bought are excellent. Homemade are,
simply, something else.

Homemade English Muffins

For 10 to 12 muffins

1 Tb dry active yeast dissolved in ¼ cup
(½ dL) tepid water

2 Tb instant mashed potatoes softened in ½
cup (1 dL) boiling water (or ¼ cup or ½ dL
grated raw potato simmered until tender in 1
cup or ¼ L water)

½ cup (1 dL) cold water (or cold milk if using
raw potato)

2½ cups (6 dL) all-purpose flour in a 3-quart
(3-L) mixing bowl

To be added after first rise: 1½ tsp salt dissolved in 3 Tb tepid water

2 to 3 Tb butter, softened

Equipment

**A heavy griddle or large frying pan, or a non-
stick electric skillet; muffin or crumpet rings or
cat-food or tunafish cans about 3 inches (8 cm)
in diameter with tops and bottoms removed; a
4- to 5-Tb ladle or long-handled cup; spatulas
(both rubber and metal); and, perhaps, pliers**

*Pikelets (top left). Oven-baked muffins (top right).
Crumpet-muffins (bottom).*

The dough

While yeast is dissolving, assemble the other ingredients. Then into the instant potatoes beat the cold milk, and stir it along with the water and dissolved yeast into the flour. (Or, if using raw potato, stir the cold milk into the potato pan, then stir both into the flour, adding dissolved yeast only after mixture has cooled to tepid.) Beat vigorously for a minute or so with a wooden spoon to make a smooth loose thick batter, heavier than the usual pancake batter but not at all like the conventional dough. Cover with plastic wrap and let rise, preferably at around 80°F/27°C, until batter has risen and large bubbles have appeared in the surface (usually about 1½ hours—it must be bubbly, however long it takes).

Stir the batter down, then beat in the salt and water, beating vigorously for a minute. Cover and let rise until bubbles again appear in the surface—about an hour at 80°F/27°C. The batter is now ready to become English muffins.

🕐 Batter may sit for an hour or more after its second rise, or you may use one of the delaying tactics suggested at the end of the recipe.

Preliminaries to cooking the muffins

When you are ready to cook the muffins, brush insides of rings or tins fairly generously with butter; butter surface of griddle or frying pan lightly and set over moderate heat. When just hot enough, so that drops of water begin to dance on it, the heat is about right. Scoop your ladle or cup into the batter and dislodge the batter into a ring or tin with rubber spatula; batter should be about ⅜ inch (1 cm) thick to make a raised muffin twice that. (Batter should be heavy, sticky, sluggish, but not runny, having just enough looseness to be spread out into the ring—if you think it is too thick, beat in tepid water by driblets.)

Cooking the muffins

The muffins are to cook slowly on one side until bubbles, which form near the bottom of the muffin, pierce through the top surface, and until almost the entire top changes from a wet ivory white to a dryish gray color; this will take 6 to 8 minutes or more, depending on the heat. (Regulate heat so that bottoms of muffins do not color more than a medium or pale brown.) Now the muffins are to be turned over for a brief cooking on the other side, and at

Batter on left has risen.

this point you can probably lift the rings off them; if not, turn them over and dislodge rings with the point of a knife, cutting and poking around the edge of rings if necessary. Cans are sometimes more difficult to remove; you may find it useful to have a pair of pliers for lifting, as well as a small knife for poking. Less than a minute is usually enough for cooking the second side, which needs only a token browning and drying out. Cool the muffins on a rack.

🕐   Fresh but cold muffins freeze beautifully and keep freshest when stored frozen, although they will stay fresh enough wrapped airtight in a plastic bag for a day or two in the refrigerator.

To serve English muffins

The muffins must be split (not cut) in half horizontally, since the inside texture should be slightly rough and full of holes (the bottoms are always solid, however). To split them, you can use a table fork, pushing the tines into the muffin all around the circumference, then gently tearing the two halves apart. Or use a serrated knife, cutting a slit in one side, then tearing the muffin apart all around and inside, using short slashes made with the point and top ½ inch (1½ cm) of the knife.

An electric toaster is not at all suitable for homemade English muffins: since the muffins are damp in texture they must be toasted very slowly under a broiler; the slow browning dries out the interior while crusting the surface. Toast the uncut side a minute or so, then turn and toast the cut side for 2 to 3 minutes, until lightly browned. Butter the cut side and return under the broiler for a moment to let the butter bubble up and sink in. Serve as soon as possible.

Remarks:

Delaying tactics and sourdough: Not much can happen to ruin this dough, as long as you have achieved the necessary bubbles. You may let it wait at room temperature for an hour or more before baking; or you may even refrigerate it overnight. If it seems to have lost its bubble, you can bring it back to life by beating in another cup of flour blended with enough tepid water to make a batter; this will give the yeast something more to feed on and in an hour or so it will rise and bubble again as it gobbles its new food.

You can even turn this batter into a sourdough. Simply let it sit at room temperature for a day or two until it has soured, then bottle and refrigerate it. You can now use it in any sourdough recipe, or you can make sourdough English muffins: blend ½ cup of it with 1 cup flour and enough water to make a batter, add 1 tablespoon dissolved yeast, and let it rise; then beat in more flour and water, or milk, and add salt (proportions make no difference as long as you get your bubbles); let it rise and bubble again; and cook your muffins. Replenish the sourdough starter by mixing it with more flour and water or milk blended into a batter, and let sit at room temperature until it has bubbled up and subsided; refrigerate as before.

To Poach an Egg

Here are three ways to poach eggs in water—and I am not talking about the electric poacher, which is really a steamer. If you are lucky enough to have very fresh eggs very recently out of the hen, you will have no trouble whatsoever; you simply break the egg into a pan of barely simmering water and in a few minutes you have the most beautiful neat perfect oval of a poached egg, the yolk cozily masked by the white all over. It is when you have store-bought eggs of uncertain date that you can at times run into exposed yolks, wispy whites, and quite unpresentable results that can be served only under a thick disguise.

However, when your eggs are reasonably fresh you can do very well as follows:
The 10-second firm-up: First prick the large end of each egg with a pin or an egg pricker, going down ¼ inch (¾ cm) into the egg; this will let the air from the pocket in the large end escape in the hot water, and prevent a burst of white from coming out of any crack in the shell. Then lower the eggs, using a slotted spoon, into a pan of boiling water, boil exactly

10 seconds, and remove at once; this gives just a little cohesion to the white, but not enough to stick it to its covering membrane or shell.

The vinegar coagulant: Vinegar coagulates the surface of the white as soon as they come in contact with each other, and although vinegar does very slightly toughen the outermost surface of the white, you are wise to use it when your eggs are not newly laid. For every quart or liter of water, pour in 2½ tablespoons of white or cider vinegar.

Timing poached eggs: The perfectly poached egg, besides being attractive, has a tender white that is just set all the way through, and a yolk that is still liquid. I find that 4 minutes in barely simmering water is just right for "large" and "extra large" eggs.

I. The whirlpool poach. Choose a rather high saucepan, 6 to 7 inches (15 to 18 cm) in both diameter and depth, add water to come ⅔ the way up, bring to the boil, and pour in 2½ tablespoons vinegar per quart or liter. Prick the eggs and boil 10 seconds in the shell. Then stir the water with a wooden spoon or spatula, going round and round the edge of the pan to create a whirlpool; quickly break an egg into the center or vortex and the swirling water

should form the egg neatly. Leave at the barest simmer for 4 minutes, then remove with a slotted spoon to a bowl of cold water.

II. The free-form free-floating egg. This is a neat trick when it works, and makes the cook feel clever. Fill a wide shallow saucepan with 1½ inches (4 cm) of water, adding the required 2½ tablespoons vinegar per quart or liter. Then, with water at the barest simmer, crack an egg and, holding it very close to the water, your fingers all but in it, swing the shell open and let the egg drop in. If you are lucky, it will form into a quite neat oval, but you can often help it, if help it needs, by rapidly rolling it over and over with a wooden spoon before it has coagulated. Set timer for 4 minutes and continue with the rest of the eggs, adding 4 to 6 in all, depending on the size of your pan; for accurate timing, start the first egg at the handle side of the pan, and move around clockwise, taking out the first egg as the timer goes off, then the second, and so forth, dropping each as it is done into a bowl of cold water.

III. The oval egg holder triumph. A most satisfactory solution to egg poaching and one which produces a handsomely shaped egg is the oval metal egg poacher with perforated bottom. (Before each poaching session, be sure to wash and wipe carefully to remove any rust or dirt in the holes.) Place the poachers in 2 inches (5 cm) of water, and proceed exactly as in the preceding directions, dropping the eggs one by one into the poachers. When your 4 minutes are up, remove the poachers one by one and very gently scoop the egg out with a dessert spoon into a bowl of cold water.

Storing poached eggs. Refrigerate poached eggs in a bowl with enough cold water to submerge them completely, but do not cover the bowl. They will keep perfectly for 2 or 3 days.

To reheat cold poached eggs. Drop into a pan of barely simmering salted water and leave for 2 minutes, then remove with a slotted spoon, and roll against a folded towel to dry them.

Eggs Benedict

For 12 eggs, 2 per serving

12 toasted and buttered English muffin halves (recipe on page 166)

12 rounds of boiled ham, lightly sautéed in butter

12 beautifully poached eggs (the preceding recipe)

About 1½ cups (½ L) hollandaise sauce (the following recipe)

Optional topping: <u>Either</u> slices of truffle <u>or</u> 1 hard-boiled egg, chopped, tossed with 3 Tb minced fresh parsley, 2 Tb minced cooked ham, and salt and pepper

Just before serving, place 2 hot toasted muffin halves on each plate and top each with a piece of ham. Heat the eggs as described in their recipe and rapidly remove from hot water with a slotted spoon, rolling each against a folded towel as you do so. Set an egg on each ham-topped muffin, spoon over a good dollop of hollandaise, and lay a slice or sprinkle on a big pinch of the optional topping. Serve at once.

A Light Hollandaise Sauce

For about 1 ½ cups

3 Tb fresh lemon juice and 3 Tb water in a small saucepan

½ tsp salt

1 whole egg and 2 yolks in a smallish stainless-steel saucepan

6 to 8 ounces (180–225 g) warm but not bubbling-hot butter in a small saucepan

Salt, pepper, and more lemon juice to taste

Shortly before serving, bring the lemon juice and water to the simmer, adding the salt. Meanwhile, vigorously beat the egg and yolks in their pan with a wire whip for a minute or so until they are pale and thick. Then set the yolk mixture over moderately low heat and whisk in the hot lemon juice by driblets. Continue whisking, not too fast but reaching all over bottom and corners of pan, until you have a foamy warm mass; remove from heat just as you see a wisp of steam rising. (Do not overheat or you will coagulate the egg yolks.) Immediately start beating in the warm butter by driblets, to make a thick, creamy, light yellow sauce. Taste carefully for seasoning, adding salt, pepper, and more lemon juice to taste.

🕐　This is such an easy sauce to make that I think it best done at the last moment. Otherwise I would suggest a regular hollandaise, and if it must wait and stay warm for any length of time, beat into it 2 tablespoons of *béchamel* (white) sauce for every 2 cups or ½ liter of hollandaise; this will help to hold it. However, any egg yolk and butter sauce can be kept only warm, not hot, or it will curdle; and remember that sauces with egg yolks are prime breeding grounds for sick-making bacteria. I would therefore not hold such a sauce longer than an hour, and would prefer to make fresh sauces as often as needed rather than risk the slightest chance of food poisoning.

Corned Beef Hash

To serve 6 to 8 people

Timing note: A good hash takes at least 40 minutes to make since it must have time to crust on the bottom, and that crust is stirred into the hash several times before the final crust is formed.

2½ cups (6 dL) minced onions

2 Tb or more butter

2 Tb or more olive oil or cooking oil

3 Tb flour

¾ cup (1¾ dL) or more bouillon (cooking liquid) from the corned beef, or chicken or beef broth

4 cups or more diced boiled potatoes (I like "boiling" or all-purpose potatoes because they keep their shape during cooking)

4 cups or more chopped or roughly ground cooked corned beef

½ tsp or so minced herbs such as sage, oregano, thyme, or a mixture

5 to 6 Tb or so minced fresh parsley

Salt and pepper

½ cup (1 dL) or so heavy cream (optional)

Equipment

A heavy frying pan or electric skillet with cover, 12 inches (30 cm) top diameter, and if you plan to unmold the hash it should be of well-seasoned iron or have a nonstick surface; an oiled pizza pan also, if you plan to unmold

The hash mixture

Sauté the onions slowly in 2 Tb each butter and oil for 6 to 8 minutes, stirring frequently, until tender, then raise heat slightly and let them brown a bit. Lower heat again; blend in the flour and a little more butter or oil if needed to make a paste; stir and cook slowly for 2 minutes. Blend in ¾ cup (1¾ dL) bouil-

lon or broth, let boil a moment, then mix in the potatoes, corned beef, herbs, and parsley. Taste carefully for seasoning, and if hash seems dry blend in tablespoons of optional cream or more bouillon.

Cooking the hash

Rather firmly, press the hash down all over with the flat of a spatula, set a cover over the pan, and cook slowly for about 15 minutes or until the hash has crusted on the bottom. Stir it up to mix some of the crust into the body of the hash, and repeat the process being careful not to overcook and dry it out (or it will not be cohesive enough to unmold properly). Taste and correct seasoning.

🕐 Hash may be cooked in advance to this point; set aside off heat, and you may cover and refrigerate it when cold. Reheat slowly, covered, then proceed.

Some 10 to 15 minutes before serving, uncover the hash, press it down all over with a spatula, and let it form its final crust over moderate heat.

Serving

You may serve the hash as is, turning each serving upside down on the plate to present a crusted surface. Or you may wish to unmold it in a half-moon shape onto a platter: to do so, start sliding the large cake of hash onto a hot platter but stop at the halfway mark, then, holding pan by its handle, your thumb underneath, quickly flip pan upside down to turn other half of hash neatly over the first, crusted bottom in full view. (This can often be a tricky business, but it does help to have the first half of the hash thinner than the other half and a small pan is far easier to control than the large one described here.) A second unmolding system is to slide the whole cake of hash out onto an oiled pizza tray; then turn the frying pan or a round platter upside down over it and reverse the two, leaving the hash crusted side up. In either case, cracks and musses can be hidden under a sprinkling of chopped parsley.

Accompaniments

Serve each helping of hash with a fried or poached egg on top, and a dollop of fresh tomato sauce or of warm ketchup or chili sauce.

Sautéed Chicken Livers

For 6 to 8 small servings

1 pound (450 g) chicken livers

Salt, pepper, and flour

2 Tb butter and 1 of oil (more if needed)

About ½ cup (1 dL) chicken stock or broth (more if needed)

4 Tb Port, Madeira, or dry white French vermouth

A sprinkling of tarragon (optional)

½ pound (225 g) fresh mushrooms, quartered and sautéed separately in butter (optional)

1 Tb or more butter as final enrichment (optional)

2 to 3 Tb fresh minced parsley

To prepare the livers for cooking, look them over to be sure no black or greenish bile spots are on the surface. If so, shave them off since they are bitter; although this is a rare occurrence, it is well to watch for it. Just before sautéing, dry the livers in paper towels; then place on wax paper and toss with a sprinkling of salt and pepper, and then of flour, to give them a light dusting. Immediately, then, get to the sautéing: set a heavy 10-inch (25-cm) frying pan over high heat, add to it enough butter to film the bottom, plus ½ that amount of oil. When the butter foam begins to subside, toss in as many livers as will fit in one layer. Turn and toss for 2 to 3 minutes until, when you press them, the livers have changed from squashy raw to just resistant to your finger. Pour in the stock and wine, the optional tarragon and mushrooms, and boil rapidly, tossing and turning the livers for a moment or two until liquid thickens lightly. Taste and correct seasoning.

🕐 May be cooked in advance; set aside uncovered.

Just before serving toss over moderately high heat, adding more liquid if you feel it necessary, a tablespoon or so of butter if you wish, and the parsley.

Sour Cream and Bread Crumb Flapjacks

Tender pancakes

For about 10 pancakes 4 inches in diameter

1 cup (¼ L) toasted fresh, nonsweet white bread crumbs

4 Tb melted butter

1 egg

½ cup (1 dL) Wondra or instant-blending flour

½ cup (1 dL) sour cream

½ cup (1 dL) or more milk

½ tsp double-acting baking powder

Salt and pepper

To make toasted bread crumbs, crumb fresh bread in a blender or processor, then spread out in a roasting pan in a preheated 350°F/180°C oven, and toss until lightly browned—15 to 20 minutes. Toss in a frying pan with the melted butter over moderate heat.

Blend egg, flour, sour cream, ½ cup (1 dL) milk, and baking powder in a 4-cup (1-L) measure; fold in the buttered crumbs and salt and pepper to taste. Stir in driblets more milk if you think it necessary (but can you tell until you have tried a pancake?).

Drop batter onto a buttered hot skillet and cook pancakes, turning when bubbles appear on the surface.

Serve with melted butter and maple syrup or honey.

Scrapple

*For an 8-cup loaf pan, serving 12
or more*

4 cups (1 L) sausage meat, preferably
homemade (see recipe following)

4 cups (1 L) pork stock or other flavorful meat
stock in a 3-quart (3-L) saucepan with heavy
bottom

1 Tb or more fragrant leaf sage

1 cup (225 g) yellow cornmeal, stone ground
preferred

½ cup (1 dL) cold water

3 eggs

Salt and pepper

Equipment

An 8-cup (2-L) loaf pan or baking dish, and a
board or plate that will fit into it for weighting
down scrapple after baking

Sauté sausage meat in a large frying pan until it
turns from pink to gray, breaking it up with a
fork as you do so—5 minutes or more. Drain in
a sieve set over a bowl, and reserve fat—which
may be used for sautéing finished scrapple
later.

Meanwhile, bring the stock to the boil,
adding sage to taste. Mix the cornmeal with
the cold water in a bowl, then whisk in a cupful of the hot stock. Return cornmeal to stock,
bring to the boil whisking slowly, and cook for
5 minutes or more until mixture is thick, like
cornmeal mush. Cover pan, set in a larger pan
of simmering water, and cook for 30 minutes.
Remove from pan of hot water and boil over
moderately high heat, stirring with a wooden
spoon, until cornmeal is thick and heavy and
holds its shape in a spoon—the thicker the better, so that it will unmold and slice easily later.

Beat the cooked and drained sausage
meat into the cornmeal, breaking it up so that
it will blend nicely, and boil, stirring and beating, for 3 to 4 minutes. Beat in the eggs. Taste
carefully for seasoning: scrapple is tradi-
tionally fragrant with sage and highly seasoned.

Butter an 8-cup (2-L) loaf pan, line bottom of pan with wax paper, and turn the cornmeal mixture into it. Cover with wax paper
and aluminum foil and bake for an hour or
more in a preheated 350°F/180°C oven, until
mixture has swelled and is bubbling hot.

Remove from oven, place a board on top
of the scrapple (over the wax paper and foil)
and a 5-pound (2¼-kg) weight (canned goods,
meat grinder, etc.), and let cool. When cold,
remove weight and board, cover airtight, and
chill.

🕐   Once baked in its pan, scrapple will keep
for at least 2 to 3 weeks in the refrigerator. It
can be frozen; however, pork products tend to
lose texture and savor after 2 months or so in
the freezer.

To serve, run a knife around inside of
mold, then set mold on top of stove to heat and
loosen bottom; unmold onto a cutting board.
Slice into serving pieces about ⅜ inch (1 cm)
thick. Dredge lightly in cornmeal, and brown
on both sides in rendered sausage fat or butter.

Serve for breakfast with fried or poached
eggs, or fried apple slices; or use as a dinner
meat, accompanying the scrapple with green
vegetables such as broccoli or cabbage, or a
green salad, or cole slaw.

Remarks:

Traditional farm scrapple is made, literally,
from pork scraps and bones that are boiled up
together for 2 hours or so with herbs and
aromatic vegetables—carrots, onions, celery.
The meat adhering to the bones is then scraped
off and chopped, along with the other pork
meat scraps. The cooking broth is strained and
boiled up with the cornmeal, then the two are
combined, and that is the scrapple. If you have
cured your own pork, as in the recipe on page
138, you can use the same system whether you
decide to bone your pork before or after salting (and soaking) it. Once you have chopped
the boiled meat, you can substitute it for the
sausage in the preceding recipe. Simply stir it
into the saucepan of cooked cornmeal, which
has been boiled up with your pork-cooking
liquid, and continue with the recipe.

Fresh Sausage Meat

For about 8 cups, or 4 pounds

8 cups (2 L) fresh ground pork—including 2 to 3 cups (½–¾ L) fresh pork fat or blanched salt pork fat—from shoulder, rib, or loin

1 Tb salt

1 Tb sage

1 tsp mace

½ tsp cracked pepper

1 tsp paprika

4 to 5 Tb white wine or vermouth

Optional other herbs: thyme, allspice

Grind pork not too fine in meat grinder or processor, beating in seasonings and wine or vermouth (to lighten the mixture). Sauté a spoonful and taste, then correct seasoning as you feel necessary.

🕐 Best made a day ahead, so that flavoring will have time to blend with meat.

To be used in the preceding scrapple, or to sauté in cakes, as breakfast sausage.

Scrapple made from fresh cornmeal and fresh sausage meat surrounding a platter of scrambled eggs.

🕐 *Timing*

Because breakfast is such a personal meal, this chapter offers you a choice of dishes from which you might like to compose your own menu. Supposing, however, that you want to take on the whole shooting match, the work could be divided up as follows:

During the party, cook pancakes and assemble eggs Benedict to order. This means having on hand a pitcher of pancake batter, a bowl of warm water (to reheat the eggs), hot toasted and buttered muffins, hot sautéed ham slices, and warm hollandaise sauce. You can prepare all of these half an hour in advance.

Scrapple, too, is fried to order, or fried just beforehand and kept warm; and the same goes for the sausage cakes.

Corned beef hash takes about 45 minutes (with some attention from you) to form a good crust; it may be kept warm over hot water. You could cook it till not quite done the night before, cool and refrigerate, and finish the crust 10 minutes before the party.

Eggs may be poached up to 2 or 3 days in advance and kept refrigerated, uncovered, in a bowl of water.

Muffins freeze perfectly; you can wait until that morning to thaw, split, toast, butter, and toast again.

Coffee and tea must be made that morning, but will keep over low heat if you don't let them get cold—or scalded—at any time.

Corned beef keeps almost indefinitely; sausage meat and scrapple can stay in the freezer for up to 2 months.

Menu Variations

English muffins: See the Postscript to this chapter for other kinds of yeast batter griddle cakes. And I need not remind you that the English muffin, known in my youth as the Garbo, can get away with almost anything, including peanut butter. Peanut Garbos! Divine.

Eggs Benedict: You can substitute Canadian bacon for the ham, and toast or little pastry cases for the muffins. Keeping only the poached egg, you can switch everything else around: with chicken livers, it's an egg Henriette; with spinach, an egg Florentine; you can sit it on a sliced grilled tomato; you can use cheese sauce (eggs à la Mornay), or tomato sauce, or a *soubise*.... Escoffier has some 19 recipes, all with resounding names.

Corned beef hash: See page 138 for how to corn pork, and try hashing that. Or add beets for red flannel hash. Or cook it in little cakes; it doesn't have to be a big pillow. Or hash leftover chicken or turkey, going a bit lighter on the seasoning and adding cream. Or hash lamb, perhaps adding cooked rice or kasha instead of potatoes.

Chicken livers: You could broil them on skewers instead of sautéing them, or use duck or other poultry livers if you like a stronger flavor. Chopped fine, combined with mushroom *duxelles*, quickly sautéed and moistened with a little leftover gravy flavored with Port or Madeira, they make a luxurious spread for hot buttered toast. Thinly sliced sautéed calf's liver is also nice with eggs for a hearty breakfast.

Pancakes: These are fairly close cousins to the muffin variants in the Postscript—to pikelets in particular. You can bake almost any batter on a griddle (buckwheat, rye, oat, barley, corn, etc.), and don't forget the charm of grated potato pancakes blobbed with sour cream, or mashed-potato pancakes (see page 191). Or lovely yeasty blini, nice with smoked fish as well as with caviar—nice with butter and honey, for that matter. Or Swedish pancakes, maybe with lingonberries. Or French crêpes, rolled around a creamed mixture and sauced, or, especially for children, rolled around a spoonful of jam and dusted with confectioners sugar. Or palatschinken, or tortillas, or...well, every nation has its pancakes.

Scrapple: You can eat it with fried tomato or apple slices; you can use pork liver and other scraps in the recipe; you can use oatmeal instead of cornmeal (in which case it's called "goetta")—but I can't really think of any variations in cooking it.

Sausage meat: For other sausage makings, check out *Mastering II* and *J.C.'s Kitchen*. And sometime try baking homemade sausage in a pastry crust.

Grated potato pancakes and sausages waiting for their blob of sour cream.

Leftovers

Poached eggs: If you have extra ones, even rewarmed, congratulations. Coat them with aspic for eggs *en gelée*—an exquisite cold appetizer. Warm them, then sauce and bed them with and on practically anything. Tuck them into a soufflé, bedded on about ⅓ of the mixture, then covered with the rest. *Ham:* I don't need to suggest what to do with extra sliced ham. *Muffins:* If you have some unsplit, they freeze (or refreeze) perfectly. *Hollandaise sauce:* If it has sat around long, I don't think it's safe to keep. If it hasn't, you can refrigerate and rewarm cautiously to tepid.

Hash and *scrapple:* Chill or refreeze any uncooked leftovers. And do likewise with uncooked *sausage meat*, although this you can combine with other meats, in meatballs (see page 105), in hamburgers, and in terrines and *pâtés*.

Chicken livers: Once they're cooked, I'd make them into a simple *pâté*—you can just run them through a processor or blender with a little cream and beat into softened butter, then chill.

Pancakes: Leftover cooked pancakes will freeze but, because it contains baking powder, the batter won't keep. However, if it's still fairly lively you could stir in enough flour to make a light dough, and bake in muffin tins.

Postscript: More on muffins

Remember the schoolbook story of how King Alfred let the poor cottager's cakes burn as he sat by the hearth worrying about the Danish invaders? Even back in the 800s, those "cakes" were probably muffins and probably made with yeast, which has been known since the dawn of history.

Most home cooks in France, where I got my culinary education, never learn bread making at all, so I came late to its ancient mysteries, which still give me a sense of awe—a sense shared, and poetically expressed, by Elizabeth David. If you too are fascinated, I refer you to her masterly account of British baking, *English Bread and Yeast Cookery* (London: Penguin Books, 1978).

Apropos muffins and crumpets, Mrs. David says, in a whole chapter devoted to them, that the distinction is rather foggy and the batter similar; but the crumpet is only half as thick and holds more butter because you don't split it. The same combination of yeast batter and griddle cooking (using all kinds of flours) gives you the pikelet (baked without a ring, flat and free-form), the girdle cake, the bannock, and the scone of Scotland. The latter two may be baked in the oven, as is the plump Scottish bap. Mrs. David says that many country kitchens in the British Isles still keep their ancient bake stones and baking irons, used right in the hearth. King Alfred would feel right at home.

At this intimate dinner you can cook right at the table and not miss a word of the conversation. And for chocolate lovers, there is a treat in store.

Chafing-Dish Dinner

Menu

Seviche of Sea Scallops with Fresh Artichokes

❧

Steak Diane
Fresh Green Peas
Real Mashed Potatoes

❧

Le Gâteau Victoire au Chocolat, Mousseline

❧

Suggested wines:
Alsatian Riesling, Chablis, or Muscadet with
the seviche; a Cabernet or red Bordeaux with
the steak. With the cake (optional), a Cham-
pagne, a sparkling Vouvray, or a Sauternes

What to do about conversations you can't bear to miss? Cook at the table, of course, says Paul, adding sagely that we'd better practice first. How right he is. Chafing-dish jokes, featuring splashes and scorches, were a staple in our parents' day, when the kitchen belonged exclusively to the cook but the family tried to play too. People nowadays do seem to use chafing dishes on buffet tables, as food warmers, but are apt to ignore their usefulness as small, real stoves, not to mention their dramatic possibilities.

Flambé dishes are fun but a bit too obviously showy. So we settle on Steak Diane, to make a party chic as well as intimate. Why Diane? Nobody remembers. Why a French name, since it's not related to the French Sauce Diane, a creamed-up version of the classic gamy *poivrade?* Anne Willan, in her Grand Diplôme series, suggests that the dish originated in Australia. Anyway, that touch of Worcestershire sauce would indicate the New World—but if the dish resembles its namesake, the mysterious Diane must have been quite a girl: good-looking, classy, brisk, and modish but not faddy. The sauce has a tangy, refreshing taste, not too overpowering before a rich dessert. The meat is pounded to make it thinner for swift searing; and for this you need a very strong heat source (see Recommended Equipment for details). We have experimented with various fuels and have found that liquid denatured alcohol is an absolute essential because of its hot, clear, odorless flame. For Steak Diane we practice such flourishes as pouring oil from on high, and turning the meat with a deft flick of the wrist—two wrists I mean, one for each fork. Great fun.

If you have friends who are chocolate addicts, do something special to indulge their passion. For instance, there used to be a chocolate cake in New York in the thirties, legendary among connoisseurs. It was made by a smart little bakery whose dour proprietress has never revealed her secret recipe. This much-discussed cake, which I unfortunately never tasted in those halcyon days, was baked in a loaf shape and had a fat and unctuous texture and intense chocolate flavor; it sank in the middle, and this trough was, accordingly, mounded with curled shaved chocolate. Fanciers were all agreed that the cake must have involved a lot of butter, egg whites and yolks beaten separately, and practically no flour (one very skillful cook, it was said, evolved a near replica using only one tablespoonful). But what effect, I wonder, would so little flour have, anyway? I made a number of serious tries, but then sailed off on a different tack. What finally came out of endless experiments was a cake I have proudly named Le Gâteau Victoire au Chocolat, Mousseline. Its components sound like custard makings, its airiness suggests a mousse, and yet, it is a cake: a cake with no butter, no flour at all, a simple

method, and an incredibly sparse list of ingredients. Sparse but sumptuous: it includes one whole pound of chocolate.

I happen to love the old-fashioned combination of peas and mashed potatoes—plain but exquisite if you have good fresh peas and Idaho potatoes, and wonderful with steak. You might think this would involve long minutes away from the table. But mashed potatoes can, in fact, be done ahead and kept warm: the trick is to cover them only partially, to give them air. (By that same token, a baked potato also acquires a dank, stifled flavor if you let it sit unopened. Slash it and give it a squeeze.) By doctoring them with cheese and whatnot, busy people can make do pretty well with dehydrated or otherwise pre-prepared potatoes; but these are not for plain mashing. You must use the real thing. Why not recoup peeling time by shelling the peas mechanically? I have found an ingenious device, something like an old-fashioned laundry mangle in miniature, which you can crank by hand or else attach to an ordinary electric beater (see page 186). You feed the pea pods into it and, with efficient little zips, it gobbles up the pods and spews them out one side while the peas—quite unharmed—bounce briskly out the other. This chapter's section on Menu Variations does not include vegetables, since almost all vegetables are good with steak; but my recommendation, if the menu seems too starchy to you, would be to substitute tomatoes, baked or *à la provençale* (with garlic, olive oil, and bread crumbs), and string beans or broccoli for the peas and mashed potatoes.

Anyway, the goloptiousness, as Winnie-the-Pooh would have said, of this menu decided us on a light first course—rather reminiscent of the *nouvelle cuisine*—which has a good deal of subtle charm. Sea scallops are sliced into a lime juice marinade which "cooks" them briefly—something to do with enzymes, I understand. Then they are arranged with sliced fresh artichoke bottoms, tomatoes, and watercress or romaine; the delicate sauce *vinaigrette* is given a little body by the addition of an egg white.

With its easy, uninterrupted flow, this kind of little dinner is usually a happy one. My own enthusiasm is divided about equally among the nimble pea sheller, the efficient, energy-saving little stove, and that super chocolate cake.

Preparations

Recommended Equipment:
For the potatoes and the peas, you'll need a potato ricer and two heavy pots. For the cake, a 10-cup (2½-L) cake pan, which must be at least 2 inches (5 cm) deep. I usually measure a new pan's capacity by pouring it full of water and measuring the amount; then I scratch "10 c" or whatever on the back of the pan. A nonstick surface is strongly recommended. You need a larger pan, also, to serve as a bain-marie (water bath) for the cake pan.

For your dinner table: see the Steak Diane recipe for the sauce set-up, which should be conveniently arranged on a tray. You'll need an electric warming tray, or trays, with room

enough for dinner plates, a small serving dish for the steaks, and a serving dish or dishes for the vegetables. The heat source should sit on a metal tray. You can use an electric skillet or a camp stove in place of a chafing dish; all you need for tabletop sautéing is strong heat and a wide pan. About chafing dishes: many pretty ones of open, leggy design, while fine for scrambling eggs or other slow-heat cookery, don't work for sautéing. This is because you need a focused flame, which you can't get unless it is enclosed at the sides with just enough air circulation to keep it burning. You could surround a leggy chafing dish with a collar of sheet metal with a few holes cut in near the top. Denatured alcohol gel won't give you enough heat; you must have liquid denatured alcohol.

And play safe: if you have to replenish the fuel (though the usual-sized container will hold enough for hours), douse the flame and let the lamp cool a bit before adding more alcohol. And in the—very unlikely—case of fire, have baking soda handy and remember that the quickest way to extinguish any blazing pan is to clap a well-fitting lid on it.

For serving your cake you will need a platter or board with flat surface large enough to hold the unmolded cake.

Marketing and Storage:
Staples to have on hand

Salt
Black and white peppercorns
Optional: bottled green peppercorns ▼
Mustard (the strong Dijon type; see Remarks, page 6)
Soy sauce
Worcestershire sauce
Olive oil
Optional: peanut oil
Flour
Cornstarch
Unsweetened baking chocolate (2 ounces or 60 g)

Semisweet baking chocolate (14 ounces or 400 g)
Sugar (about ½ cup or 1 dL)
Optional: confectioners sugar
Pure vanilla extract
Eggs (7 "large")
Butter
Heavy or whipping cream (at least 2 cups or ½ L)
Milk
"Baking" potatoes (3 or 4 large) ▼
Parsley
Shallots or scallions
Limes (1)
Lemons (3 or 4)
Beef bouillon (1 cup or ¼ L)
Instant coffee
Cognac
Port or Madeira
Dark Jamaica rum

Specific ingredients for this menu

Steaks (4; see recipe)
Fresh sea scallops (8 to 10 large)
Artichokes (2 or 3 large fine)
Fresh green peas (about 2 pounds or 1 kg) ▼
Watercress or romaine
Tomatoes (2 or 3) or cherry tomatoes

▶ ## *Remarks:*
Staples

Green peppercorns: buy them "au naturel," meaning they are packed in lightly salted water. They will keep several weeks in the refrigerator; for longer storage freeze them.
Potatoes for mashing: you want floury potatoes so that they mash fluffily; you don't want new potatoes or waxy potatoes, which mash lumpily, and even glue-ily.

Ingredients for this menu

Store-bought fresh *peas* can be perfectly good, although not always as fresh and as young as you would like. But properly cooked, they're so much better than frozen or canned. Be sure the pods are fresh and crisp and neither too full (meaning the peas are large and old) nor too flat (meaning the peas have not formed). If in doubt, discreetly tear open the package a little bit and taste—right there in the supermarket.

Seviche of Sea Scallops with Fresh Artichokes

Sea scallops have a lovely freshness of taste and texture when sliced thin and marinated raw in lime juice, salt, parsley, and minced shallots or scallions—the lime juice cooks them, as it were. For a light first course you need only 2 or 3 per serving, and half a large artichoke bottom plus a little fresh tomato and watercress or romaine for decoration.

For 4 servings

8 to 10 large fresh sea scallops
1 fresh lime
Salt and white pepper
½ Tb minced shallots or scallions
2 Tb minced fresh parsley
2 Tb flour
2 or 3 lemons
2 or 3 large fine artichokes
1 tsp Dijon-type mustard
1 Tb raw egg white
4 to 5 Tb light olive oil
For decoration: watercress or shredded romaine, sliced tomatoes or cherry tomatoes

The scallops

Wash and drain the scallops to remove possible sand. Dipping a sharp knife in cold water for each cut, slice them crosswise (across the grain) into pieces 3/16 inch (¾ cm) thick.

Toss in a bowl with the juice of the lime, a sprinkling of salt and pepper, the shallots or scallions, and the parsley. Cover and marinate (let sit) in the refrigerator for half an hour, or until serving time.

The artichokes

To make a *blanc* or cooking liquid that will keep the artichokes white, place the flour in a medium-size saucepan, gradually beat in 1 cup (¼ L) cold water, stir in 2 more cups (½ L) water, a tablespoon of lemon juice, and 1½ teaspoons salt; bring to the boil, stirring, then remove from heat. One by one, break stems off artichokes and bend leaves back upon themselves all around to snap them off the base until you come to the bulge at the top of the artichoke bottom; cut off crown of leaves at this point, and trim base all around to remove greenish parts—rubbing frequently with cut lemon to prevent darkening. Drop each as done into the cooking water. Simmer 30 to 40 minutes, until tender when pierced with a knife, and leave in cooking water until ready to serve.

🕑 Will keep 2 to 3 days under refrigeration.

Wash under cold water, scoop out chokes with a teaspoon, and cut into 3/16-inch (¾ cm) slices going from top to bottom. Fold gently in a bowl with the following dressing.

Vinaigrette Liée:

(lightly thickened French dressing)
For about ⅓ cup dressing, beat ½ teaspoon salt with 1½ tablespoons lemon juice and the teaspoon of mustard, beat in the egg white, and then, by dribbles, the oil. Taste carefully for seasoning, adding pepper to taste—dressing should not be too strong or it will mask the taste of the artichokes.

Assembling

Line individual small plates or shells with watercress or shredded romaine. Then arrange slices of artichoke interspersed with tomato, for instance, around the edges of the dishes and a rosette of scallop slices in the middle, with a central dot of tomato for accent. Cover with plastic wrap and refrigerate until serving time.

🕑 May be prepared up to an hour ahead.

Steak Diane

For 4 people

4 steaks (about ½ pound or 225 g trimmed) cut ½ inch (1½ cm) thick from the top loin strip (or tenderloin, or Delmonico, or rib-eye steaks)

1½ Tb green peppercorns packed in water, or freshly ground pepper

Drops of soy sauce

Olive oil or peanut oil

The Sauce Set-up for the Dining Room:

A small pitcher of oil and a plate with a stick of butter

¼ cup (½ dL) each minced shallots or scallions and fresh parsley, in small bowls

A pitcher or bowl containing 1 Tb cornstarch blended with 1 Tb Dijon mustard and 1 cup fragrant beef bouillon

Worcestershire sauce

A lemon cut in half

Cognac and Port or Madeira

Equipment

A heavy frying pan about 12 inches (30 cm) top diameter for tabletop sautéing; a strong heat source; 2 large forks for turning and rolling up steaks; 2 dessert spoons, 1 for stirring and 1 for tasting; a butter knife; matches; 4 hot dinner plates

Preliminaries

Trim steaks of all fat and gristle—especially the piece of gristle at large end of loin under fat. One at a time, pound steaks between pieces of wax paper to enlarge them and reduce them to an even ¼-inch (¾-cm) thickness; use a wooden mallet, metal pounder, rubber hammer, rolling pin, bottle, or other handy object. Crush drained green peppercorns with the back of a spoon and spread a little on one side of each steak (or rub into steaks a grind or two of regular pepper) along with a few drops soy sauce and oil. Roll up each steak like a rug from one of the small ends and arrange on a platter; cover and refrigerate until serving time.

Prepare ingredients for the sauce set-up.
🕐 May be done several hours in advance. Cover shallots or scallions and parsley with dampened paper towels and plastic wrap and refrigerate; refrigerate the bouillon mixture.

Sautéing Steaks Diane at the table

Preheat frying pan in the kitchen to a reasonably hot temperature and bring it and the steaks with you to the table. The sauce set-up should be already in place near the chafing-dish burner.

The steaks are sautéed two at a time as follows: Pour 1 tablespoon oil into the pan as it heats on the flame and add 2 tablespoons butter. Butter will foam up, gradually foam will subside, and just as butter begins to brown, unroll one steak and immediately a second in the pan. Sauté 30 to 40 seconds on one side, turn with forks, and sauté on the other side—steaks will barely color and will just become lightly springy to the touch—for rare. Rapidly roll them up with your forks and replace on the platter. Sauté the other two steaks in the same manner, and roll up beside the first.

Add another spoonful or two butter, and when foaming stir in a big spoonful of shallots or scallions and parsley, let cook for a moment, then stir in the pitcher or bowl of bouillon mixture. Stir about for a moment, then add a few drops of Worcestershire and the juice of half a lemon (pierce lemon with fork, picking out seeds first, and squeeze with flourish). Add droplets of Cognac and Port or Madeira, taste, and add droplets more—again with flourish. Finally with forks and fanfare, and one by one, unroll each steak and bathe in the sauce, turning and dipping with your two forks, before placing it on a hot dinner plate.

When the other steaks are sauced and in place, spoon the rest of the sauce over them and serve.

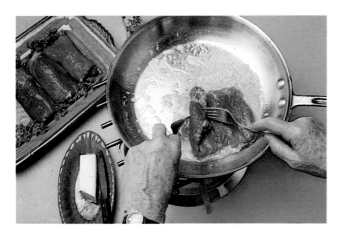

Fresh Green Peas

(the store-bought kind)

For 4 people

3 cups (¾ L) shelled fresh peas (about 2 pounds or 1 kg large fresh peas in the shell)

Salt

2 or more Tb butter

1 or more tsp sugar

Pepper

2 Tb minced scallions (optional)

Drop the peas into a large saucepan containing at least 3 quarts (3 liters) rapidly boiling salted water and boil slowly, uncovered, for 5 minutes or more, until just cooked through—taste several to make sure. Immediately drain and refresh for several minutes in cold water to set the green color and preserve the fresh texture.

🕐 May be precooked several hours in advance; cover and refrigerate.

Half an hour or so before serving, smear a heavy saucepan with butter, pour in the peas, and toss with 1 teaspoon sugar. Several minutes before serving, toss with salt, pepper, and the optional scallions and add several tablespoons water. Cover and bring to the rapid boil, tossing, to warm through. Taste carefully for seasoning—you may wish a little more sugar, just enough to give the illusion of fresh-picked sweetness. Toss with more butter if you like, turn into a hot dish, and serve immediately.

The mechanical pea-sheller.

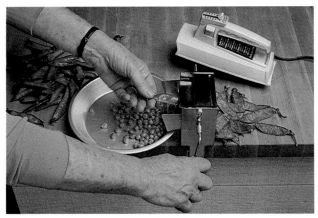

Real Mashed Potatoes

For 4 people

3 or 4 large "baking" potatoes

Salt

Milk and/or cream

Butter

White pepper

Equipment

A potato ricer

Wash and peel the potatoes, cut into lengthwise quarters, and set in a saucepan with lightly salted water to cover. Boil for 15 minutes or so, until potatoes are tender when pierced with a knife—cut a piece in half and taste to be sure. Immediately drain and put through ricer into a heavy-bottomed saucepan. Stir with a wooden spoon over moderate heat for a minute or more until potatoes begin to film bottom of pan, indicating excess moisture has been evaporated. Beat in several tablespoons milk and/or cream to lighten them slightly, then a tablespoon butter, and salt and white pepper to taste. If you are serving immediately, beat in milk and/or cream until the potatoes are the consistency you wish, and more butter if you like, then turn into a hot dish and serve at once.

🕐 You may cook them an hour or so ahead. In this case, add only a minimum of milk and/or cream and butter and set pan of potatoes in another and larger pan of hot but not simmering water. Cover the potato pan only partially—hot potatoes must not be covered airtight or they develop an off taste. At serving time, uncover, raise heat, and beat the potatoes with a wooden spoon, beating in more milk and/or cream and butter to taste.

Le Gâteau Victoire au Chocolat, Mousseline

Chocolate mousse dessert cake

Here is a very tender, moist, and delicate, and very chocolaty, dessert confection that is more like a cheesecake or custard than a cake, yet it is a cake—almost. However, it is cooked in a bain-marie—a pan of barely simmering water —in the oven, and it contains no flour or starch and no baking powder, only chocolate, a little sugar, eggs, and whipped cream. It is best served tepid, or at least at room temperature.

For a 10-cup (2½-L) cake pan, such as a square one 9 by 9 by 2 inches (23 x 23 x 5 cm), serving 8 to 10 or more

1 Tb instant coffee
4 Tb hot water
4 Tb dark Jamaica rum
14 ounces (400 g) semisweet baking chocolate
2 ounces (60 g) unsweetened baking chocolate
6 "large" eggs
½ cup (100 g) sugar
1 cup (¼ L) heavy or whipping cream, chilled
1 Tb pure vanilla extract
Confectioners sugar
Equipment

A 10-cup (2½-L) cake pan, preferably with nonstick lining, buttered, bottom lined with buttered wax paper, and floured; an electric mixer with round-bottomed bowl or a hand-held mixer or a large whisk and a metal bowl of the same type

Preliminaries

Preheat oven to 350°F/180°C and place rack in lower-third level. Prepare cake pan. Choose a roasting pan large enough to hold cake pan easily, fill with enough hot water to come halfway up cake pan, and set in oven. Assemble all ingredients and equipment.

The chocolate

Swirl the coffee and hot water in a medium-size saucepan, add the rum, and break up the chocolate into the pan. Bring 2 inches (5 cm) of water to the boil in a larger pan, remove from heat, and set chocolate pan in it; cover and let the chocolate melt while you continue with the recipe.

The egg and sugar mixture

Break the eggs into the beating bowl, add the sugar, and stir over hot water for several minutes until eggs are slightly warm to your finger—this makes beating faster and increases volume. Then beat for 5 minutes or more, until mixture has at least tripled in volume and forms a thick ribbon when a bit is lifted and falls from the beater; the eggs should be the consistency of lightly whipped cream. (You must have beating equipment that will keep the whole mass of egg moving at once, meaning a narrow rounded bowl and a beater that circulates about it continually.)

The whipped cream

Pour cream into a metal mixing bowl. Empty a tray of ice cubes into a larger bowl, cover them with cold water, then set the cream bowl into the larger ice-filled bowl. Beat with a hand-held mixer or large balloon whisk, using an up-and-down circular motion to whip in as much air as possible, until cream has doubled in volume and holds its shape softly. Whip in the vanilla.

Assembling and baking

Beat up the melted chocolate with a whisk; it should be smooth and silky. Scrape it into the egg-sugar mixture, blending rapidly with a rubber spatula, and when partially incorporated, fold in the whipped cream, deflating cream and eggs as little as possible. Turn batter into prepared cake pan, which will be about two-thirds filled. Set it at once in the pan of hot water in the preheated oven. Cake will rise

some ⅛ inch (½ cm) above edge of pan, and is done when a skewer or straw comes out clean—after about 1 hour of baking. Then turn off oven, leave oven door ajar, and let cake sit for 30 minutes in its pan of water, so that it will sink evenly. Remove from oven, still in its pan of water, and let sit for another 30 minutes so that it will firm up before unmolding and serving. Cake will sink down as it cools to about its original volume.

🕐 This cake is at its most tender and delicious when eaten slightly warm; however, you may cook it even a day or two in advance, leave it in its pan (covered when cool, and refrigerated), then set it in a 200°F/95°C oven for 20 minutes to warm gently.

Serving suggestions

Unmold the cake and decorate with a sprinkling of confectioners sugar, or with pipings of whipped cream, or with a soft chocolate icing (semisweet chocolate melted and beaten with a little soft butter). You may wish to pass a custard sauce or sweetened and vanilla-flavored whipped cream with the cake.

Remarks:

Since this is a most delicate confection with only enough body to hold itself together, it does not always cut neatly like a regular cake. Furthermore, once unmolded it cannot be lifted and transferred from one serving platter to another unless you reverse it again into its pan.

🕐 *Timing*

Coming into the dining room, your guests should feel like first nighters at a magic show. There, carefully disposed, are the props: dinner plates on their warming tray and an array of condiments and implements. Under the chafing dish, the alcohol lamp is ready for flaming: what next? But first, the appetizer. When this is eaten, there is a pause.

After removing the used plates to the kitchen, you start heating the steak pan on the stove, to speed things up in the dining room. You toss the blanched peas in their buttered pot and give a quick stir to the potatoes. In moments, you return with the vegetables to the dining room, set them on the warming tray, fetch the steaks and the hot pan, set it on the chafing dish, and begin. The actual job of making Steak Diane is a matter of 2 minutes in all for searing the steaks, which you do two at a time—it goes fast on such a hot, wide cooking surface—and then 2 minutes more for combining and reducing the sauce, and 1 minute for bathing the steaks in it. However, with your warming tray at hand, you have no reason to rush, and a suave performer never looks hurried.

In a second brief pause, you remove the dinner and serving dishes, and decorate the cake with the whipped cream you have standing ready (in the refrigerator in a sieve lined with cheesecloth, so it won't get watery while standing).

The cake can be made in the morning, or even the day before, but don't unmold it. Half an hour before dinner, warm it (if you wish) to tepid (see recipe), and unmold it just before you call in your guests.

In principle, the potatoes should be done as late as possible, but you'd be surprised how long they keep their goodness, partly uncovered over hot water.

All the appetizer elements can be prepared in the morning, for assembly not more than an hour before serving. You can blanch, drain, and chill the peas in the morning, and, that afternoon, set them in their buttered pot. During the day, pound the steaks and refrigerate till just before serving.

Well in advance and at leisure, carefully arrange your dinner table. For chafing-dish meals, I even make a check list, for an omission is almost as ignominious as forgetting the salt on a picnic!

Menu Variations

The appetizer: Before a hearty, tangy main course and a rich dessert, you want something light, like oysters or a variant of the little shellfish salad (see "Lo-Cal Banquet," page 40, or "Birthday Dinner," page 6), or a piquant consommé (see "Dinner for the Boss," page 123). *Gravlaks* (see kitchen "Cocktail Party," page 104) would be appropriate in flavor and texture, but perhaps too simple-looking. Before dishes like steak and cake, it's nice to have something "composed."

The main course: See "Menu Alternatives," page 235, for chafing-dish food that is cooked slowly. The parameters, or ground rules, here are: something sautéed, with or without deglazing sauce; something not so redolent as to argue with dessert, and some-

Crêpes Suzette being bathed in orange butter and folded into a triangle before being flamed in Cognac and orange liqueur.

thing handsomely and quickly done. Many kinds of scallopini are practical; pounded steaks are a kind of scallopini anyway. Veal, chicken, turkey, pork tenderloin? And you can do these with the same Diane sauce. High heat is for delicate things. You could blanch and slice brains or sweetbreads beforehand, dredge with flour, and finish them at table with browned butter and capers; or dredge thinly sliced calf's liver and sauté, adding thin onion slices halfway through; or do chicken livers with sliced mushrooms. Shad roe is a chafing-dish classic, as are veal kidneys.

The vegetables: As noted earlier, anything goes with steak. What's good today in the market?

The dessert: I hate to commend any other cake to you until you have tried the Victoire. But if you want a chocolaty one with no last-minute worries, you might consider the almond-rich Reine de Saba ("Queen of Sheba") or Le Marquis, a chocolate sponge cake, both in *Mastering I,* or the all-chocolate layer cake, Le Glorieux, in *Mastering II,* where you will also find a chocolate-filled cake, La Charlotte Africaine, made with slices of yellow or white leftover cake. In *J.C.'s Kitchen,* there is a section on working with chocolate, and one remarkably light though buttery chocolate cake called L'Eminence Brune. This particular name is a small joke: on *l'éminence grise,* the "gray eminence," as Père Joseph du Tremblay, Cardinal Richelieu's secret counselor, was nicknamed in the seventeenth century—and also on the name of a certain beautiful, green-eyed Persian pussycat. Christening a cake in the fanciful French style is almost as much fun as creating it.

And then, of course, you might want to save your performance at the chafing dish for dessert. One thinks automatically of cherries jubilee (or ice cream with other hot, liqueur-flavored sauces, some of which are flamed), and of crêpes Suzette, or the many other dessert pancakes in *Mastering I* and in *J.C.'s Kitchen;* or you can make sweet omelets, stack them on a warm side dish, and create a sauce in the pan.

Leftovers

The smaller your party, the more precisely you can plan quantities; so, unless a guest can't make it at the last minute, you won't have much left over. If you should have one raw *steak,* for some such reason, you can put it to good use (and stretch it to feed two) in beef Stroganoff or in one of those pleasant Oriental dishes like sukiyaki or beef with pea pods. Or split it between the two of you next morning, in a good old steak-and-eggs.

Mashed potatoes, though, are worth making in an overlarge quantity for the sake of two nice by-products. In the proportion of 2 cups mashed potatoes to 3 egg yolks, beat the mixture smoothly to make *pommes duchesse,* which, piped through a large rosette tube, makes a handsome border for a platter or for ramekins. Or beat 1 egg yolk into 1 cup *warmed* mashed potatoes, beat in 1 tablespoonful each parsley and chives, and fold in 1 beaten egg white to make an excellent mixture for mashed-potato pancakes. If you have just a small amount of mashed potatoes left, use them to thicken a soup or add to a bread dough.

You could rewarm the *cake* to tepid (back in its mold, of course), or eat it cold and call it a mousse or a super-rich brownie.

Postscript: Cooking in public

Preparation is everything, as the length of this chapter's Timing section suggests. At our TV studio, we have a backstage kitchen, where we prepare our stand-in dishes and those which must emerge in finished form seconds after the star has been prepared before the cameras. Careful charts are made of the cooktop and working surfaces so that every implement and ingredient is on hand and in place. Bottle tops are unscrewed beforehand, wastebins—out of camera range–are strategically placed (everybody asks me, "When you fling scraps over your shoulder like that, where do they land?"), and shallots, scallions, tomatoes, etc., are chopped and measured beforehand. What I do for the cameras looks easy because it *is* easy, with all the dirty work out of the way. At home, it's not a cinch for anyone; and then the telephone rings just as the aspic jells or the soufflé gasps and sinks.

In private or public cooking, broad, firm gestures are the most efficient. Wallop your steaks! Whoosh up your egg whites! And, behind your chafing dish and before your guests, act with assurance and decisiveness. Let every move accomplish something, and don't twiddle. As brevity is the soul of wit, spareness or "line" is the basis of bravura. And "line" is a matter of practice and preparation, which really is not dirty work for those who love to cook.

Let it rain! This no-fuss, no-muss barbecue can be given indoors just as well.

Indoor Outdoor Barbecue

We love to eat out on a flowery terrace above a fragrant garden with a little breeze keeping everything astir; an occasional zesty whiff from the grill doesn't at all interfere with the roses and heliotrope. But in our part of the world there's an old saying, "If you don't like the weather, wait a minute," and, unfortunately, it works the other way too. Just as we have the coals ready, just as we take our grand big hunk of meat from its marinade, dark clouds herd up and cover the sun, a sudden evil wind flips the leaves inside out... and blam: here it comes, and in we go.

But all those good smells and sizzles, so appetizing in the open air, can be just a bit much inside with the windows shut against a downpour. By using a leg of lamb boned and flattened out, which can be grilled out of doors or roasted indoors with only a final browning under the broiler, we have solved the problem to our great satisfaction. And this method solves three other problems as well. Boning makes it possible to cook this big cut, whose flavor adapts so beautifully to marinating and grilling, over coals in a reasonable time, getting it cooked through without charring and without searing its odd shape unevenly. It makes carving a matter of seconds. And it produces glorious leftovers—which can't be said for shish kebab.

The heavy, complicated structure of tail, hip, and shank—almost half the weight of a lamb leg—is hard to carve around but easy to extract before cooking. If you've never boned meat before, a lamb leg would be ideal as a practice victim; nothing much can go wrong. Calling it a butterfly, as butchers do, is a joke like naming your bloodhound Fifi. Far from being fluttery or ethereal, the lamb is hearty, richly flavored from its marinade, and something like a beef *filet* in texture. The meat firms up as it cooks into a thick juicy slab. We like it rare, firm and dark-brown outside and an even bright peony-pink within and we cut it in thick slices. It's an American technique to butterfly and grill a lamb leg and one which delights and surprises our French guests, who don't even recognize their old friend the *gigot*.

A perfect accompaniment to grilled lamb, and a convenient one since it's good hot or cold, is a dish of topinambours, a vegetable which gardeners tell me grows like a weed and which markets have begun to offer regularly. The word is French, adapted from the Portuguese, which is in turn an alteration of *tupinamba*—short for *batata tupinamba* or tupinamba potato, according to the big Webster's. And according to a French source, the Tupinamba are a small native tribe in Brazil who presumably nourished themselves on the vegetable that bears their name. The vegetable is related to the sunflower family, and since sunflower in French is *girasol*, it is probable that the nickname "Jerusalem artichoke" is a corruption of what was originally "*girasol artichaut*." But the topinambour vegetable is neither potato, nor is it artichoke. "Sunchoke," as the topinambour is sometimes called, is a modern publicity-stunt name invented to intrigue the buyer and only adds to general confusion. When this delightful vegetable is not available for a barbecue menu, I cook artichokes in a particularly flavorful way (since they too can be served hot or cold and suit lamb very well); see the bonus recipe in the Menu Variations section.

Speaking of names, the Zabaione Batardo Veneziano, which sounds like Iago badmouthing Otello, *basso profondo,* is called "Venetian" because it is based on a lovely concoction we first ate at a hotel in Venice; "Zabaione" because it involves egg yolks beaten with Marsala; and "Batardo" because it is bastardized by being stabilized with gelatin and served cold. Real *zabaione* is just egg yolks, wine, and sugar and is served still warm in a wineglass the moment it's made.

We don't have too leafy a salad, since so many guests enjoy stuffing theirs into a pita pocket: a mixture of bite-sized vegetables with just enough foliage for texture seems to work best. We always did like store-bought pita; but then we tried making our own and got addicted. Homemade pita, which you can attend to unhurriedly, permitting two rises and a rest before baking, has a fuller flavor than the store kind and a pleasing tender chewiness—even though it looks like the makings of a snow-

boot, suede-smooth outside and fleecy inside. If you and your guests have had to move indoors, and especially if some of them are teenagers, do take a few unbaked pita disks and some grated cheese from your freezer, add some herbs and some Italian tomato sauce (the store-bought kind can be very good), and give them homemade pita pizzas as an effortless extra. Or, if you have a glass-fronted oven or can borrow one of the portable electric ones, you might feature pita baking as a rainy-day double feature. About one minute after the inert white disks go into the oven, at highest heat, they begin to stir mysteriously, swelling and heaving from side to side. At full inflation, the edges lift right off the baking surface and the pita stand on tiptoe as if aspiring to flight. The moment is brief, the striving too strenuous, and they sink back, but only a little: still unbowed, I like to think.

In a similarly poetic mood, my husband one day christened a beautiful and potent emerald-green cocktail of his own invention. Remember the doggerel ballad by one J. Milton Hayes about the dashing young subaltern in Inscrutable India, who stole "The Green Eye of the Yellow God" to gratify the whim of his love, the Colonel's daughter? Alas for impetuous youth! In the rhythm of "Polly-Wolly-Doodle," the verses trot to a melancholy conclusion, for the god took his revenge.

There's a one-eyed yellow idol to the north of Khatmandu,
There's a little marble cross below the town;
There's a broken-hearted woman tends the grave of Mad Carew,
And the Yellow God forever gazes down.
Paul's delicious creation is luckily not so malevolent as its namesake; but be warned. It's every bit as powerful.

Preparations

Recommended Equipment:
If you don't own a charcoal grill, or if you plan to improvise one, I suggest you take a look at the detailed and practical section on outdoor cooking in *Joy of Cooking*, a book that surely needs no introduction. The only equipment specifically needed for doing butterflied lamb over coals is a hinged two-sided rack with a long handle for easy turning. See the pita recipe for a discussion of alternative baking methods.

For the cocktail, the wine, and the dessert, note that you will need 18 goblets.

Marketing and Storage:
Quantities for 6 people
Staples to have on hand

Salt
Peppercorns
Hot pepper sauce
Dry mustard
Rosemary
Cream of tartar
Pure vanilla extract
Soy sauce
Red wine vinegar
Cooking oil
Olive oil for optional marinade and for salad (or use another fine salad oil)
Plain unflavored gelatin (1 package)
Granulated sugar
All-purpose flour (2¾ cups or 390 g), unbleached recommended
Plain bleached cake flour (¾ cup or 105 g)
Recommended: Wondra or instant-blending flour (⅓ cup or 50 g)
Dry active yeast (1 Tb or 1 package)
Butter (1 stick)
Heavy cream (1 cup or ¼ L, plus more if using for dessert decoration)

Eggs (4)
Lemons (2)
Garlic (2 heads)
Parsley and/or chives
Shallots and/or scallions

Specific ingredients for this menu

Leg of lamb (note that a big, 7-pound or 3½-kilo leg will serve 12 to 14 when butterflied)

For optional lamb stock: 1 carrot, 1 onion, 2 or more celery ribs, 1 leek, and an herb bouquet

Topinambours (Jerusalem artichokes or sunchokes), 14 to 18

Romaine (1 medium-size head)

Watercress (1 or 2 bunches)
Red onions (1 medium-size)
Green and/or red sweet peppers (2)
Cherry tomatoes (12 to 18)
Fresh herbs (if possible): tarragon, chervil, basil
Feta cheese (½ pound or 225 g)
For *zabaione* decoration: cocoa or grated chocolate, or home-candied orange peel
Sweetened bottled lime juice (Rose's recommended)
Green crème de menthe (mint liqueur)
Gin
Marsala wine (best quality), ⅛ bottle
Peanuts, to serve with the cocktail

Buddha's Eye

A gin and lime cocktail with green crème de menthe

A strong clean drink to be served in small upstanding stemmed glasses

5 parts gin

2 parts sweetened lime juice (Rose's recommended)

2 parts green crème de menthe (mint liqueur)

Stir all ingredients together in a pitcher with ice cubes and, as soon as well chilled, pour into the glasses.

Butterflied Leg of Lamb

For barbecuing or roasting

To butterfly a leg of lamb means to bone it so that the meat may be spread out in one large piece. You can then barbecue it or roast it, and not only does it cook in half the time of an unbutterflied leg, but carving is wonderfully easy.

Fat removal and bone location

To prepare the lamb, first cut off as much outside fat as you can from all sides of the meat, then shave off the fell (membrane on top side of leg), and it is ready for boning. The whole leg of lamb contains the hipbone and tail assembly at the large end, the main leg bone that slants crosswise from the socket of the hipbone to the knee, and the shank bone from the knee to the ankle at the small end. All the boning takes place on the underside of the leg, not on the top or fell side.

Hipbone

The first and the worst bone to tackle is the hipbone-tail assembly, a complicated and convoluted structure if there ever was one. Lay lamb so its large end faces away from you and plunge fearlessly in with a very sharp, rather short knife; and by always cutting against the bone rather than against the flesh in any boning operation you are doing the right thing. Start at the exposed cut end of the hip that sticks out in the upper middle of the underside at the large end. Cut around under it (the side of the bone facing you, and the small end of the leg), branching out both right and left as well as down, and you will find that it attaches itself at about its middle to the main leg bone: you will gradually uncover the round ball end of the leg bone that fits into the socket of the hip. By cutting around the ball end you will detach its tendons from the hip socket, and then as you follow on down the hip and cut around under it, you can quite easily detach it from the meat.

Leg bones

With the hip out of the way, do the shank bone next, at the small end of the lamb, starting again on the underside. Cut the meat from the sides of the bone and under it, and proceed up to the knee joint but do not cut around it yet. Now you will make a frank cut in the meat, still from the underside of the lamb, going from the knee joint in a direct line to the ball joint where you removed the hip. Cut around the main leg bone thus exposed and the knee, being careful not to pierce the flesh on the top side of the meat (although there is no great harm done if you do), and you will free the leg and shank bones in one piece. Cut out the white cartilaginous disk that is the kneecap, as well as all chunks of interior fat.

Final rites

Lay the meat out, boned surface up, on your work surface, and you will note that it forms two large lobes. (If you have a large leg and are serving only 6 people, you may wish to cut off one of the lobes and freeze it for another roast or for shish kebabs.) For even cooking, I always slash the lobes in 2 or 3 places, making long cuts about 1½ inches (4 cm) deep; otherwise these thick pieces of meat will take longer to cook than the rest. Then, to keep the roast in shape, I like to push long skewers through the wide sides of the meat, one through the top third, and the other through the bottom third.

⏺ Lamb may be boned and prepared for roasting a day in advance; wrap in plastic and refrigerate.

Optional Marinade:

3 to 4 Tb olive oil
2 Tb soy sauce
The juice of ½ lemon, plus the grated peel if you wish
½ tsp or so rosemary
1 or 2 cloves garlic, puréed (optional)

Rub the unboned side of the lamb with a tablespoon of olive oil and place, oiled side down, in a baking pan. Rub the rest of the oil and the soy, lemon juice and optional peel, rosemary, and optional garlic into the top side. Cover with plastic wrap and marinate until you are ready to cook the lamb—an hour or more, if possible.

Lamb leg (underside) before trimming and after. Note the ball of the leg bone and the socket of the hip.

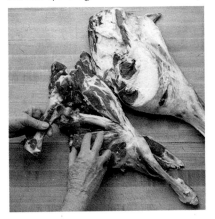

To barbecue the lamb

When the coals are just right, place the lamb in an oiled, hinged (double-sided) rack and barbecue, turning every 5 minutes or so and brushing with oil, for 45 minutes to an hour, depending on the heat of your coals and the way you like your lamb. If you want it rosy red, it is done when it begins to take on resistance to your finger, in contrast to its soft raw state. A meat thermometer reading would be 125°F/51°C. Remove the lamb to a carving board and let it sit for 8 to 10 minutes, allowing juices to retreat back into the meat before carving. To carve, start at either of the small ends and, to make attractively largish slices, begin somewhat back from the edge, angling your knife as though carving a flank steak (or even a smoked salmon).

To roast in the oven

I prefer to roast the lamb and then finish it off under the broiler. To do so, place the marinated lamb flat, boned side up, in a roasting pan in the upper middle of a preheated 375°F/190°C oven and roast for 20 to 25 minutes, or to a meat thermometer reading of 120°F/49°C. (I do not turn the lamb on its other side.) Then baste with oil and set for 2 to 3 minutes under a preheated broiler to brown lightly. Always let it sit for 8 to 10 minutes outside the oven before carving and carve as suggested in the preceding paragraph.

Save All Bones for Soup or Sauce:

You can make a wonderfully hearty broth out of lamb bones and meaty scraps. Whack the bones into convenient pieces with your cleaver, then brown bones and scraps in a 450°F/230°C oven in a roasting pan with a quartered onion and carrot. Drain off accumulated fat and dump contents of pan into a large saucepan with water to cover. Then deglaze the roasting pan: set it over heat with a cup of water, scrape up coagulated juices, and pour them into the saucepan. Simmer, skim, add a couple of celery ribs, a little salt, an herb bouquet, a leek if you have one, and a clove or two of garlic. Cover partially and simmer 3 hours or so, then strain, degrease, and that's all there is to it. Recipes for sauces are in *Mastering I*, and for soup see *J.C.'s Kitchen*.

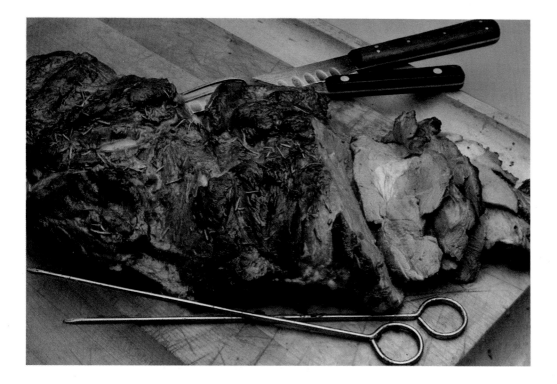

Pita Bread

Armenian, Syrian, or Israeli flat bread
Pita bread, the flat pale bread-dough Near Eastern pancakes that you can separate into two layers, is easy indeed to make when you have constructed yourself a simulated baker's oven. That means you have quarry tiles or a stoneware griddle to set on your oven rack, onto which you slide the dough to bake. Although you can cook pita on top of the stove, the complete puff is not always achieved, and the bottom layer remains thicker than the top layer. And although you can also bake pita on cookie sheets in the oven, it is not as satisfactory as the griddle. Griddles, by the way, are available via many country store catalogues. They are often sold as pizza sets and include a wooden sliding board or baker's peel; the rectangular griddle is the one to order since it is a more useful shape than the round one for breads, rolls, and pita, as well as for pizza. Pita dough makes wonderful pizza, too.

Like homemade English muffins, your own-made pita cost you less than half the price of store-bought ones, in addition to being fun and dramatic to make.

For 12 pita 6 inches in diameter

1 Tb (1 package) yeast dissolved in ½ cup (1 dL) tepid water

About 1 pound (450 g) of flour as follows:
   2¾ cups (390 g) all-purpose flour, unbleached recommended
   ¾ cup (105 g) plain bleached cake flour

2 tsp salt

1 Tb olive oil or tasteless salad or cooking oil

1 cup (¼ L) tepid water; droplets more as necessary

Equipment

Best, a tile or stoneware baking surface to fit your oven rack; second best, an aluminum baking sheet. A wooden sliding board, shingle, or peel. A long-handled pancake turner. A cake rack or racks for cooling baked pita. A rolling pin

Making the dough

When yeast is thoroughly dissolved, combine it with the ingredients listed, kneading in enough of the water to make a moderately firm dough. When well blended, let rest for 2 minutes, then knead vigorously until dough is smooth and elastic and does not stick to your hands—5 minutes or more. Place in a clean, fairly straight-sided 4-quart (4-L) bowl, cover, and let rise at 75°F to 80°F (24°C–27°C) until slightly more than doubled in bulk—2 hours or so. Deflate by pulling dough inward from sides of bowl, cover, and let rise again to slightly more than double—about 1½ hours.

🕐 Second rise may be completed in the refrigerator, and when risen, you may punch down dough, cover with a weight to keep it down, and leave for 24 hours—or you may freeze it.

Forming the pita

Turn dough out onto a floured work surface and lengthen it by rolling it back and forth under the palms of your hands, forming a thick sausage shape about 16 inches (40 cm) long. Cut even portions all the same size by halving the dough crosswise, halving the 2 halves, then cutting each of these 4 pieces into thirds. Then, to make the pancake shape more even, first form a cushion out of each piece of dough by bringing the 4 corners together and pinching to seal them, then turn seal side down and roll under the palm of one hand to make a ball; set each aside, as you form it, on a floured corner of your work surface, and cover with a lightly floured sheet of plastic.

These balls of dough are now to be rolled into pancake-size disks which are to rest either on a floured wooden surface or on floured towels for 20 minutes or so while the oven heats. Proceed as follows: one at a time, with a rolling pin on a quite heavily floured surface, roll each ball into a disk ¼ inch (¾ cm) thick

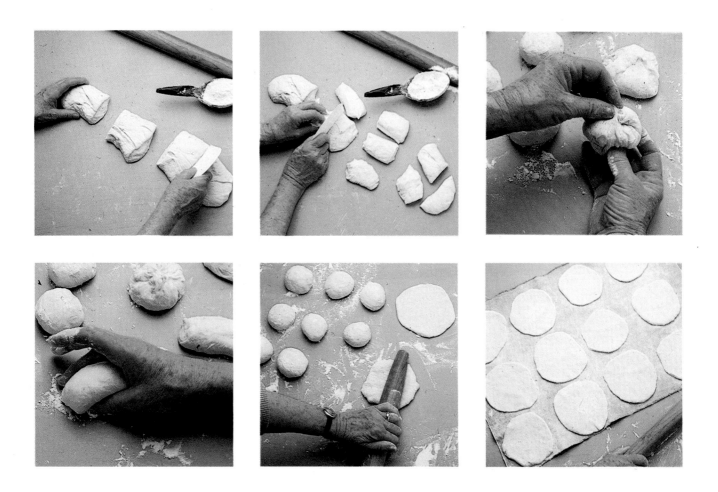

and 6 inches (15 cm) across. Place disk on prepared resting surface, cover with floured plastic, and continue with the rest.

Baking the pita

Set quarry tiles, griddle, or bake sheet in lower middle level of oven, and preheat to 500°F–550°F (260°–270°C)–highest heat! When oven is ready, lightly flour the sliding board, place on it 2 or 3 pita, and slide then onto the hot baking surface. In about 1 minute, large bubbles will appear on surface of the pita and they will then quickly and dramatically puff up like pillows, reach their maximum, and subside slightly. Leave for a moment (baking should take about 2 minutes in all) and remove with a pancake turner before they have time to color or harden. Continue with remaining pita. Let cool completely; they will gradually collapse.

🕐 Leave on rack for an hour or two, then stack together, pressing out air, and store in a plastic bag; refrigerate for 2 to 3 days, or freeze.

Manufacturing Notes:

You may find, as I did, that although pita are easy to make, it does take a session or two to perfect your techniques. It seems important to watch that the dough is fairly firm, since if it is too soft the disks are sticky to roll and limp to handle. They must be smooth, unwrinkled, and at least ¼ inch (¾ cm) thick, too, or the pita may not puff up into the proper pillow shape.

Pizza:

Roll the pita dough to any size you wish, but the 6-inch (15-cm) pita shape is just right for individual servings. When oven is ready, place 3 or 4 dough disks on lightly floured sliding board, rapidly garnish with the pizza topping of your choice, and slide onto hot baking surface in oven, exactly as though you were baking pita. Topping will prevent dough from puffing, and when bottom is lightly browned, in about 5 minutes, the pizza is done.

Notes on Freezing:

You can roll out the dough into disks, flour the disks, stack each between sheets of plastic wrap, and freeze in a bunch. You can then take them singly from freezer to oven; although they will bake into pita, they do not puff quite as much as when fresh—and whether you bake a pita solidly frozen or thawed seems to make little difference. I find the frozen disks just fine for pizza, however, either frozen or thawed before baking.

Serving Suggestions:

Pita pocket sandwiches. Cut the baked pita in half crosswise, gently pull the two halves apart, and fill with any kind of sandwich mixture, such as a salad, hamburger and trimmings, scrambled eggs, a cooked eggplant and tomato mixture, and so forth. Or make your filling and bake it in the pita pocket.

Toasted pita triangles. Split the pita breads—it is often easiest to cut all around the circumference with scissors to make an even split—and cut into triangles of whatever size you wish. Brush with melted butter and, if you wish, a sprinkling of mixed dried herbs and/or grated Parmesan cheese. Arrange buttered side up on a baking sheet and place for a few minutes in a preheated 350°F/180°C oven to crisp and brown lightly. Serve with soups, salads, cheese, or with drinks.

Topinambours

Also called Jerusalem artichokes or sunchokes

These little knobby roots grow underground like potatoes and do remind one in taste of artichokes, yet they are crisp like water chestnuts when raw, and have a very special and mildly pungent taste of their own when cooked. Hot, buttered, and tossed with parsley or chives, they go nicely indeed with roast lamb—or with roast pork, turkey, or beef, for that matter. Cooked and cold, they make an attractive salad vegetable. Since they discolor rapidly, they should be cooked in a *blanc* (a thin solution of flour and water with salt and lemon), the same way you would boil artichoke bottoms or salsify.

For 6 people as a vegetable course

⅓ cup (¾ dL) flour, preferably the instant-blending kind

6 cups (1½ L) cold water; more if necessary

3 Tb lemon juice

2 tsp salt

14 to 18 topinambours

If serving hot—3 Tb or more butter, salt, pepper, and minced parsley and/or chives
If serving cold—minced shallots, salad or olive oil, fresh lemon juice, salt, pepper, and parsley and/or chives

To make the *blanc* liquid, place the flour in a saucepan and beat in the water gradually, to prevent flour from lumping. Add the lemon juice and salt and bring to the simmer. Set the pan by your work surface, and peel the topinambours one by one (using a small knife and simply removing the little knobs along with the peel). Cut the topinambours into ¼-inch (¾-cm) slices and drop the slices into the *blanc* liquid as you proceed. When all are sliced, bring to the boil and simmer 15 to 20 minutes or until just tender when pierced with a knife. (You will notice a remarkable change in taste, from crisp and raw with no pronounced flavor to cooked and with a definite yet subtle taste that is reminiscent of artichoke, yet utterly and uniquely topinambourish.)

🕐 May be cooked in advance. Leave them in their liquid until you are ready to proceed.

To serve hot

Drain (reserving the cooking liquid for a soup base) and toss gently in a sieve under cold running water. Then melt the butter in a saucepan, add the topinambours, and toss gently to coat with the butter and to heat through. Taste carefully for seasoning, then toss with the herbs and serve.

To serve cold

Drain and wash as described in preceding paragraph, then toss with minced shallots, oil, lemon, salt, pepper, and herbs.

Seasonal Salad

Of romaine, watercress, red onion rings, green and/or red peppers, cherry tomatoes, and feta cheese

This is a salad of the season and needs no formal recipe. One suggestion is to tear the romaine into bite-size pieces, stem the watercress, wrap them together in a damp towel, and place in the refrigerator in a plastic bag several hours before serving. Also some hours before serving, slice the red onions and, to minimize their sting, place the slices in a sieve and run boiling water then cold water over them; drain thoroughly and toss in a bowl with a spoonful or two of your salad dressing. Halve, seed, and slice the peppers; refrigerate in a covered bowl. Cut the feta cheese into ½-inch (1½-cm) dice and taste; if salty, soak 10 minutes or so in a bowl of cold water and drain. Toss with freshly ground pepper, thyme, oregano, or a mixture of herbs, and a tablespoon or two of olive oil; let macerate for several hours, tossing once or twice. Shortly before serving, wash, stem, and halve cherry tomatoes; sprinkle lightly with salt. At serving time, toss all ingredients except the cheese together in a big salad bowl with your dressing (see next recipe and index for suggestions) and with fresh herbs if you have them. Taste, correct seasoning, then fold in ¾ of the cheese cubes, strewing the remainder on top.

Vinaigrette Salad Dressing

I have found the following a useful base for salad dressing made in quantity for a large gathering. Use the best and freshest of everything for success!

For 30 people or more, 3 ½ cups (1 scant liter) dressing

4 Tb minced shallots or scallions

2 Tb dry mustard

5 to 6 shakes hot pepper sauce

Grinds of fresh pepper to taste

1 tsp salt, or to your taste

5 Tb red wine vinegar; more as needed

2 Tb or more fresh lemon juice

3 cups best-quality olive oil, new fresh peanut oil, or other oil of impeccable quality

Fresh herbs of your choice, such as tarragon, chervil, or basil

Beat all ingredients together in an electric mixer or shake in a large screw-topped jar. Taste carefully, and correct seasoning. After you dress your salad, taste a leaf or two and toss in more salt and pepper if needed.

The following proportions would be about right for 6 to 8 people. Simply reduce accordingly for a smaller number.

2–3 tsp minced shallots or scallions

½ tsp dry mustard

Grinds of fresh pepper to taste

¼ tsp salt, or to your taste

1 Tb red wine vinegar

1 Tb fresh lemon juice

½ cup best-quality olive (or other) oil as above, plus fresh herbs

Beat together with a whisk or shake in a screw-top jar. Correct seasoning to your taste both before and after dressing your salad.

🕐 May be made somewhat in advance, but it is never a good idea to let salad dressing sit around for more than a day or two; it loses its freshly made quality.

Zabaione Batardo Veneziano

Mock zabaione

This turns out to be, actually, a Marsala-flavored Bavarian cream. One friendly warning is to watch out when you combine the Marsala custard with the whipped cream at the end: if the custard is warm it will deflate the cream, yet if it is too cold the chilled cream will cause the gelatin in it to set and get lumpy before you complete the folding process.

For about 6 cups, serving 6 to 8

⅓ cup (¾ dL) plus 1 Tb sugar

¾ cup (1 ¾ dL) best-quality sweet Marsala wine in a 6-cup (1 ½-L) saucepan

1 ½ level tsp plain unflavored gelatin

4 egg yolks in a 2-quart or -liter stainless-steel saucepan

1 Tb pure vanilla extract

2 egg whites in a clean dry beating bowl

A pinch of salt and ⅛ tsp cream of tartar

1 cup (¼ L) heavy cream for whipping in a 2-quart or -liter stainless-steel bowl

A large bowl with a tray of ice cubes and water to cover them

Decoration

Whipped cream and/or cocoa or grated chocolate, or home-candied orange peel

Combining
Marsala custard ingredients

Stir ⅓ cup (¾ dL) sugar into the Marsala, sprinkle the gelatin on top, and set aside to soften while you assemble the rest of the ingredients listed. Then, with a wire whip, vigorously beat the egg yolks in their saucepan for a minute or two until they are thickened slightly and pale yellow. Now set the

Marsala over moderate heat (but do not bring it to the boil) and stir to dissolve both gelatin and sugar completely, looking carefully to be sure there are no unmelted granules of either in the liquid. Finally, beating the egg yolks with your whip, slowly dribble in the hot Marsala.

Heating the Marsala mixture

The Marsala and egg yolk mixture is now to be thickened over heat like a custard. To do so, set it over a moderately low (but not too low) burner, and beat with your wire whip as it slowly warms. As you beat and heat it the mixture will start to foam, and in a few minutes it will be entirely foamy throughout—keep testing with your impeccably clean finger. When it is too hot for that finger you should almost at the same time see the first wisp of steam rising from the surface, and the custard is done. Remove from heat, and beat vigorously for a minute or two to stop the cooking; beat in the vanilla, and set aside.

Beating egg whites and whipping cream

Beat the egg whites slowly until they begin to foam, then beat in the salt and cream of tartar; gradually increase speed to fast and continue until they form shining peaks, then sprinkle on the tablespoon of sugar and beat vigorously to stiffen them more. Delicately fold them into the warm Marsala custard.

Then whip the cream, setting it in the ice cubes and water, until it has doubled in volume, beater leaves light traces on its surface, and cream holds its shape softly—this is now *crème Chantilly,* or lightly whipped cream.

Combining the elements

Set custard pan in the ice cubes and fold custard delicately (so as not to deflate it) with a rubber spatula, testing continually with your finger just until custard is cool but not cold or chilled. Immediately remove pan from ice and at once fold in the whipped cream to make a beautifully smooth, creamy pale yellow ambrosia. Turn it either into a serving bowl or into individual goblets, cover, and chill for 2 hours or more.

🕐   May be completed a day or two in advance.

To serve

Decorate with swirls of whipped cream and/or cocoa or grated chocolate—or with a julienne of home-candied orange peel.

Timing

This meal could hardly be easier to plan for. Just before serving time, dress and toss the salad, whip the cream, if you're using it, for the dessert decoration, and reheat the topinambours if you're having them hot. Remember to give the lamb a 10-minute sit after it's cooked; and, if you're cooking indoors, it needs watching during its 3 minutes in the broiler. Oven roasting, with an occasional baste, takes 20 to 25 minutes.

If you're outside, allow an hour, with frequent basting and turning, for the lamb to grill. At least an hour before cooking, set the lamb in its marinade. At that stage start your fire. Any time during the day, wash, dry, and trim the salad makings, prepare the dressing, and cook the topinambours.

You can bone the lamb the day before. The *zabaione* can be made one or two days before, and the pita, two or three. (Or you can freeze the pita dough, made long before; but they don't puff quite so high.)

Menu Variations

The barbecued meat: Other large cuts of meat to marinate and grill would include beef, both steak and roasting cuts, not more than 2 inches (5 cm) thick. You can of course grill chops, and there is always chicken; but, if you are forced indoors, they will have to be done under the broiler and given close attention.

The salad: There are several salad recipes in this book; with full-flavored meat and wine, have something rather assertive and oniony.

The zabaione: See the Menu Variations in "Informal Dinner" for other custardy desserts you can make ahead of time.

The topinambours: The only other vegetable that remotely resembles topinambours in flavor is the artichoke. See the recipe for preparing artichoke bottoms on page 183. Or forget that flavor altogether and do one of the eggplant recipes in *Mastering II*. Lamb and eggplant go beautifully together.

Sauté of Fresh Artichoke Hearts with Onions and Garlic

Onions and garlic and a whisper of wine vinegar give a special taste to this sauté of artichokes. Serve it hot with roast or barbecued meats, cold as an hors d'oeuvre, or with sausages, or with hard-boiled eggs and sliced tomatoes.

For 6 people as a vegetable accompaniment

6 to 8 fine fresh artichokes
1 lemon
4 Tb or so olive oil
1 head garlic
4 large onions
Salt and pepper
Thyme or mixed dried herbs
2 Tb or so butter
1 to 2 Tb wine vinegar
Minced fresh parsley
Equipment
A heavy deep frying pan or an electric skillet

Preparing the artichokes

Artichoke hearts include the artichoke bottom and the tender part of the inner cone of leaves. When artichokes are very young and fresh, you can use the whole cone without removing the choke; however, it is rare indeed to find such quality outside the artichoke-growing regions. I prepare the usual store-bought artichokes as follows, one at a time. Cut the stem off an artichoke, close to the base. Then bend the leaves at right angles to the base until they snap close to their large end; pull down toward the base to snap the leaf off, leaving the tender part of its base attached to the artichoke bottom; continue rapidly until you reach the pale creamy cone of leaves covering the choke. Shave the tough green from around the base of the artichoke, using a small knife at first, then a vegetable peeler. Frequently rub cut portions of artichoke base with half a lemon as you go to prevent discoloration. After trimming you will usually have to cut off the top part of the cone, down to where you judge the tender part begins. Cut the heart in half lengthwise and, if large, in quarters. Scoop out the choke (hairy portion covering bottom) with a small knife, and rub the quarters again with lemon. As soon as one heart is prepared, drop it into your frying pan with the olive oil and set over low heat, tossing to cover with the oil. Continue rapidly with the rest of the artichokes.

The sauté

With the artichokes still over low heat and being tossed now and then (toss by swirling and shaking pan by its handle), separate the cloves of garlic and drop them into a pan of boiling water for a moment to loosen the skins. Peel the cloves, halve or quarter them lengthwise if large, and add to the artichokes. Peel, halve, and slice the onions lengthwise; toss them into the pan with the artichokes and garlic. Season with salt, pepper, and herbs; add 2 tablespoons butter and toss to melt it. Cover the pan and cook slowly until artichokes are just tender when pierced with a knife—20 minutes or so—and toss once or twice. Pour in the vinegar, toss, cover, and cook 5 minutes more. Correct seasoning.

🕐   May be cooked in advance; set aside uncovered and reheat, tossing and adding a little more oil or butter if you wish.

To serve hot
Toss with minced parsley.

To serve cold
Let cool after their initial sauté and, if you wish, chill. Before serving, toss with a little lemon juice, a little olive oil, salt and pepper to taste, and fresh minced parsley.

Leftovers

The barbecued lamb: This is as good cold as it was hot, in slices or sandwiches. If you have only scraps, think of curry, shepherd's pie, hash, or add to a hearty soup based on lamb stock made from the bones (see recipe).

There's little to be said about the other elements in this meal, except to warn you not to keep any eggy mixture, like the *zabaione,* for more than four days unless you freeze it.

Postscript: On eating

In planning meals for company, we all think carefully about our resources of money, kitchen equipment, serving possibilities, and, especially, time. And at the shopping stage we are careful about quality and flexible (if what we wanted isn't there) about varying our menus. Feasible preparation, graceful service, good food: can one ask any more than that?

Yes. One ought, in planning menus, to ponder the act of eating as much as the food itself. One of the nice things about this barbecue, for instance, is the agreeable option for guests of stuffing a pita pocket with salad, mingling moist and dry, crunchy and chewy, sharp and bland for that first alligator-size bite. Instruments and gestures matter: the light supple grasp of chopsticks, for instance, affords a sensation different from the stab and leverage of a fork: which one suits your menu? What happens to a mouthful? A cannelated tube doesn't merely make a purée prettier; the tongue delights in smoothing the little corduroy ridges to velvet.

Eating wasn't done with the fingers when I was young, except with bread, corn on the cob, and, in some parts of the country, asparagus. I have come to wonder if all the *do*'s and *don't*'s about eating, rather than the anxiously cramming mothers the shrinks love to belabor, weren't the reason why so many children had "feeding problems" then. How *could* anybody not love to eat, unless it had always been made a penance?

I agree, of course, that table manners are important. Dribblers, twiddlers, spillers, garglers, smokers at meals, and panters are unwelcome company. And such legerdemain as filleting a sautéed trout or carving a squab (a bird I really prefer, however, to eat in gluttonous solitude) is as pleasant to watch as to perform. During one stay in Rome, Paul and I went daily to the same little trattoria expressly to watch one of their regular client's beautifully deft way with the peeling of whole oranges and pears, and the neat dismemberment of small spit-roasted birds; his awareness of our admiration seemed to stimulate him to heights of virtuosity.

But it would have been a pointless performance if the old gentleman hadn't eaten with such relish. Food like love is a deeply emotional matter. Intrusive or assertive displays aside, do you really mind, do you find indecent, the sight of intense bliss, of a child's pointed pink tongue molding the ice cream in a cone, of a friend's half-closed eyes and expanded nostrils as he inhales the scent of your good brandy? Isn't there joy in the sound of a fork's first break into a puff pastry, and a doomsday note in the expiring gurgle of a chocolate soda's last drop on its way up the straw?

I like to watch my guests eat and to imagine their pleasure in the lobster's clawlets as they suck, or in something so simple as the smoothness, form, and heft of a hard-boiled egg. I think of Muriel Spark's loving glimpse in *Memento Mori* of a grandmother feeding a baby, her mouth moving in unconscious sympathy as he eats. Nominally about death, that novel is about the preciousness of life, and so, however modestly, is every honest cookbook.

Bon appétit, then... and *vive la compagnie!*

Essay

Cooking to Bring

Here are a few thoughts for those happy occasions when everybody brings something: a cake for, say, a bake sale; a festive aspic for a summer weekend; a wondrously convertible stew/salad/casserole for any friend who is faced with a big crowd; an elegant egg dish you can bring to a lunch party and reheat; and, finally, an unabashedly fancy fish assemblage that could be the *pièce de résistance* at a cooking-club get-together. Since it has an alluring relative, the golden, feathery brioche loaf, I've included the recipe for that, too.

Chocolate-Chip Spice and Pound Cake

When they know you're coming, bring them a cake! And this one with its nicely spiced flavor and generous sprinkling of chocolate bits will go with fruits, ice cream, or just coffee and tea.

Manufacturing Notes:
Whenever you put something like candied fruits or nuts into a cake batter, you want them to stay put and not fall down to the bottom of the pan. That goes for chocolate chips, too. It turns out that the best kind of cake batter for this purpose is the pound cake formula, which is moistly buttery yet solid enough to hold fruits or chocolate in place; and you also moisten and flour these items to encourage their suspension.

This is a recipe that calls for whole eggs and sugar beaten until they are thick and heavy like a mayonnaise, so you must beat them in a rounded bowl, one so shaped that the whole mixture is in motion at once; if your machine is equipped with a large flat-bottomed bowl—and I don't know why anyone continues to design mixers that way—substitute another bowl. My old mixer, as an example, came with the wrong kind of bowl. It now works nicely with a stainless-steel bowl 4¾ inches deep that is 7¾ inches across the top and 3 at the bottom (or 12, 19, and 8 cm, respectively). Now, after that bit of mechanical lore, here is the recipe.

Proportions for a 6-cup (1½-L) loaf pan about 10 inches (25 cm) long, serving 10 to 12

4 "large" eggs
⅓ cup (¾ dL) packed-down, dark brown sugar
½ cup (1 dL) white granulated sugar
Pinch salt
1 tsp powdered mace
1½ sticks (6 ounces or 180 g) unsalted butter
1¼ cups (175 g) all-purpose flour (measure by dipping dry-measure cups into flour container and sweeping off excess with the straight edge of a knife)
1¼ tsp double-action baking powder
6 ounces (1 cup or 180 g) semisweet chocolate chips (bits, morsels), in a bowl
Drops of rum, whiskey, or coffee
1 Tb pure vanilla extract
Other items
Soft butter, flour, and wax paper to line a loaf pan; a metal bowl for beating butter; the right bowl for your mixer—see discussion preceding recipe

Preheat oven to 350°F/180°C and place rack in middle or lower-middle level.

Beating the eggs and sugar

Place the eggs, sugars, salt, and mace in bowl of mixer and stir over hot water for a minute or so to take off chill. Then set on stand and beat at high speed for 5 minutes or more, until eggs are doubled in volume, form the ribbon, and are the consistency of lightly whipped cream or of heavy mayonnaise.

Other preliminaries

Meanwhile, cut up the butter, if chilled, and stir over hot water to soften it; then beat until light and fluffy (setting in cold water if it has softened too much)—it must be the consistency of the egg-sugar mixture. Set aside and beat up again later, if necessary. Butter the loaf pan, line bottom with wax paper, butter that, then dust with flour, knocking out excess. Measure out the 1¼ cups flour into a sifter and set on a piece of wax paper, then stir the baking powder into the flour. Toss the chocolate bits with a few drops of rum, whiskey, or coffee, just to coat them (pour out excess), then toss with a tablespoon or two of the flour, again just enough to coat them. You are now ready to combine the elements of the cake batter.

Finishing the cake batter

Being sure that the eggs are a thick mayonnaise-like consistency and are at room temperature (beat over hot water if not, or they will congeal the butter), beat in the vanilla. Check also that the butter is soft and fluffy, then beat a dollop—⅓ cup (¾ dL) or so—of the eggs into the butter. By fourths, and with a rubber spatula, delicately and rapidly fold the flour into the eggs, deflating them as little as possible until last addition of flour is almost incorporated; then scoop the butter into the eggs. Rapidly spread it out and then fold it in with your spatula until almost incorporated; fold in the flour-covered chocolate bits. Immediately scoop batter into pan, which will be filled by about two-thirds.

Baking, cooling, serving, and storing

Set at once in preheated oven and bake for 50 to 60 minutes. Cake should rise to fill pan and will brown nicely on top; it is done when top feels springy, when you can gently pull cake from sides of pan, and when a skewer plunged into center comes out clean (except for traces of melted chocolate). Remove from oven, set pan right side up on a rack, and let cool for 10 minutes. Then unmold on rack, peel paper off bottom of cake, and carefully, with the aid of a long spatula, turn cake right side up. May be served warm or cool; but if wrapped and chilled after cooling, it is best served at room temperature to bring out the texture and flavor of both cake and chocolate.

❶ May be wrapped airtight when cold and refrigerated, or may be frozen.

Ring Mold of Eggs in Aspic

Les Oeufs en Gelée à la Carrousel

Rather than preparing jellied eggs individually, do them all together in a ring mold and bring them along as a first course or as the star main course for a summer luncheon. You can fill the center of the unmolded aspic ring with sprigs of watercress tossed in an oil and lemon dressing, or a mayonnaise of shellfish, or a salad of fresh mushrooms and asparagus tips. The whole dish may be assembled and refrigerated a day or even two days in advance of serving.

Luxury Note:

The following recipe calls for truffle and *foie gras* because this is a very special dish—and besides, I've not used them at all in this book. However, a decoration of shrimp, lobster, or crab, or nicely cut ham slices, or fancifully shaped cooked vegetables would be equally appropriate.

For 6 servings

A 1-ounce (30-g) canned truffle and its juices

4 Tb Port or Madeira

2 envelopes (2 Tb) plain unflavored gelatin

4 cups (1 L) excellent clarified meat stock or consommé, in a saucepan

6 slices *foie gras* ⅛ inch (½ cm) thick, and egg shaped, or about ½ cup (1 dL) excellent liver mousse

6 small or medium poached eggs (page 169), chilled

Filling or sauce for serving (optional), such as the suggestion in the introductory paragraph, or a bowl of homemade mayonnaise

Equipment

A 4-cup (1-L) ring mold; a bowl large enough to accommodate mold with 2 trays of ice cubes and water to cover them; a small saucepan for chilling aspic; a chilled round serving platter

Cut the truffle into 6 slices and return to the can with its juices and enough Port or Madeira to fill it; let macerate until needed.

To make the aspic, sprinkle the gelatin over the cold stock or consommé, let soften 2 to 3 minutes, then stir over gentle heat until gelatin has dissolved completely. Assemble the rest of the ingredients listed. (If you are using liver mousse rather than *foie gras*, taste carefully for seasoning: you may wish to beat in a few drops of truffle juice, some pepper, a little soft butter, and a pinch of allspice.) Pour the truffle juice and remaining wine into the aspic; chill the truffle slices.

Pour a ⅜-inch (1-cm) layer of liquid aspic into the ring mold and chill in the bowl of ice 10 to 15 minutes or until set. Pour a little liquid aspic into the saucepan, stir over ice to cool, remove from ice, and dip truffle slices into it to coat them; arrange over the aspic layer in the mold—each slice marks the place for each of the 6 eggs. Cover each truffle with a slice of *foie gras* (or a spoonful of liver paste).

Trim eggs evenly and lay upside down over the *foie gras*. Pour a cup of liquid aspic into saucepan, chill over ice until syrupy and almost set, then pour a ½-inch (1½-cm) layer into mold around the eggs; chill mold in ice to set the aspic and hold the eggs in place. Chill remaining aspic in saucepan; when syrupy, pour around the eggs to fill the mold. Cover the mold and chill at least an hour in the refrigerator.

To unmold, fill a large bowl with very hot water. Run a knife between the aspic and mold, both outside and inside edges. Dip into hot water for 6 to 8 seconds, remove, and turn the chilled serving dish upside down over mold. Reverse the two, giving mold a sharp downward jerk to dislodge aspic. Remove mold, cover aspic with inverted bowl, and refrigerate until serving time; then fill center with whatever you have chosen. You may wish to decorate outside with chopped aspic or aspic cutouts. Pass mayonnaise separately, if you wish.

The eggs in this photograph were jumbo, so that the aspic on the inside of the ring did not quite cover them. Use small or medium eggs and you will not have to hide them with parsley and greens as we did here.

Turkey Wine Stew–
Turkey Salad–
Turkey Casserole

If you are bringing a main dish to a party, try a turkey salad or a turkey casserole for a change, either of which you can make from a turkey wine stew—and that means simmering the turkey in pieces, whereby it cooks much faster than whole turkey and the meat is moist and tasty.

Turkey Wine Stew

Note:
If turkey is frozen, thaw in its original plastic wrapping either in the refrigerator for several days or in a sinkful of cold water for several hours.

For about 3 quarts (3 liters) of cooked turkey meat

A 12- to 14-pound (5½- to 6¼-kg) turkey

2 large onions, peeled and quartered

1 large carrot, scrubbed and roughly chopped

1 large celery stalk, washed and roughly sliced

1 large leek, quartered, washed, and sectioned (optional)

1 large herb bouquet (10 parsley sprigs, 2 bay leaves, 1 tsp thyme or sage, tied together in washed cheesecloth)

2 bottles dry white wine (Chablis, white table wine, or anything that tastes fresh, strong, and healthy)

Chicken broth or water, as needed

Breast meat marinade (optional)

Salt and white pepper, 2 Tb Cognac or lemon juice, 1 tsp minced shallot or scallion, 2 Tb olive oil or salad oil

1 Tb salt, or to taste

Cutting up the turkey

Disjoint the turkey as follows. Remove leg and thigh sections in one piece, along with the nuggets of dark meat at the small of the back and from thigh joint to tail; separate drumsticks from thighs. Cut off wings close to body. Remove each breast-meat half in one piece, scraping it from ridge of breastbone and down rib cage to backbone; remove the white tendon that runs almost the length of the underside of each breast—scrape down each side and then draw it out. Pull and cut the skin off the breast meat, drumsticks, thighs, and as much of it off the wings as you easily can—the rest can be removed from the wings after cooking. (I discard the skin.) Chop the carcass into pieces that will easily fit into your stew pot.

Assembling the turkey in the pot

Arrange the carcass pieces in the bottom of your pot with the turkey neck, gizzard, and heart (reserve the liver for another dish). Place the drumsticks, thighs, and wings over the carcass pieces, add the vegetables and the herb bouquet, and pour in the wine and enough chicken stock or water to cover ingredients by 2 inches (5 cm). Bring to the simmer over moderately high heat. Meanwhile, place the breast meat in a bowl and, if you wish, add marinade: sprinkle with salt and pepper, the Cognac or lemon juice, shallot or scallion, and oil; turn the meat about in the bowl to cover with the marinade, then cover the bowl and refrigerate until it is time to add the breast meat to the stew pot.

Stewing the turkey

2 to 2½ hours

Skim off the gray scum which will continue to rise from the simmering turkey for several minutes. Salt lightly to taste, then cover partially and let simmer slowly for 1 hour. Add the breast meat and its optional marinade and a little more stock or water, if needed, to cover the meat; simmer about 45 minutes more, until breast meat is tender and cooked through (slice one in half lengthwise to see, if you are not sure). Remove the breast meat when done and dip out other pieces, such as the wings and second joints, if they are tender before the drumsticks; place removed pieces in a bowl and cover with turkey cooking stock to keep moist. When all the turkey pieces are done, return everything to the pot and let cool, uncovered, for half an hour or more, so that the turkey meat will remain juicy and will pick up the flavor of the cooking liquid.

Finishing the turkey

Dip the turkey pieces from the pot and remove meat from bone. If you are serving the turkey in a salad or casserole, cut the large pieces of meat into big-bite-size pieces. Discard skin from wings and remove as much wing meat as possible. When cool, refrigerate the turkey meat in a covered bowl. Return bones to pot and simmer them in the cooking liquid another hour, then strain, degrease, and save the stock for soup or sauces.

Turkey Pot-au-Feu— Turkey Boiled Dinner

I can't leave turkey stew without remarking that this turkey meat, boned or not, makes a fine simple meal served with the usual boiled-dinner vegetables cooked or steamed with the turkey stock—carrots, onions, turnips, parsnips, potatoes—and you could even add a sausage or two to liven things up. (See the Corned Beef and Pork Boiled Dinner on page 138 for ideas.)

Turkey Salad

Serving 16 or more

| The preceding 3 quarts (3 L) of cooked turkey meat |
| Salt and white pepper |
| 1 cup (¼ L), more or less, finely minced mild onion |
| 2 cups (½ L), more or less, finely diced celery |
| 4 Tb, more or less, capers |
| ½ cup (1 dL), more or less, fresh lemon juice |
| 4 Tb, more or less, light olive oil or salad oil |
| ½ cup (1 dL) lightly pressed down, minced fresh parsley |
| 6 hard-boiled eggs, diced |
| 2 cups (½ L), or more, homemade mayonnaise |
| Decorative suggestions |
| Hard-boiled eggs, green or red peppers sliced into rings, capers |

Toss the turkey in a very large mixing bowl with salt and pepper to taste, then toss with the onion, celery, capers, lemon juice to taste, and several spoonfuls of oil. Let stand, tossing several times and checking on seasoning, for 20 to 30 minutes before folding in the parsley, hard-boiled eggs, and just enough mayonnaise to coat the turkey lightly. Pile into a serving bowl, mask the surface with a light coating of mayonnaise, and decorate the top with sliced or quartered hard-boiled eggs, peppers, capers, and/or whatever other good ideas you have. Cover with plastic wrap and refrigerate until serving time.

Turkey Casserole

Turkey gratinéed in white wine sauce with mushrooms and onions

This is the kind of old-fashioned recipe that always makes good eating and is useful indeed when you have a crowd to feed since you can assemble the whole thing the day before.

Serving 16 or more

| The preceding 3 quarts (3 L) of cooked turkey meat |
| Salt and pepper |
| 2 quarts (2 L) fresh mushrooms |
| 4 Tb minced shallots or scallions |
| 2 Tb fresh lemon juice, or more if needed |
| 2 quarts (2 L), more or less, strained and degreased turkey cooking stock, heated in a saucepan |
| 1½ quarts (1½ L) sliced onions |
| 1½ sticks (6 ounces or 180 g) butter |
| ½ cup (70 g) flour |
| 3 egg yolks blended in a mixing bowl with 1 cup (¼ L) heavy cream |
| 3 cups (¾ L) lightly packed, grated cheese (Swiss, Parmesan, mild Cheddar, or a mixture of all three) |

Toss the turkey meat in a very large bowl with salt and pepper to taste. Trim the mushrooms, quarter or halve them, wash rapidly, and drain. Toss them in a large saucepan with the shallots or scallions, lemon juice, and a cup (¼ L) of the turkey stock; cover the pan, bring to the boil, and simmer, tossing once or twice, for 3 minutes. Drain thoroughly, reserving liquid, toss with a sprinkling of salt and pepper, and add the mushrooms to the turkey. Return cooking liquid to pan, fold in the onions, a sprinkling of salt and pepper, and add 4 tablespoons of butter; cover and cook slowly until the onions are very tender, about 20 minutes. Drain thoroughly, reserving juices, and add onions to turkey and mushrooms.

Meanwhile, prepare the White Wine Sauce.

White Wine Sauce:

For 5 to 6 cups or 1 ¼ to 1 ½ liters
First, make a *roux:* melt 1 stick of butter in a large heavy-bottomed saucepan, blend in the flour, and stir with a wooden spoon over moderate heat as the flour and butter cook and finally foam and froth together; cook, stirring, for 2 minutes, not letting the *roux* turn more than a buttery yellow color. Remove from heat and, when it has stopped bubbling, pour in about 4 cups (1 L) of hot turkey stock, beating vigorously with your wire whip to blend. Beat in any mushroom/onion cooking juices. Set sauce over moderately high heat, stirring slowly with your whip, and bring to the simmer, thinning out with additions of stock to make a quite thick sauce. Let simmer, stirring with a wooden spoon and reaching all over bottom and corners of pan, for 5 minutes.

Remove from heat and, beating the egg yolk and cream mixture with your whip, dribble in 2 to 3 cups (½ to ¾ L) of the hot sauce, then beat the egg yolk mixture back into the sauce. Set over moderately high heat and stir slowly with a wooden spoon until sauce comes back to the simmer; simmer 2 to 3 minutes, stirring. Remove from heat and taste very carefully for seasoning, adding salt, pepper, and drops of lemon juice if needed.

Assembling and baking

Fold the turkey meat with the onions, mushrooms, more salt and pepper to taste, two thirds of the grated cheese, and two thirds of the sauce. Butter a 5- to 6-quart (5-L) baking dish and turn the turkey mixture into it. Spread the remaining sauce and cheese over the surface.

🕐   May be prepared in advance to this point. When cool, cover and refrigerate.

About an hour before serving, set in upper middle level of a preheated 375°F/190°C oven and bake until contents are bubbling hot and surface has browned nicely. If you are not serving soon, keep warm on an electric hot plate or over simmering water—do not overheat or you will ruin the texture and quality of the turkey.

Eggs Interalliés

Scrambled eggs and mushrooms gratinéed with cheese

I ran across this recipe way back in the early 1960s when doing an article for *House and Garden* on renowned Washington hostesses and their favorite recipes. Mme Hervé Alphand contributed the idea for this dish, which she served at diplomatic luncheons in the French Embassy, and I have always loved it. It is simple yet unusual, as well as easy to make, and it can be reheated. It would make a welcome contribution to a lunch or brunch or breakfast.

For 8 servings

1 pound (450 g) fresh mushrooms
About 1½ sticks (6 ounces or 180 g) butter
2 Tb minced shallots or scallions
Salt and pepper
6 Tb flour
About 2 cups (½ L) milk, heated in a small pan
About 1 cup (¼ L) heavy cream
Drops of fresh lemon juice
12 to 16 eggs
½ cup (1 dL) grated Parmesan cheese, or a mixture of Parmesan, Cheddar, and/or Swiss

Equipment

A 9-inch (23-cm) frying pan, preferably non-stick, for both mushrooms and eggs; a lightly buttered fireproof baking and serving dish, such as an oval 9 x 12 x 2 inches (23 x 30 x 5 cm)

The mushrooms

Trim the mushrooms, wash rapidly, dry, and cut into quarters. Sauté in 3 tablespoons butter over high heat for 5 to 6 minutes or until they are barely beginning to brown. Then stir in the shallots or scallions and toss over moderate heat for 1 to 2 minutes. Season to taste with salt and pepper, and set aside.

The sauce

For about 3 cups

Melt 5 tablespoons butter in a heavy-bottomed saucepan. Blend in the flour with a wooden spoon and stir over moderately low heat until butter and flour froth together for 2 minutes without coloring. Remove from heat and vigorously beat in the simmering milk with a wire whip to blend thoroughly. Beat in half the cream and salt and pepper to taste. Boil slowly, stirring, for 4 to 5 minutes. Then thin out the sauce with additional cream, beaten in by driblets. Sauce should coat a spoon nicely but not be too thick. Correct seasoning and beat in drops of lemon juice to taste. Clean off sides of pan with a rubber spatula, then float a tablespoon of cream on top of sauce to prevent a skin from forming.

Scrambling the eggs

Note that the eggs must be very soft and creamy, or slightly underdone; they will finish cooking under the broiler. Beat the eggs and seasonings in a bowl until just blended. Smear 3 tablespoons of butter in the skillet with a rubber spatula. Pour in the eggs and stir over moderately low heat. When eggs slowly begin to thicken, in 2 to 3 minutes, stir rapidly until they scramble into very soft curds. Immediately remove from heat and stir in, if you wish, a tablespoon or two of additional butter. Season to taste.

Assembling and serving

Spoon a thin layer of sauce into the bottom of the oval dish and sprinkle over it 2 tablespoons of cheese. Spread on half the eggs. Fold a cup (¼ L) of the sauce into the mushrooms and spoon over the eggs, sprinkling on 3 more tablespoons of cheese. Cover with the rest of the eggs, then the rest of the sauce. Sprinkle with the remaining cheese, and dot with butter.

◗ May be prepared an hour or so in advance; set aside at room temperature.

Shortly before serving, preheat broiler to very hot and place dish so surface is an inch (2½ cm) from heating element for a minute or so, until lightly browned. Serve at once.

Fish en Croûte

Loup en Croûte—Whole striped bass, salmon, or trout baked in a brioche crust

Fish in a crust was conceived in France by, I think, Paul Bocuse, but the first time I had it was with my French colleague Simone Beck, at Louis Outhier's restaurant, L'Oasis, in La Napoule, on the Mediterranean. The *loup* was a large sea bass, and this one came to us in a fish-shaped crust—enormous, brown, and glistening. The headwaiter cut around the edges of the crust, lifted it off, and there lay the fish—steaming, fragrant, and ready to serve, a really remarkable sight. With each serving of fish we received a portion of the crust, a big spoonful of creamy, buttery sauce, and another of fresh tomato nicely flavored with shallots and herbs. Fortunately, it is actually an easy way to cook a whole fish, and one in which the flesh retains its juices and delicate flavor.

This is the kind of dish to bring to a small informal party where everyone enjoys cooking and eating, and where you can have access to the kitchen, since you will have to assemble and bake it on the spot. I would suggest that you have everything ready at home, such as the fish all cleaned, oiled, iced, and the dough made and chilled. You bring fish and dough with you (as well as the tomato fondue, if you want to serve it), your rolling pin, baking pan, serving board, and other minor accessories. Assembly will take less than 10 minutes, and baking about 45. If you're making the butter sauce, it will take but a few minutes, and you can whip that up just before serving the fish.

For a 3-pound (1½-kg) fish, serving 8 as a first course

A 3-pound (1½-kg) fresh striped bass, salmon, or trout (weighed whole) cleaned, scaled (but with head on, if possible), and brushed with olive oil

Salt and pepper

6 to 8 fresh parsley sprigs

½ tsp fennel seed, or a handful of fresh fennel or dill

Brioche dough, risen and chilled (the following recipe)

Egg glaze (1 egg beaten in a cup with 1 tsp water)

Optional: white butter sauce (page 225) and fresh tomato fondue (page 143)

Equipment

Brown paper to make a fish template; a buttered jelly roll pan large enough to hold the fish diagonally; the metal tube from a pastry bag or scissors to make decorations; a platter or board to serve the fish on, plus a side dish for scraps and bones

An hour before you plan to serve, preheat oven to 400°F/205°C and set rack in middle or lower middle level. Wash and dry the fish, salt and pepper it inside, and tuck the parsley and fennel or dill in cavity. Cut a brown paper silhouette of the fish. Roll the dough into a rectangle and cut in half. Chill one piece. Roll the other out rapidly about ⅛ inch (½ cm) thick. Using template, cut into a fish shape (see page 222), roll up on pin, and unroll it in place on the jelly roll pan. Refrigerate dough scraps. Lay the fish on the dough. Rapidly roll out second piece of dough and cut ½ inch (1½ cm) larger all around than template; roll up on pin and unroll over fish; press the 2 layers together all around and tuck under fish. Working rapidly, roll out scraps of dough to form mouth, eyes, back fin, and tail decorations; paint those areas with egg glaze and affix the decorations. Paint fish with egg glaze; let dry a moment, and paint again. Using metal tube end or scissors, cut upstanding snips in surface of dough to simulate scales. Fish should now be baked immediately, before dough has a

chance to rise, so that it will remain thin and crusty.

Bake about 45 minutes. Fish is done at an internal thermometer reading of 160–165°F/71–74°C—or just when juices begin to escape into the pan. Crust will be brown and slightly puffed. Serve as soon as possible, accompanied, if you wish, with the white butter sauce and the tomato fondue.

To serve, cut all around outside edge of crust and lift it off. Peel skin off top of fish, and serve pieces of fish from topside of bone. Then remove bone, and serve bottom side of fish. Cut a strip or two of the top crust for each serving. (The soggy bottom crust is discarded.)

Remarks:

You could, if you wished, use the giant crepe described for the Choulibiac, page 82, rather than brioche dough for the bottom crust. You would cut it into a fish shape, following the template, and tuck half an inch (1½ cm) or so of the top covering brioche dough under the crepe.

The fish we got for this picture was too big to fit on the pan so we had to cut off its head.

Plain Brioche Dough

Pâte à Brioche Commune—
Made in a mixer or processor

This is the dough for fish *en croûte*, beef Wellington, *coulibiac,* or best-quality bread for sandwiches, toast, and canapés.

Brioche dough—rich, buttery, eggy, light in texture, and almost cakelike in taste—is fast and easy to produce in either a heavy-duty mixer or a food processor; but in both cases I think it needs a few minutes' rest after making, then a few minutes of hand work just to be sure it is kneaded enough. For best taste and texture, any yeast dough, in my opinion, benefits from two risings before it is formed; while the first and most important rise is long, slow, and supervised, the second may take place in the refrigerator. (By the way, the food processor recipe is my adaptation of James Beard's method, which appeared in the April 1978 issue of *Cooking,* the Cuisinart magazine.)

Note: The following proportions will make a little more dough than you need for a 3-pound (1½-kg) fish *en croûte,* but you can turn the extra amount into a loaf of bread. Start the dough the day before you plan to use it; or even several days in advance, and freeze it. (The whole recipe will make the equivalent of 4 loaves of bread baked in 4-cup or 1-liter pans.)

For about 8 cups (2 liters) of dough

2 packages (2 Tb) dry active yeast dissolved in ½ cup (1 dL) warm water (100°F/38°C)
2 sticks (½ pound or 225 g) butter
½ cup (1 dL) milk
2 pounds (7 cups or 900 g) all-purpose flour—measure by scooping flour into cup and sweeping it off level with lip of cup
1 Tb salt
3 Tb sugar
8 "large" eggs (1⅔ cups or 3¾–4 dL)

Making the dough in an electric mixer
(A large heavy-duty mixer is best for this; use the dough hook and put on the splatter shield, if your machine is equipped with one. For a smaller mixer, do the dough in 2 batches and then combine them for the final kneading.) Prepare the yeast; cut the butter into smallish pieces and melt in a small saucepan with the milk. Measure all but 2 cups of the flour into the mixer bowl, add the salt and sugar, the melted butter and milk, and the eggs. Mix to blend; the mixture, which the eggs will have cooled, should be just warm to the touch; if too hot, wait for several minutes before adding the yeast. Beat at moderate speed for 2 to 3 minutes, gradually adding the rest of the flour. Continue (lifting beater out of dough to unclog the blades as necessary, if you have no dough hook), mixing until dough is elastic enough to retract back into shape when a piece is pinched away from the mass. Turn dough out onto a lightly floured board, let rest 2 minutes, then knead vigorously by hand for a minute or two until dough is smooth. (It will be a soft dough.)

Making the dough in a food processor
(This goes very fast indeed, but you will have to make the dough in 2 or 3 batches, depending on the size of your processor container: for the 2-quart [2-L] size, make 3 batches; for the larger container, make 2 batches. As each batch is made, a matter of less than 2 minutes, turn it out onto your work surface, then combine for the final kneading.) Dissolve the yeast, stir it up, and divide it into 2 (or 3) portions. Cut the butter into smallish pieces and divide into 2 (or 3) portions. Measure 3½ cups (⁴/₅ L) flour, for 1 of 2 batches (2⅓ cups or 4 dL, for 1 of 3 batches) into the container of the processor and add ½ (or ⅓) of the salt and sugar. Break the eggs into a metal bowl, add the milk, and stir over hot water to take off the chill; pour into a quart or liter measure. Turn on the processor and blend several seconds and then in spurts until butter is completely broken up into the flour—30 to 45 seconds. Pour in ½ (or ⅓) of the eggs; process several seconds and then in spurts until dough masses on the blades and revolves against the top of the container; continue processing for 30 seconds or so—this is the kneading action. Remove the dough to your work surface and, without cleaning out the processor, continue with the next 1 or 2 batches. Let rest 2 minutes, then mass the batches together and knead vigorously on a lightly floured surface until dough is smooth. (It will be a soft dough.)

The rising of the dough
Place dough in a clean, fairly straight-sided 8-quart (8 liter) bowl, or divide into 2 bowls. Cover with plastic wrap and a towel and let sit at 72–75°F/22–24°C. (In hot weather, let the rise start, then refrigerate dough from time to time to slow the rise.) When tripled, in 3 hours or more, the dough will feel spongy and springy; turn it out onto your work surface. Pat into a rectangle with the palms of your hands, and fold dough in 3; repeat and return to cleaned bowl—this redistributes yeast cells throughout the dough to make a finer grain. Cover and let rise again, this time to slightly more than double (1½ to 2 hour).

❶ You may wish to complete this rise in the refrigerator overnight; but if dough has already started its rise, cover with a plate and a weight to prevent its over-rising.

When second rise is complete, if you are doing the fish recipe, turn dough out onto work surface, flatten with palms of hands, and place on a lightly floured tray; flour lightly, cover with plastic, a board, and a weight. It must be chilled before you proceed with the fish recipe—or for making similar dough-wrapped creations like beef Wellington or *coulibiac*.

❶ To delay the rise you can always refrigerate the dough; for a long delay, weight it down when it has chilled. To stop the rise, freeze the dough—up to 10 days; to continue, either thaw overnight in the refrigerator or set in a warm place until thawed and the rise has started up again, then proceed where you left off.

Brioche Sandwich Bread

Pain Brioché

A fine loaf of bread is always a welcome gift, and the preceding brioche dough makes perfect sandwich bread or toast for *foie gras*, smoked salmon, and other such delicacies. Rather than baking it in an open pan, you can cover the pan so that your loaf will be contained in an even rectangular shape. Although you can sometimes find covered pans known as Pullman pans or *pain de mie* pans in professional stores and import shops, you can easily improvise your own, as illustrated.

For 1 brioche loaf baked in an 8-cup (2-liter) pan

⅓ the preceding brioche dough, fully risen

Equipment

A buttered 8-cup (2-L) bread pan, as straight-sided as possible, to make a rectangular shape; a sheet of very smooth aluminum foil, buttered on the shiny side (to cover bread pan); a baking sheet and a heavy heat-proof weight of some sort like a brick, a big stone, or an axe head

Flatten the dough into a rectangular shape slightly shorter than the bread pan, fold in half lengthwise and pinch the two edges together, then fit seam side down into the pan, pressing dough in place with your knuckles. Dough should fill pan by slightly less than half. Cover loosely and let dough rise to fill pan only by about three quarters; it will rise to fill pan later while baking. (Preheat oven to 450°F/230°C and set rack in middle level before dough has completed its rise of about an hour.) Cover the pan with the foil, buttered side down, and set in oven. Place baking sheet and weight on top, and bake 35 to 40 minutes—do not peek or remove baking sheet and weight for 30 minutes. Bread is done when nicely browned on top, when the loaf has shrunk very slightly from sides of pan, and when it unmolds easily.

Let cool on a rack. When thoroughly cold, in several hours, wrap airtight and refrigerate or freeze. For easy sandwich slicing, bread should be a day old.

White Butter Sauce with Herbs

Beurre Blanc aux Fines Herbes

This is a more classic version of the lemon butter sauce on page 53, and I like it lightened with a little cream and brightened with a sprinkling of herbs. Unless you are familiar with it and know the tricks of making it ahead and keeping it, you're wise to make the sauce only at the last minute, although there are directions for ahead-of-time preparation at the end of the recipe.

For 1½ to 1¾ cups (3½ to 4 deciliters)

4 Tb white wine vinegar
2 Tb lemon juice
4 Tb dry white vermouth
2 Tb finely minced shallots or scallions
Salt
White pepper
2½ sticks (10 ounces or 285 g) chilled butter, cut into ¼-inch (¾-cm) slices
4 to 8 Tb heavy cream
Minced parsley and/or dill

Simmer the vinegar, lemon juice, vermouth, shallots or scallions, ½ teaspoon salt, and ⅛ teaspoon pepper in a 6-cup (1½-L) enameled or stainless-steel saucepan until liquid has reduced to 1½ tablespoons. Remove saucepan from heat and immediately beat in 2 pieces of the chilled butter with a wire whip. As butter softens and creams, beat in another piece. Then set pan over very low heat and, beating constantly, continue adding more pieces of butter as each previous piece has almost been absorbed into the sauce. Sauce should become thick and ivory colored, the consistency of hollandaise sauce. Remove from heat, add more salt and pepper to taste, and beat in the cream by spoonfuls to lighten the sauce. Beat in the herbs, turn into a warm (not too hot) sauce bowl, and serve.

🕐   If you wish to make the sauce ahead, omit cream and herbs and set sauce near a gas pilot light, or near a warm burner, just to prevent butter from congealing; at serving time, heat the cream and beat by driblets into the sauce to warm it, then beat in the herbs.

Metric Conversions

Some day we shall convert from our illogical system of pounds, ounces, feet, and inches to metrics, where all will be in easy divisions of 10 rather than a mishmash of 2's, 4's, 12's, 16's. In anticipation of that happy metric day, all the recipes in this book give both versions, and clumsy though this is at times, at least it will remind us that 350°F is 180°C, that 1 cup is ¼ liter, and that 9 inches is 23 centimeters.

At this writing there seems to be some agreement among metric consultants about some of the terms and abbreviations that should be used in this country. However, there is disagreement about whether the metric cup measure should be ¼ of a liter (250 milliliters) or 240 milliliters to correspond to our present 8-ounce cup. Should the tablespoon and teaspoon be retained as terms? Or should those measurements be expressed in milliliters? But why use milliliters at all? say I. The Europeans, who have been cooking in metrics for generations, don't ever use any milliliters in cooking, only the large fractions of the liter down to deciliters (1/10 of a liter) and centiliters (1/100 of a liter). I suppose our metric people want to be utterly logical, and if we are using grams, which are 1/1000 of a kilogram, we must then use milliliters, which are 1/1000 of a liter. However, is it logical to launch out on a new system when the rest of the metric users do not agree? After all, the point of our going metric is that we be able to communicate with the rest of the world.

Since, then, there is as yet no established plan, I am using the European system for liquid measures. No milliliters! I think the large fractions of the liter are far easier; besides, ¼ liter is just about the same as our 1 cup. And why use milliliters for our easy-to-measure tablespoon and teaspoon? You will note, in the charts to follow, that there is not always perfection in conversion since the deciliter does not fit as easily into our cup measures

as could be wished—for instance, while ½ cup makes for convenience 1 deciliter, 1 cup makes 2½ deciliters, or ¼ liter. However, these slight discrepancies make no appreciable difference in home cooking. What I am looking for is reasonable accuracy and easy measurement.

By the way, there have been worry rumors that once we convert to metrics all of us will have to buy kitchen scales. Not so! Everything will be measured in cups and spoons as before; it is up to the recipe writers to figure out how many cups of flour 140 or 190 grams make, how many prunes fit into a ½ liter, how much sugar to a deciliter, and so forth and so on. In addition, recipes and cookbooks will have to include both systems, as this one does, for many years to come.

Liquid Measure Conversions

Cups and Spoons	Liquid Ounces	Approximate Metric Term	Approximate Centiliters	Actual Milliliters
1 tsp	1/6 oz	1 tsp	½ cL	5 mL
1 Tb	½ oz	1 Tb	1½ cL	15 mL
¼ c; 4 Tb	2 oz	½ dL; 4 Tb	6 cL	59 mL
⅓ c; 5 Tb	2⅔ oz	¾ dL; 5 Tb	8 cL	79 mL
½ c	4 oz	1 dL	12 cL	119 mL
⅔ c	5⅓ oz	1½ dL	15 cL	157 mL
¾ c	6 oz	1¾ dL	18 cL	178 mL
1 c	8 oz	¼ L	24 cL	237 mL
1¼ c	10 oz	3 dL	30 cL	296 mL
1⅓ c	10⅔ oz	3¼ dL	33 cL	325 mL
1½ c	12 oz	3½ dL	35 cL	355 mL
1⅔ c	13⅓ oz	3¾ dL	39 cL	385 mL
1¾ c	14 oz	4 dL	41 cL	414 mL
2 c; 1 pt	16 oz	½ L	47 cL	473 mL
2½ c	20 oz	6 dL	60 cL	592 mL
3 c	24 oz	¾ L	70 cL	710 mL
3½ c	28 oz	4/5 L; 8 dL	83 cL	829 mL
4 c; 1 qt	32 oz	1 L	95 cL	946 mL
5 c	40 oz	1¼ L	113 cL	1134 mL
6 c; 1½ qt	48 oz	1½ L	142 cL	1420 mL
8 c; 2 qt	64 oz	2 L	190 cL	1893 mL
10 c; 2½ qt	80 oz	2½ L	235 cL	2366 mL
12 c; 3 qt	96 oz	2¾ L	284 cL	2839 mL
4 qt	128 oz	3¾ L	375 cL	3785 mL
5 qt		4¾ L		
6 qt		5½ L (or 6 L)		
8 qt		7½ L (or 8 L		

To convert:

Ounces to *milliliters:*
multiply *ounces* by 29.57
Quarts to *liters:*
multiply *quarts* by 0.95
Milliliters to *ounces:*
multiply *milliliters* by 0.034
Liters to *quarts:*
multiply *liters* by 1.057

Temperatures

Fahrenheit degrees are here converted to the most convenient Celsius term, with actual Celsius degrees in parentheses. (Note that by international agreement the term "Celsius" has been substituted for the term "Centigrade"; however, the degrees are the same whichever term you use. This decision was evidently made because both Celsius and Fahrenheit were men, which is not the case with Centigrade. We must be logical!

Fahrenheit°/Celsius°	(Actual Celsius°)
−5°F/−20°C	(−20.6°C)
32°F/0°C	(0°C)
37°F/3°C	(2.8°C)
50°F/10°C	(10°C)
60°F/16°C	(15.6°C)
70°F/21°C	(21.1°C)
75°F/24°C	(23.9°C)
80°F/27°C	(26.7°C)
85°F/29°C	(29.4°C)
100°F/38°C	(37.8°C)
105°F/41°C	(40.6°C)
110°F/43°C	(43.3°C)
115°F/46°C	(46.1°C)
120°F/49°C	(48.9°C)
125°F/52°C	(51.7°C)
130°F/54°C	(54.4°C)
135°F/57°C	(57.2°C)
140°F/60°C	(60°C)
150°F/66°C	(65.6°C)
160°F/71°C	(71.1°C)
165°F/74°C	(73.9°C)
170°F/77°C	(76.7°C)
180°F/82°C	(82.2°C)
190°F/88°C	(87.8°C)
200°F/95°C	(93.3°C)
205°F/96°C	(96.1°C)
212°F/100°C	(100°C)
225°F/110°C	(107.2°C)
228°F/109°C	(108.9°C)

Fahrenheit°/Celsius°	(Actual Celsius°)
238°F/115°C	(114.4°C)
250°F/120°C	(121.1°C)
275°F/135°C	(135°C)
285°F/140°C	(140.6°C)
300°F/150°C	(148.9°C)
325°F/165°C	(162.8°C)
350°F/180°C	(176.7°C)
375°F/190°C	(190.6°C)
400°F/205°C	(204.4°C)
425°F/220°C	(218.3°C)
450°F/230°C	(232.2°C)
475°F/245°C	(246.1°C)
500°F/260°C	(260°C)
525°F/275°C	(273.9°C)
550°F/290°C	(287.8°C)

To convert:
Fahrenheit to *Celsius:*
subtract 32, multiply by 5, divide by 9.
Celsius to *Fahrenheit:*
multiply by 9, divide by 5, add 32.

Inches to Centimeters

Inches ("in")	Centimeters ("cm") (Nearest equivalent)
1/16 in	¼ cm
⅛ in	½ cm
3/16 in	"less than ¼ in/¾ cm"
¼ in	¾ cm
⅜ in	1 cm
½ in	1½ cm
⅝ in	1½ cm
¾ in	2 cm
1 in	2½ cm
1½ in	4 cm
2 in	5 cm
2½ in	6½ cm
3 in	8 cm
3½ in	9 cm
4 in	10 cm
5 in	13 cm
6 in	15 cm
7 in	18 cm
8 in	20 cm
9 in	23 cm
10 in	25 cm
12 in	30 cm
14 in	35 cm
15 in	38½ cm
16 in	40 cm
18 in	45 cm
20 in	50 cm
24 in	60 cm
30 in	75 cm

To convert:
Inches to *centimeters:*
multiply *inches* by 2.54
Centimeters to *inches:*
multiply *centimeters* by 0.39

Ounces to Grams

Ounces	Convenient Equivalent	Actual Weight
1 oz	30 g	(28.35 g)
2 oz	60 g	(56.7 g)
3 oz	85 g	(85.05 g)
4 oz	115 g	(113.4 g)
5 oz	140 g	(141.8 g)
6 oz	180 g	(170.1 g)
8 oz	225 g	(226.8 g)
9 oz	250 g	(255.2 g)
10 oz	285 g	(283.5 g)
12 oz	340 g	(340.2 g)
14 oz	400 g	(396.9 g)
16 oz	450 g	(453.6 g)
20 oz	560 g	(566.99 g)
24 oz	675 g	(680.4 g)

To convert:
Ounces to *grams:*
multiply *ounces* by 28.35
Grams to *ounces:*
multiply *grams* by 0.035

Pounds to Grams and Kilograms

Pounds	Convenient Equivalent	Actual Weight
¼ lb	115 g	(113.4 g)
½ lb	225 g	(226.8 g)
¾ lb	340 g	(340.2 g)
1 lb	450 g	(453.6 g)
1¼ lb	565 g	(566.99 g)
1½ lb	675 g	(680.4 g)
1¾ lb	800 g	(794 g)
2 lb	900 g	(908 g)
2½ lb	1125 g; 1¼ kg	(1134 g)
3 lb	1350 g	(1360 g)
3½ lb	1500 g; 1½ kg	(1588 g)
4 lb	1800 g	(1814 g)
4½ lb	2 kg	(2041 g)
5 lb	2¼ kg	(2268 g)
5½ lb	2½ kg	(2495 g)
6 lb	2¾ kg	(2727 g)
7 lb	3¼ kg	(3175 g)
8 lb	3½ kg	(3629 g)
9 lb	4 kg	(4028 g)
10 lb	4½ kg	(4536 g)
12 lb	5½ kg	(5443 g)
14 lb	6¼ kg	(6350 g)
15 lb	6¾ kg	(6804 g)
16 lb	7¼ kg	(7258 g)
18 lb	8 kg	(8165 g)
20 lb	9 kg	(9072 g)
25 lb	11¼ kg	(11,340 g)

Flour and Sugar Measurements

Flour equivalents are for flour scooped and leveled: scooped into cup; leveled off even with lip by knife-edge sweep.

Flour Measurements	Ounces	Nearest equivalents
1 Tb	¼ oz	7½ g
¼ c; 4 Tb	1¼ oz	35 g
⅓ c; 5 Tb	1½ oz	50 g
½ c	2½ oz	70 g
⅔ c	3¼ oz	100 g
¾ c	3½ oz	105 g
1 c	5 oz	140 g
1¼ c	6 oz	175 g
1⅓ c	6½ oz	190 g
1½ c	7½ oz	215 g
2 c	10 oz	285 g
3½ c	16 oz; 1 lb	454 g
3¾ c	17½ oz	500 g

Sugar Measurements	Ounces	Nearest equivalents
1 tsp	1/6 oz	5 g
1 Tb	½ oz	12-15 g
¼ c; 4 Tb	1¾ oz	50 g
⅓ c; 5 Tb	2¼ oz	65 g
½ c	3½ oz	100 g
⅔ c	4½ oz	125 g
¾ c	5 oz	145 g
1 c	7 oz (6¾ oz)	190-200 g
1¼ c	8½ oz	240 g
1⅓ c	9 oz	245 g
1½ c	9½ oz	275 g
1⅔ c	11 oz	325 g
1¾ c	11¾ oz	240 g
2 c	13½ oz	380-400 g

Menu Alternatives

To give you a wider choice in planning menus than this book would otherwise afford, here is an addendum for each chapter, suggesting other food that will fit the same requirements. Where the situation is unique, as in "Holiday Lunch," I've given a list of possibilities; otherwise I have created a menu for 11 of the 13 occasions, drawing recipes out of each one of my books. Here, recipe titles are usually given in French because that's the way my earlier books were set up, but there is sufficient description of each recipe in English to tell you what the dish is all about.

A Birthday Dinner Menu from *Mastering the Art of French Cooking, Volume Two*

Bisque de Crabes, Crab Bisque, page 36
Gigot Farci, en Croûte, Boned Stuffed Lamb Baked in Pastry, page 189
Gratin d'Épinards aux Oignons, Spinach Braised with Onions, page 360
Le Succès; Le Progrès; La Dacquoise, three names for the same cake: a meringue-nut layer cake with butter-cream frosting and filling, page 497
Suggested wines: a red Bordeaux–Saint-Emilion or Cabernet Sauvignon with the lamb; Champagne with the cake

Ideas for a Holiday Lunch from *Mastering the Art of French Cooking, Volume Two*

Main-dish soups
Soupe Catalane aux Poivrons, Catalonian Pepper and Leek Soup, page 21
Soupe à la Victorine, Purée of White Bean Soup, eggplant and tomato garnish, page 22

Pâtés and terrines
Terrine de Foie de Porc, Pork-Liver *Pâté,* page 320
Pâté de Campagne, Pork and Liver *Pâté* with Veal or Chicken, page 321
Pâté de Foie et de Porc en Brioche, Pork and Pork-Liver *Pâté* baked in *brioche* dough, page 322
La Terrine Verte; Pâté sans Porc, A Porkless *Pâté,* page 324
Pâtés en Croûte, Pâtés Baked in Pastry Crust, page 326
Luncheon stews
Boeuf en Pipérade, Beef Stew with a Garnish of Peppers and Tomatoes, page 152
Tripes à la Niçoise, Tripe Baked with Onions, Tomatoes, Wine, and Provençal Seasonings, page 244 (Must be served very hot, but can be repeatedly reheated)
Cold meat
Langue de Boeuf, Bouillié ou Braisé, Beef Tongue, Boiled or Braised, in several fashions, pages 232–42
Poitrine de Veau, Farcie, Breast of Veal Stuffed and Braised, page 216 (May be served hot or cold)
Jambon Persillé, Mold of Parsleyed Ham in Aspic, page 310 (Best made with home-cured pork—see recipes in *Mastering II* and in this book)
One-dish main courses
Chou Farci, Stuffed Whole Cabbage, page 379
-or-
Feuilles de Chou Farcies, Stuffed Cabbage Leaves, page 384
Feuilletée au Fromage; Jalousie au Fromage, Cheese Tart of French puff pastry, page 140 (This one is made with slats or Venetian-blind effect on top.)
Vegetables
Tian de Courgettes au Riz, Gratin of Zucchini, Rice, and Onions with Cheese, page 371
Oignons Farcis au Riz, Onions Stuffed

with Rice, Cheese, and Herbs, page 376
   Gratin de Potiron d'Arpajon, Purée of Pumpkin or Winter Squash and White Beans, page 404
   Purée Freneuse, Purée of Rice and Turnips with Herbs and Garlic, page 405
   Salade de Poivrons, Provençale, Peeled and Sliced Sweet Bell Peppers in Garlic and Oil, page 411
   Garnish
   Petits Oignons Aigre-Doux, Sweet-Sour Onions Braised with Raisins, page 410 (May be served hot or cold)
   Desserts
   Le Marly; La Riposte, Strawberry Shortcake Made with Rum-soaked *Brioche,* page 448
   Pain d'Épices, Spice Cake, page 481
   Mille-Feuilles, Napoleons, page 462 (Layers of puff pastry and pastry cream or whipped cream, iced on top)
   Bourbon-soaked Chocolate Truffles (in this book)
   Couques and *Palmiers,* Caramelized Cookies Made from Puff Pastry Dough, pages 477 and 478

Lo-Cal Banquet Suggestions from *The French Chef*

   Clams *en Gelée,* Clams in Aspic on the half shell, page 222
   Choice of
   Poularde Demi-désossée (or Half-Boned Chicken) poached in wine, unstuffed, with aromatic vegetables, page 389,
   -or-
   Saumon Poché, Whole Poached Fish, page 350 (Use the recipe for poached salmon, substituting any fish. Salmon is rather high in calories.)
   -or-
   Potée Normande; Pot-au-Feu, French Boiled Dinner, page 61 (Use chicken only, if you wish.)

   Boiled Asparagus (in this book)
   Grilled Tomatoes (in this book)

An Informal Dinner Menu *From Julia Child's Kitchen*

   Soupe au Pistou Verte, Green Zucchini Soup with a Garlic and Basil Garnish, page 8
   Filets de Sole Dugléré, Poached Filets of Sole with White Wine Sauce and Tomatoes, page 138
   Steamed Rice (in this book)
   Chopped Cooked Spinach, page 420, or Green Beans (in this book)
   Broccoli Flowerettes (in this book), or Asparagus (in this book)
   Crêpes, Flambées, Sainte Claire, French crêpes with apricot flavor, flamed, page 537
   Suggested wines: white Burgundy or Chardonnay

A VIP Lunch Menu from *Mastering the Art of French Cooking, Volume One*

   Filets de Poisson en Soufflé, Fish Soufflé Baked on a Platter, page 170, with Hollandaise Sauce, page 79
   Épinards Étuvés au beurre, Spinach Braised in Butter, page 470
   Oranges Glacées, Glazed Oranges, served cold, page 629, with *Reine de Saba,* Chocolate and Almond Cake, page 677
   Champagne throughout is suggested.

Ideas for a Cocktail Party *From Julia Child's Kitchen*

   Cheese appetizers
   Croque Madame and *Croque Monsieur,* Ham and Cheese Sandwiches, the former baked, the latter sautéed, pages 42–44; *Petites Fondues Frites,* Cheese Croquettes, page 45; cheese tarts, tartlets, covered tarts, and turnovers large and small, made from pie dough, mock puff pastry, and regular puff pastry.
   Quiches
   Lorraine, with cream and bacon, page 59; *au Gruyère,* with Swiss cheese, page 61; *au fromage,* with mixed cheeses, page 61; or with

smoked salmon, eggplant, broccoli or spinach, with various other vegetables, and with shell-fish, pages 62–64.

Homemade pizza, topped with tomatoes, cheese, and mushrooms, page 483; or *à la Niçoise,* with onions, olives, anchovies, and cheese, page 486; and—not a pizza, but similar—*Socca,* a baked pancake of chick-pea flour, page 486. Eggplant "pizza," page 398, has pizza topping, but the base is eggplant slices instead of dough—to be eaten with a fork.

Pâtés, terrines, and homemade sausage

A *pâté* of pork and liver with veal or chicken, page 368; a *pâté pantin* (free-form *pâté en croûte,* baked in a crust), page 372; a terrine of duck, page 369; a terrine of pork and veal with sweetbreads, page 371; and homemade sausage baked in a crust, page 364.

Fish and shellfish

Pain de Poisson, Loaf-shaped Fish Mousse, page 159, served cold and eaten with a fork. A similar mousse made with shrimp, page 155. Shrimp in a quiche, or *à la Grecque* (simmered in aromatic broth), or sautéed with lemon, page 64, 163, or 164. Scallops grilled on skewers, page 122. Two ways of broiling oysters in the half shell, pages 168–69 (must be served very hot, to eat with fork). The humane way to boil lobsters, page 174; serve the meat on toothpicks, with homemade mayonnaise (in this book).

Brochettes

Beef tenderloin, chicken breasts and livers, lamb, or scallops on skewers, page 287, 211, 292, or 122. Or braised ham, cubed, on toothpicks.

Vegetables

Homemade Potato Chips, page 413; *Caviar d'Aubergine,* Eggplant Caviar, page 400, or Eggplant Pizza, page 398; Mushrooms or Onions *à la Grecque,* page 407 or 408.

Eggplant caviar is generally used as a dip or a spread. Others: *Tapénade,* a Provençal combination of olives, capers, and anchovies, page 86; or two *brandades* (garlicky purées)—one of salt cod *(de morue),* page 179, the other of white beans *(à la Soissonaise),* page 342.

These dips can be used to flavor stuffed hard-boiled eggs. Other ways: with puréed asparagus, artichokes, smoked salmon, and shrimp, pages 85–86.

Garnish

Try recipes for preparing and storing the imported salt-packed large capers and whole anchovies one can find here in Italian markets, pages 437–38 and 49–53. I warmly recommend them.

A Dinner for the Boss Menu from *Mastering the Art of French Cooking, Volume Two*

Potage aux Concombres, Cream of Cucumber Soup, page 17 (May be served hot or cold)

Melba toast (in this book), made from *Pain de Mie,* Homemade White Sandwich Bread, page 74

Filet de Boeuf en Croûte, Tenderloin of Beef in Pastry—Beef Wellington, page 181 (This version, with a *brioche* crust, uses pre-sliced beef, and the mushroom stuffing lies between the slices. Another, equally good, is in *The French Chef Cookbook,* with a prebaked bottom crust and a mock puff pastry topping. Beef Wellington is another splendid dish that has lost its once-fine reputation through sloppy cooking, but again, as with Veal Orloff, it can be just as marvelous to eat as it is exciting to look at...and interesting to prepare.)

Sliced Fresh Asparagus Spears Tossed in Butter (in this book). Cut the asparagus on a diagonal, with the knife blade at a 20° angle to the stalk, for elegantly elongated slices.

Fresh green peas (in this book) or broccoli flowerettes (in this book)

La Surprise de Vésuve, French Baked Alaska, Flamed, page 432

Suggested wines: a red Bordeaux-Médoc or Cabernet Sauvignon with the beef; Champagne with dessert.

Do-It-Yourself Parties for All Ages for Sunday Night Supper

A Pizza Party
From Julia Child's Kitchen

Your Own Homemade Pizza, page 484
Tomato topping, page 484
Niçoise topping (onions, anchovies, olives, and cheese), page 486
Tranches d'Aubergine à l'Italienne, Pizza with an Eggplant Base instead of dough, page 398
Caesar Salad, page 433 (As Caesar made it)
Le Gâteau des Trois Mages, Le Gâteau Deblieux, Cake in a Cage, page 553 (A layer cake with whipped cream and fruits, enclosed by a floor and a dome of hard caramel)

An Omelette Party from *The French Chef*

Two-egg omelettes, each serving one person
Sliced sautéed mushrooms, a cheese sauce, and grated cheese, to use separately or combine for an *Omelette gratinée aux Champignons,* page 105
Pipérade for filling, page 419 (A mixture of tomatoes, peppers, onions, and ham)
To make some of the classic fillings listed by Escoffier, you could set forth bowls of:
Minced parsley and herbs (*omelette aux fines herbes*)
Minced parsley and minced sautéed onion (*omelette à la Lyonnaise*)
Diced ham (*omelette à la fermière*)
Diced sautéed potato with onions and chopped parsley (*omelette Parmentier*)
Diced sautéed chicken livers (in this book) (*omelette aux foies de volaille*)
Skewered Salad (in this book)
Croquembouche, A Tower of Cream Puffs, filled or not, stuck together with cara-

mel, page 359 (You could set out a tray of puffs, a bowl of whipped cream for filling, and keep the caramel stickily warm on a heating tray, so your guests can build the tower together.)

A Buffet for 19 from *Mastering the Art of French Cooking, Volume One*

Gratins, which can be prepared in advance and presented in baking dish
Gratin of Potatoes, with Ham and Eggs and Onions, page 153
with Onions and Anchovies, page 154
with Onions and Sausages, page 155
Gratin of Leeks and Ham, page 155
Gratin of Endives and Ham, page 156
Gratins of creamed mixtures, of fish, chicken, brains, or sweetbreads, pages 156–57
Gratins of *quenelles* made of fish, shellfish, veal, chicken, or turkey, pages 188–89
Gratins of canned salmon or tuna, or fish leftovers, page 189
Thon à la Provençale, Tuna or Swordfish Steaks with Wine, Tomatoes, and Herbs, page 219
Coq au Vin, page 263
Beef stews
à la Bourguignonne (in red wine), page 315; *Carbonnades à la Flamande* (with beer), page 317; *en Daube,* page 322; *Paupiettes de Boeuf* (Braised Stuffed Beef Rolls), page 318
Lamb in a *Navarin Printanier* or *Moussaka,* page 345 or 349
Veal, *Prince Orloff,* page 355; or *Sauté Marengo,* A Brown Stew with Tomatoes and Mushrooms, but not with last-minute fried eggs, page 360
Jambon Farci et Braisé, Ham Sliced, Stuffed, and Braised in Madeira, page 394 (This can be done in a pastry crust.)
Cassoulet, French Baked Beans with Pork, Sausages, Duck, etc., page 399
A useful list of cold main dishes
Poulet en Gelée à l'Estragon, Tarragon

Chicken in Aspic, page 549 (You can cut up the chicken after cooking, before jelling.)

Suprêmes de Volaille en Chaud-froid, Blanche Neige, Breast of Chicken in a Special Stock-and-Cream Jellied Sauce, page 551 (This is not made with the usual jellied *béchamel*.)

Crab or lobster *en Chaud-froid,* page 553

Volailles en Escabèche, Cold Fowl or, especially, Game in Lemon Jelly, page 554

Boeuf Mode en Gelée, Aspic of Sliced Cold Braised Beef, page 556

Cold jellied mousses of chicken, turkey, duck, game, ham, or fish, pages 558–64

Desserts

Among the many classic tarts, I recommend the lime or lemon (cold) soufflé-filled one, page 645. And among the cakes, the Savarin (a *baba* ring mold, soaked in rum and filled with fruit and whipped cream, page 662).

Charlotte Malakoff, page 607

Diplomate, Custard, unmolded, with Glacéed Fruits, page 612

Charlotte Chantilly, A Strawberry or Raspberry Cream, page 608

Crème Plombières Pralinée, Caramel Almond Cream, in a bowl not in a mold, with variations, page 594

Bavarian creams: orange, chocolate, strawberry or raspberry, pages 596–600

Riz à l'Impératrice, Molded Custard with Rice and Glacéed Fruits, page 601

Unmolded caramel custard, with variations, pages 610–11

Chocolate Mousse, page 604, and Orange Mousse, page 603

Charlotte aux Pommes, Apple Charlotte, page 623 (Don't forget to use Golden Delicious apples or another firm kind; see notes in this book.)

Pommes Normande en Belle Vue, An Applesauce Caramel Mold, page 624

Aspic de Pommes, Rum-flavored Apple Aspic, unmolded, page 627

Pêches Cardinal, A Compote of Fresh Peaches with Raspberry Purée, page 630

A Chafing-Dish Dinner Menu *From Julia Child's Kitchen*

Potage Crème de haricots, White Bean Soup with Herbs and Lemon, page 14 (May be served hot or cold)

Truites Meunière, Whole Trout Sautéed in Butter, page 126

Zucchini en Pipérade, Grated Zucchini Sautéed with Onions, Peppers, and Herbs, page 427

Petits Pains: Galettes ou Champignons, Homemade French Rolls: Round or Top-Knotted (nicknamed "mushrooms"), pages 468 and 469

Pommes Rosemarie, Apples Rosie, page 494 (A version of apple Betty)

Suggested wines: Pouilly-Fuissé, Pouilly-Fumé, Chablis, dry Riesling, or Chardonnay with the trout; Vouvray Mousseux or a domestic sparkling white wine with dessert

An Indoor/Outdoor Barbecue Menu *From Julia Child's Kitchen*

Brandade de Morue, Purée of Salt Cod with Potatoes, Olive Oil, and Garlic, page 179 (Used as a dip for crackers or potato chips)

Les Crudités, Assorted Raw Vegetables

Crevettes à la Grecque, Shrimp, either boiled in salted water or simmered in court bouillon, page 163

Homemade Mayonnaise (in this book)

Brochettes (skewers) of scallops or chicken breasts and livers, page 211, or beef tenderloin, page 287, or lamb, page 294

Pommes de Terre Sautées à l'Ail, Potatoes Sautéed with Garlic and Herbs, page 417

Courgette Géante en Barquette, Bellesoeur, A Giant Cooked Zucchini as a Container for a Vegetable Mixture, page 427

Bombe Glacée au Chocolat, Molded Vanilla and Chocolate Ice Cream, homemade or best-quality store-bought, page 543

Suggested wines: red and white jug wines

Index

This book is set in Sabon, designed in 1967
by Jan Teischold, and is a face based on
early fonts engraved by Garamond and
Granjon.

The book was photoset on the
Merganthaler VIP by TypoGraphics
Communications, Inc., New York,
New York.

Designed by Chris Pullman and Gaye
Korbet of WGBH-TV, Boston, Mass.

Photography by James Scherer, with additional photographs by Michael Peirce and
Lou Sardonis.

Separations by Offset Separations Corp.,
New York, New York, and Milan, Italy.

Printing and binding by R. R. Donnelley
and Sons, Willard, Ohio.